PENGUIN

ARKANA

RIVER'S WAY

A key figure in the field of dream and bodywork, psychological interventions in psychiatry and in conflict resolution, Arnold Mindell is the author of *Dreambody*, *Working with the Dreaming Body*, *River's Way*, *City's Shadows*, *Working on Yourself Alone*, *The Year I*, *The Dreambody in Relationships* and with Amy Mindell, *Riding the Horse Backwards* and *Coma: The Dreambody Near Death*. Many of his books are published by Arkana. He is an analyst in private practice, co-founder of the Centre for Process Oriented Psychology, Zurich and Portland, and analyst and teacher at these centres. He has been a resident teacher at Esalen Institute, Big Sur, California, and lectures and teaches throughout the world.

1 *Oregon badge on emperor's surcoat showing the primal dragon, symbol of the creative element behind change (Royal Ontario Museum)*

Arnold Mindell

RIVER'S WAY

The process science of the dreambody

Information and channels in dream and bodywork, psychology and physics, Taoism and alchemy

ARKANA
PENGUIN BOOKS

To Marie Louise von Franz

ARKANA

Published by the Penguin Group
Penguin Books Ltd, 27 Wrights Lane, London W8 5TZ, England
Penguin Books USA Inc., 375 Hudson Street, New York, New York 10014, USA
Penguin Books Australia Ltd, Ringwood, Victoria, Australia
Penguin Books Canada Ltd, 10 Alcorn Avenue, Toronto, Ontario, Canada M4V 3B2
Penguin Books (NZ) Ltd, 182–190 Wairau Road, Auckland 10, New Zealand

Penguin Books Ltd, Registered Offices: Harmondsworth, Middlesex, England

First published by Routledge & Kegan Paul 1985
Published by Arkana 1989
10 9 8 7 6 5 4 3 2

Printed in England by Clays Ltd, St Ives plc

CONTENTS

ACKNOWLEDGMENTS

There are many real and dream people who helped me to develop process science. Jung's voice for example stirred me towards increasing empiricism. He became a model for me of someone who recognized and respected limitations and then transcended their restrictiveness. His attitude towards dreamwork, namely of returning to the dream's night-time journey for orientation and guidance is reflected in the present work in the concept of following the many-channeled process. He introduced me to alchemy and Taoism and together with his collaborator, M.L. von Franz, led me to the historical foundations behind process work.

Fritz Perls encouraged me through his games with the hot seat to extravert the unconscious and try to get away with it. Behaviorists such as Grinder and Bandler challenged me to discover the unconscious in their behaviorist's reality. Modern physicists like Richard Feynman indirectly helped me to understand that non-causal phenomena such as synchronicity require new concepts such as time reversal and anti-matter and that physics needs the psychology of the observer. Physicists such as Bohm and Finkelstein amazed me by implying that science was also searching for process theory. Einstein instigated my field theories and relativization of channels. Swami Muktananda made me realize that my fascination for process was equivalent to his worship of Shakti. I was just as surprised to find a verification and foundation for the idea of process work in Muktananda's Siddha Yoga as I was in finding this foundation in alchemy, Taoism and the mythology of time. Furthermore, Muktananda opened my eyes to the mythical emptiness of western body work.

Process science rests upon Jung's teleological attitude towards the collective unconscious, gestalt-oriented process work, Buddhist meditation, electronic communication theory and the phenomenological attitude of theoretical physics. Without these religions, psychologies and physical sciences, I could not have done my work. The present work has also grown out of the research presented in my *Dreambody* and *Working With the Dreaming Body* on the connections between dreams and body phenomena.

I am especially grateful to certain special seminar participants and co-workers in the Zürich, Switzerland, and Denver, Colorado, areas who joined me during the experimental phases of this work. Some of these people were Barbara Croci, Joe Goodbread, Nora Mindell, Max and Debbie Shüpbach, Carl Mindell, Roy Freeman, Pearl Mindell, Marilyn Raff, Glen and Jean Carlson, Amy Kaplan, Jean Claude and Giesela Audergon, Dawn Menken, Elke Müller, Julie Diamond, Urs Buttikoffer, and Victoria Herman. Special thanks to Jan Dworkin for her suggestions and critical reading of this work and to M.L. von Franz for her tireless interest in discussing the connection between psychological theory and empirical reality.

Part I
PROCESS AND CHANNELS

Chapter 1
INTRODUCTION

This text attempts to assemble the empirical events appearing in dream, body, relationship and synchronicity phenomena within one theoretical framework and related technique. The thesis of this book is that accurate observation of the dreaming process interweaving the background of these phenomena together with the ability to sensitively follow these observations allows processes to unfold in the richest and most useful manner as judged by the observer. *River's Way* suggests that information process concepts may be used as a basis for dealing with a wide spectrum of events now separately considered by the various forms and schools of medicine, physics and psychology.

In the first part of the book, basic information channels of human processes are discussed and related to recent developments in physics. Part II traces the roots of process ideas in mythology, alchemy and Taoism. The resulting development of observational, theoretical and practical techniques, called process-oriented psychology, should be considered as one possible suggestion for approaching psycho-physical events without changing professionals, schools of thought or nations.

An example
Consider a typical wide-spectrum human problem. Think of a woman who came to see me because she was terrified about dying from a breast tumor. The content of her conversation, the verbs she used and her body gestures

3

indicated that her process was flowing at the moment through her body. 'I feel this lump in my breast and am scared of the pain,' she said. But instead of feeling or experiencing this pain further, she decided to quickly pull up her blouse so that I could examine her tumor. When I hesitated and asked her why she was so quick to show me her breast she told me that doctors always asked her to take off her clothes. I asked, 'Why do you believe other people's ideas more than your own feelings about yourself?'

She immediately launched into a painful story about how she had always overvalued others' opinions about herself, and how she had tried a lot to gain the approval of men because she did not believe in herself. Spontaneously she told me a dream about a pair of lovers who had been beaten up, in part because they did not ask the world around them for approval. One of these dream lovers was apparently wounded in the chest. We then talked about the conflict between her own love feelings for herself and the disapproval of the world around her. We spoke about the possible connection between the dream and her tumor and then she put her hand on her chest to feel her conflict and wounding.

The next day her husband appeared for a session and attacked me for wanting to see her breast. He wanted to know if I wanted to sleep with her. In the midst of this session, his wife walked in and we continued the conversation as a threesome. After assuring him that I was not interested in his wife as a sexual partner, we worked on his affects and it turned out that he was interested in flirting with women but that his (inner) mother was angry at him for having sexual fantasies. The work focused upon him. As he worked she was moved to express many locked-up feelings about him. Something like a family-oriented psychotherapy evolved. They left very happily.

Now, let us go back to her once again, and examine her process. She first focused upon a somatic channel, her body problem. Then her relationship with me became an issue for both of us. She then moved into a visual channel and told me a dream and finally returned to her body at the end of the first session. In the next session, her husband appeared, and her problems reappeared, this time reversed and mirrored in him. Finally their communication became the focus of our work.

This woman's process moved through various channels in a typical wide spectrum of behavior. She would have lost something by sending her body to a surgeon (by the way, her tumor, probably a cyst, disappeared by itself several weeks after the session) one part of her to a family therapist, another part to a dream analyst and another part still to a massage salon. She had one process with many interconnected aspects.

I want to point out here that the various aspects of personal life which psychology has referred to until now as dreams, body life, relationship conflicts and illness, can be re-evaluated in terms of sensory-oriented channels such as proprioception, kinesthesis, visualization, audition and compositions of these channels. Instead of talking about terms such as psychotherapy, body work, dream work, analysis, family therapy, we can now speak of process work.

I would expect any well-trained psychologist to be able to deal with a multitude of situations. I would also expect him to let things transform as they want to and not try to organize them himself. To do this he will have to discover the pattern behind the process of a given individual situation and base his work upon the nature of this pattern and its flow. The process worker no longer needs preprogrammed psychotherapeutic strategies or other routine methods of dealing with people. As a process scientist he can follow any given individual or family situation by using observational accuracy to discover the nature of processes. He uses a wide-spectrum analysis which applies to situations in which he is alone, with one or more people or events. He listens to the verbs people use, watches their body motions, notices his own reactions, discovers those he tends to neglect and determines experiences and follows processes according to their distance from individual or collective awareness, the channels which they manifest and their time patterns. Thus he not only lets the river flow but appreciates its exact nature. Experience with a wide range of people both normal and 'psychotic', healthy and dying, children and adults, individuals and families indicates that empirically following individual and group processes can be learned and substituted for 'pre-packaged' therapeutic programs.

Sound like Taoism? Process work is modernized Taoism in the sense that the process worker tries to appreciate the flow of the river and to help clients adjust to this flow. In fact, as I was developing process science, I felt a bit Chinese myself. I understood Lao Tsu who wrote in Chapter 21 of this three thousand year old *Tao Te Ching*, that the greatest virtue is to follow the Tao even though it seems dark, dim and elusive. For within the Tao, there is reality and reason. Process is deep and essential in its orientation. Like Lao Tsu, the process worker is also in the dark about the ultimate origin of change, though unlike the great old master, he has modernized Taoism so that it can be applied to life in an exact and empirical way.

No wonder I dreamed the other night of Lao Tsu, who was staying up late working behind a printing press. The idea of the Tao is very old, and appears again and again wherever an effort is made to unify the sciences upon the basis of energy concepts and empirical observations.

UNIFYING MODERN PSYCHOLOGY

Already, many years ago the need for unifying psychology was felt and the hope for reconciliation expressed. Over thirty years ago Jung said the following.:

> I would remind you of the Liebault-Bernheim-Kreich method of suggestive therapy, reeducation de la Volonté; Babins Kils 'persuasion'; Dubois' 'traditional psychic orthopedics,'; Freud's psychoanalysis, with its emphasis on sexuality and the unconscious; Adler's educational method, with its emphasis on power drives and conscious fictions; . . . Each of them rests on special psychological assumptions and produces special psychological results, comparison between whom is difficult and often well-nigh impossible. Consequently it was quite natural that the champions of any one point of view should, in order to simplify matters, treat the opinions of the others as erroneous. Objective appraisal of the facts shows, however, that each of these methods and

theories is justified up to a point, since each can boast not only of certain successes but of psychological data that largely prove its particular assumption. Thus we are faced in psychotherapy with a situation comparable with that in modern physics where, for instance, there are two contradictory theories of light. And just as physics does not find this contradiction unbridgeable, so the existence of many possible standpoints in psychology should not give grounds for assuming that the contradictions are irreconcilable and the various views merely subjective and therefore incommensurable.[1]

Jung's early intuitions about the connections between psychology and physics and his amazing tolerance towards apparently contradictory psychotherapies are shared by many therapists today. It seems clear to me that as we approach the end of the twentieth century, the modern client's growing need to experience and understand the most extreme aspects of the personality is slowly being followed by the therapist's attempt to develop integrative process and energy theories in psychology. I expect this attempt to continue for a long time, for it is sorely needed.

Energy and process ideas in physics and psychology have been employed sporadically since the late 1960s to bridge the gaps in psychology created by nationality, sex and typology. We are not meditators or analyzers, with or without bodies, masculine or feminine, thinkers or feelers, dead or alive, but in varying degrees and at different times some impossible mixture of all these things. Stressing one aspect of the personality such as the development of the 'body' or the 'feminine' is obviously important at a given time in life. But stressing one aspect of the personality over long periods of time impoverishes another aspect and separates the individual as well as psychology into parts. This book should be understood as an effort at bridging unnecessary divisions in psychotherapy, medicine and physics.

This is also a good point to mention that after much reflection, I have chosen to use the unfortunate term 'he' in the sentences where I speak generally. I have done this because a simpler, neutral he/she term does not yet exist.

This is a sign, to me at least, that process concepts have not yet entered into our language. Future writers will certainly improve such linguistic defects.

The need to develop process concepts, however, is not based upon merely academic or theoretical considerations. Process is an empirical reality. Work with clients shows clearly that specific psychotherapies and medical rituals are definitely commensurable. In fact they are spontaneous creations which arise by amplifying events in given channels of the 'therapist-client' interaction even when the two are unfamiliar with these therapies. For example, if the process worker (kinesthetically) amplifies a client's repeated tendency to stretch, yawn and groan, specific postures from ancient yoga and modern bioenergetics appear as part of a fluid flow of events.[2] If he works verbally with the repressed sexual life of a theologian he will soon find proprioceptive experience which encourages the client to let himself enjoy pleasure along the lines of Wilhelm Reich.[3] If he works with the slow kinesthetic activity of a paralyzed person, processes mirroring the work of Feldenkrais appear.[4] A shy woman who visualizes violent encounters may have a process which switches from fantasy to violent interaction which one can find in restructuring processes used by Ida Rolf.[5] A client who uses her fingers to explain a migraine is indicating the specific proprioceptive process typical of acupuncture.[6]

If the process worker amplifies the tendency of a dreamer to speak to a particular dream figure during a dream report, then he develops a type of Black Elk dream ritual,[7] psychodrama[8] or active imagination.[9] A process worker observing the breathing of a homosexual man trying to cope with sexual excitement may rediscover Taoist Alchemy's transformation of energies.[10] A young person burdened by social conventions and parental complexes who tends to 'lose his mind in order to come to his senses' unravels the gestalt psychology of Fritz Perls.[11] A reflective woman in need of exact information about her behavior and conflict with her husband can create transactional analysis.[12]

A dying person's proprioceptive channel may use a binary system of communication with pain typical of the neurolinguistic programmer's 'reframing' method.[13] If you study the way parents talk about their kids you can develop behavioral psychology with its causal orientation and stimulus-response theory.[14] Let your clients bring their family members to their sessions, study their relationship channels and you create family therapy.[15] Trace a man's interest in connecting his dreams with his conscious problems, study the legends and myths typical of his dreams and you begin to rediscover Jungian psychology.[16] Follow parapsychology and you enter theoretical physics.[17] Move with your client, encourage his non-verbal expressions and you begin to develop dance therapy.

Thus it is useful but insufficient in process work to know the hundreds of therapy rituals because each of them appears spontaneously when the client's signals and therapy situation are followed. Process work cannot be described in terms of events because its structure and evolution are created from changing signals, channels and amplifications. Process work begins with whatever presents itself, the client's questions, problems in relationship, medical symptoms, stories of the day before, dream experiences or even the therapist's problems, and uses verbal processes, language content, body signals and environmental situations to determine the nature and evolution of the client-therapist interaction. Process work, accurately carried out, often reveals the meaning of dreams before they have been reported because the work deals with the living unconscious, that is dreaming phenomena occurring at the edge of the client's awareness.

Process work or any other psychotherapy succeeds only when the therapist is able to function in the client's momentary channel, and not because of the general validity of the therapist's education about that channel.

The therapist's successful feelings are not enough. Process science checks on the validity of its work by assessing the verbal feedback, the client's body responses and dreams.

As we approach the end of the twentieth century, psychology is blossoming in a dramatic fashion. Increasing understanding of the personality together with powerful therapeutic techniques are making it necessary for therapists trained in one specialty to increase their ability in other forms of work. It seems almost essential that a process orientation develops in psychology to unify research and practice. However, as energy theories become increasingly popular throughout the world of psychology, clarity and theoretical fundamentalness should also increase to prevent psychology from regressing backwards to shamanism.

The necessity for developing an accurate process work, though apparently obvious, will be a continuous challenge for therapists because it is not simple to have a beginner's mind and create or adjust the work to the flow of information occurring between client and therapist. Years of experience in training students and therapists from various schools of psychology have convinced me in the advantages and disadvantages of educational systems favoring one particular channel.

For example, 'process oriented' dance therapists tend to ignore relationship issues which arise with their clients, and are usually not strong in supporting a client's intellectual needs. Massage therapists are powerful in relating to the proprioceptive channels of their clients but are usually not trained to encourage verbal feedback or spontaneously arising movement processes. Dream-centred therapies often neglect dance and body experiences. Classical gestalt therapists will not support research; behaviorists do not listen to fantasies.

Thus specific belief systems, typological variations and previous education allow the therapist to become aware of only some of his client's signals. Knowing this limitation should help us remain humble and also to retain a beginner's mind when working with signals and channels which are different from the ones we may have studied. It is useful to remember that great advances in science have always occurred whenever new channels were added to accepted and predetermined categories in the face of empirical evidence which did not fit these categories. Today, there's so much of this evidence clustering around dying, physical illness, mental disturbances, parapsychology and relationship issues that we should feel free to doubt what we now know and to open up to more comprehensive frameworks of reference.

Chapter 2
ELEMENTS OF PROCESS SCIENCE

In this chapter I wish to give the reader a concise and general view of process theory.

PROCESS
I use the word process to refer to changes in perception, to the variation of signals experienced by an observer. The observer's personality determines which signals he picks up, which he is aware of and which he identifies himself with and therefore which he reacts to. The interaction between the observer and signals is discussed in greater detail in chapter 5.

A useful and naturally incomplete analogy in thinking about the term process is to compare it to a train and its stations. Process refers to the travels of this train. Sometimes observations begin with signals coming from Sick City, or Troublesville, sometimes from Happiness Town, sometimes from Death's corner. The observer gets on the train at these and other places and rides the train to wherever it takes him. Process is like a special train whose destination can not always be predicted. The observer follows the signals in his real life or in a fantasy trip as they reveal life to him.

PROCESSES AND STATES
The very idea of process contrasts with the idea of a fixed state, which is a static picture, an unchanging description of a situation which has been broken up into parts. Saying that the train process is in the state called Headache City or

Relationship Junction tells us that the process is in a certain state with a certain name. States are useful descriptions of processes. Claiming that a process is in Headache City, however, only tells us one of its states. If we get on the train where it is, in Headache City, it will go anywhere, anyplace its locomotive driver will take it.

Personal temperament of the researcher or client determines whether one focuses upon states, processes or both. Its seems essential to develop a process-oriented psychology which includes both. In process work, static unchanging conditions are defined as specific processes so that theory and practice closely follow living change and evolution. State-oriented psychology reduces living material to fixed patterns and programs. Thus, pressing a client's language into 'here and now' vocabulary, deciding to be helpful before meeting a client, wanting to heal without reference to the symptoms, or deciding relationships should be harmonious, then you are a state-oriented therapist who does not work with the changing processes which your patients may really have.

Of course, state-oriented psychology can be very valuable because its fixed routines give people the feeling of safety and predictability. Everyone needs at one time or another this stability. Thus your process may be, for a short time or even over a long period of time, working within a very exact and routine framework. State work becomes inadequate and inapplicable however, when stationarity gives way to flow and when given routines begin to inhibit experience.

PRIMARY AND SECONDARY PROCESSES

Processes can be static or moving. They can also be described as being closer or further from awareness. If I look at a train for example, I can see that it is, as a whole, running smoothly. Let us say that it has six cars and that at first sight all are moving nicely together. However at closer inspection we see that one of the cars has smoke coming out of one of its windows. We tend to ignore the smoke and say that the train is fine unless the smoke gets so heavy that it disturbs the whole train. Steady forward movement of the train is its primary process; its smoking caboose is its secondary process. People identify themselves with their intentions or primary processes. Secondary processes are experienced as being foreign and distant. For example, you may be a very sweet and decent person, as a whole. You identify yourself with your sweetness and decency. But every now and then you become a monster. This monster is something which happens to you. You feel it is not characteristic of you. As far as you are concerned, it just pops out of you every now and then. Being a monster is your secondary process. Being sweet is the primary one.

CONSCIOUS AND UNCONSCIOUS

It has been practical until now to use the terms conscious and unconscious for primary and secondary processes. Process science has to redefine these earlier terms because they are not always useful empirically in their present form. For example, in psychotic states, near death phenomena and deep body experiences the terms 'conscious and unconscious' become meaningless. So let us say that from now on consciousness refers only to those processes of which you are completely aware. When you are conscious, you notice the signals you are receiving, you are not simply receiving them but are aware of your awareness. In other words, you not only feel or see something, you are aware of the fact that you are feeling or seeing this something.

Unconsciousness refers to all other types of signal processes. Thus if I am absolutely aware of how I experience and know I am sweet and decent, then I am conscious of this process. Otherwise sweetness and decency cannot be controlled, I may even say that I know that I am sweet and decent, and yet be unconscious of how sweetness processes really overtake me. Then they are primary processes, they happen outside my control and are unconscious.

Nevertheless getting in touch with sweetness is going to be easier for me than getting in touch with my monster for it is secondary, it is much further away from my awareness. I do not identify myself with the monster. Hence every secondary process presents us with a sort of identity crisis.

However, the more aware and conscious we are the more we realize that we are a combination of many processes which may be occurring simultaneously or one after the other.

CHANNELS

Thus processes can be identified in terms of their being static or moving and also in terms of their being close to or far from our self identity. Another very typical and powerful way of differentiating processes is in terms of the signals in which they appear to us. For example, the ancient Chinese, whose culture was based upon the Tao or process of change, said that the Tao could manifest itself in essentially three channels, Heaven, Earth and Man. Modern psychologists have spoken about the personality in terms of mind, matter, psyche and more recently, relationships. Buddhist meditators speak in terms of senses which perceive specific signals, in terms of smelling, tasting, touching, hearing and seeing.

There is no one way of differentiating processes in terms of channels. It is important to realize that given channels reflect specific individuals and/or cultures. In this book, several types of channel systems will be discussed. The process scientist does not fasten himself to one particular channel system but is, theoretically, able to observe himself and a given situation and discover what channels his client or family situation is operating with. Thus he becomes fluid in his observational system and does not try to make a situation fit his categories of mind or body, especially when phenomena themselves may relativize his dimensionalizations. Thus for example, psychosomatic problems and parapsychological events make channels such as mind and body, matter and psyche look mystical because they are inappropriate tags put on events which come with other tags already on them.

The most common sensory channels appearing in one-to-one work with clients appear to be visualization, audition, body feeling or proprioception and body movement or kinesthesis. Other channels such as relationships are mixtures of these basic ones. In this book we shall focus mainly upon the basic channels and the amazing ability of processes to switch almost unpredictably from one channel to another. In a future work, I focus on the channels of couples, families and groups.

BASIC CHANNELS
Signals may be differentiated according to the perception sense which picks them up. Signals and processes are therefore channeled by our senses. We can therefore visualize, hear, we can feel with our bodies, we can sense movement, we can smell, taste and use combinations of these senses to apprehend signals and processes.

Channels are like the tracks upon which the process train moves, the potential directions of the river. We get on our train upon a certain track. If it leaves from Track 1, then our process may be manifesting itself through the channel of visualization. Track 2 is frequently hearing. Track 3 is body feeling, or proprioception and Track 4 for Americans and Europeans is usually kinesthesis, that is the sense of movement. Tracks 5 and 6 are generally compositions of the first four tracks. Smell and taste do not often play a significant role in the majority of processes and hence will not be discussed in detail in this work.

In any case your process may begin by getting on your train on Track 2, at Headache's Corner. At some point outside of town the train probably switches to Track 3 before it arrives in Peaceville. In other words, you began to follow your process when you got a headache. Internal dialogue may have been in the foreground of your awareness before you began to feel the pounding of your head and before your process began to give you some peace.

VISUALIZATION
Now let us look at the main channels which come up most frequently in one to one process work and discuss them in some detail. We shall be dealing with the basic channels, visualization, audition, proprioception and kinesthesis, the detailed or 'fine structure' of these channels and their combinations.

The visual channel is usually best developed and most familiar to us. We use our sight more than our taste or hearing. Vision gives us the ability to know things at great distance, it allows us to gain emotional distance from phenomena, it organizes what we normally call insight. The modern founders of psychology began their studies with what we are now calling the visual channel. Freud felt that the royal road to the unconscious was dreams. Jung pioneered in the study of images and the use of active imagination, a purposeful confrontation with these images which also includes audition that is listening to these images. Perls centered his work around dreams as well.

The process worker amplifies signals according to their channel and nature. Thus if a dream report stresses the color of an image, its intensity, content or story he will work with intensification of the color, intensity, amplifying its content with mythological images or encouraging the dreamer to tell more about the drama in the dream thereby gaining more courage to let the story unfold. He may also play a part of the dream and ask the dreamer to view the drama while he, the process worker, acts it out. In other words, the dream work depends very much upon how the dreamer tells the dream and what methods he uses while telling it.

The existence of process in the visual channel can be determined by the fact that the client's eyes or head move upward, by the client's use of sentences such as 'do you see', 'I need insight', or 'I am seen' or 'they look at me', or by the predominance of breathing movements located in the upper chest.

AUDITION

When the eyes move to the right or left, when sentences and statements such as 'listen to me, hear me, speak more loudly please, I can not hear you, that sounds nice, etc.' appear, or when body posture 'freezes' without the head going down, processes in the auditory channel are occurring.

Amplification of these processes occurs by increasing focus upon the tone in which sounds are being emitted, becoming aware of their tempo and rhythm, their musical nature, their verbal content, by determining the nature of internal dialogues, according to whether it is connnected to human or inanimate sources, etc.

PROPRIOCEPTION
Visual and auditory processes have been discussed in the literature more than proprioceptive and kinesthetic signals. The next chapter will therefore concentrate upon proprioception and kinesthesis.

Proprioception is usually indicted by predominance of stomach breathing, eyelid flutters (with closed eyes) or when the signaler speaks of feeling, pressure, depression, pain, joy, being turned off or on. This channel usually lies in the foreground of awareness when there are long periods of no talking coupled with eyes looking downwards; when the head drops, when people speak of falling or when hands touch painful areas. Amplification in the proprioceptive channel occurs according to the nature of the signal. The individual in a proprioceptive channel can intensify focus upon an inner feeling such as a stomach ache, sleeping foot or sexual excitement by not moving. Or the therapist can amplify pressures and pains by pushing, rolling, vibrating or lifting a body area, and observing how proprioception deepens and flows into other channels such as movement.

KINESTHESIS
Process work deals with kinesthetic activity by perceiving the nature of the movement or lack of movement in the face hands, legs and torso. Body energy often evolves from one motion into a posture, into other movements and dance or into other channels. Amplification may accur through mirroring movement, encouraging it verbally, actually touching and propelling the dancer, not talking or looking at him, or even by temporarily interrupting his movement.

THE FINE STRUCTURE OF THE BASIC CHANNELS
The signals which appear in the form of seeing, hearing propriocepting and the sense of movement differentiate

themselves in terms of what we may call, the 'fine structure of channels.' [I am thankful to Dr Joe Goodbread of Zurich for recommending this term to me.] People spontaneously tell you that they see things 'inside,' hear 'real' or 'outer' voices, experience other people 'feeling for them' or find that they can mix channels and see with their bodies for example. We can generalize these experiences by referring to signals as being introverted, extraverted, referred or mixed. Let me explain these terms in greater detail.

INTROVERTED SIGNALS
The introverted seer looks up into the air, gazes off into the distance or closes his eyes and says, while holding his breath, that he is visualizing some internal scene not necessarily seen by others. A person gifted in this mode of perception considers himself a fantasiful person, an artist or even photographer. He claims to see through things, may be a medium or mystic.

Introverted hearing picks up internal dialogue, particular voices from the past, though music and strange internal sounds often fill this channel as well. The introverted proprioceptor is highly aware of his internal body experiences and orients himself according to these. He knows when he is uncomfortable and adjusts himself accordingly. Introverted kinesthesis picks up dream-like movements and is aware of the tendency to move even before a limb has begun to tighten up or relax. Introverted kinesthesis refers to the experience of moving without actually having done anything with the body and is usually referred to as 'out of the body experience.'

EXTRAVERTED SIGNALS
Extraverted signals refer to information which is usually part of what the people around one call reality. The extraverted seer for example notices the colors and shapes of other people's clothes, he notices how people look when they are happy and sad. He can develop this function to pick up double signals in people's movement, and may use his internal visualizing capacity to even imagine what sort of

dream is being portrayed by movement which is not directly explained by the other person.

The extraverted hearing channel focuses upon the content of what others say, and is aware of the sounds of the natural environment. Thus function may be developed to also pick up the tempo and tonality of sound as well. Extraverted proprioception picks up the body experience of others through the medium of one's own touch. The masseur has usually developed the proprioceptive ability of his hands or elbows. Extraverted proprioception and kinesthesis usually are necessary for all non-verbal contact and sexual experience. Extraverted kinesthesis gives you a sense and ability to move in a congruent and graceful manner. Someone with little extraverted kinesthesis cannot throw a ball or may appear very awkward while walking and running. This person may not be able to follow someone else while dancing. This function is usually developed in early childhood, and later left untouched by conscious focus.

COMPOSITE SIGNALS
Physiology refers to the most common mixed signals as synaesthesia. Thus people on LSD sometimes hear with the bones in their legs, sometimes people say that they can see through their shoulders or the back of the head. Others claim to be able to dance with their eyes, visualize while simultaneously dancing and hearing internal music. The process worker may deal with these mixed phenomena by encouraging them to occur by using the same language with which they are described. In this way he deals with psychosomatic and parapsychological phenomena without having to call these phenomena by such complicated names.

Thus besides the fundamental channels called seeing, hearing, feeling, moving and their fine structures, there are other important channels which are compositions of these fundamental sensory perceptions. The special natures of these compositions may vary from person to person, yet the general quality of these compositions is that they can not be broken down into more fundamental components without disturbing the overall perception.

For example, you may say that you are highly aware of other people and that this awareness is based upon love without being able to say how you love in terms of seeing, hearing, moving, etc. Your loving awareness of people, or your ability to sense and relate to the natural environment are composite channel experiences, that is you can not break down your sense of awareness into more fundamental sensory perceptions without destroying your ability to perceive.

The layman's use of terms like 'awareness' and 'consciousness' frequently refer to composite channel experiences. Thus individual channels such as seeing, hearing and feeling may all be inextricably combined in such a way that they are insufficient to explain the overall composite perception.

Jung further differentiated these irreducible composite channel experiences in terms of the special abilities of consciousness he called, thinking, feeling, intuition and sensation.[1] Thus some people typically function with their thinking in perceiving others and the world around them, they tend to discover logical structures while other people feel the patterns as beautiful or awful in their environment. Intuitives sense the whole of something but cannot discover its parts while the sensation type apprehends the details, the objects and parts of a whole without being able to grasp the whole. The reader interested in the complete study of Jung's typology should refer to literature on this topic.[2] For the moment, let it suffice to mention only that all channels are a function of time and that at any given moment a new channel may be characteristic of the foreground of awareness.

RELATIONSHIP

The composite channel which I have termed, 'relationship' is referred to in discussions where people talk about another person with whom they are familiar as if this person were the central object of awareness. 'My husband is my big problem,' 'My girlfriend adores me,' 'My boss is constantly on my mind,' are statements which refer to extraverted aspects of relationships. The process worker deals with the extraverted relationship channel on the grounds of its basic nature and works together, where ever and whenever possible, simultaneously, with the outer person who is the focus of attention, together with the person making these statements.

Awareness in the relationship channel can be increased by noticing the client's behavior in the midst of relating to his partner. Alternatively the partner may be considered to be a channel for the client, or both partner and client may be understood as being channels for the relationship as a whole.

Introverted relating appears in dreams where one feels badly or is dealing with a dream figure in an inappropriate manner. Introverted relationship is then a function of gestalt imaginations or active imagination where one imagines or plays with the dream person as if it were a real person. A real outer person can be either an introverted or extraverted situation or process depending upon the client's experience of this person as being an inner problem, outer one or both. Trying to get a client to introvert a figure or work with the outer real person is thus a matter of the moment.

THE WORLD

When focus pays attention to the outer world, the universe, unfamiliar people, foreign objects and events, then we might speak of a world channel. Introverted relationship to the world occurs when people 'sense' outer events, communicate with others at a distance, or feel influenced by the universe without actually moving outside their bedroom. These people may also say that trees speak to them, that rocks and animals can be their friends and that the mother earth is their relative.

Extraverted relationship to the world is based upon actually working with outer events, objects and people, jobs and money problems, being able to fix machines, care for plants, and be interested in the ecology of the earth. Obviously, the world channel is not well developed by most Americans or Europeans who have little conscious experience, either internally or externally of the world around them, its suffering and needs. Probably this is why many people feel the world is negative or chasing them.

DIAGRAMS OF THE CHANNELS
It is fun and also instructive to place the main channels next to one another in the form of diagrams or lists. If we look at the first diagram on the next page we notice for example how channel theory makes it possible to differentiate and be more exact with earlier and vaguer terms such as mind, body and matter or world. The earlier term, 'mind' usually refers to seeing and hearing. The idea of body is usually a composition of feeling and moving. The universe is some composite channel which has meant the perception of family, nations and earth. Moreover, what has been referred to in general as consciousness and awareness either is a composition of this diagram or a specific aspect of it.

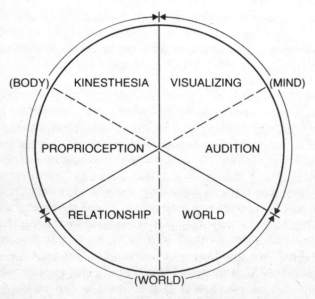

Diagram 1 *The channels*

MAIN AND UNOCCUPIED CHANNELS
What happens to the channels not occupied by your awareness? They are often filled in by other people or objects or bodies! Often people experience others as

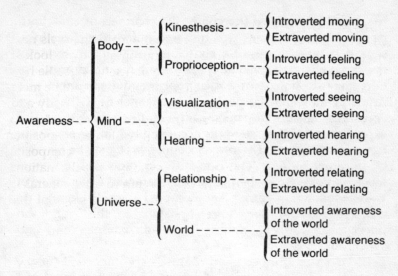

Diagram 2 *The fine structure of channels*

listening or seeing them. Other people are said to be able to feel for you, or they can move and do your activities when you feel paralyzed. If you make any of these statements then your hearing, seeing, body feeling and movement are 'unoccupied', that is you experience these channels as if they were in other people or objects. People who do not consciously use their eyes or ears usually experience these organs as if they were located in their friends or enemies. 'He sees me as I really am,' 'Only she can hear what I am truly saying,' 'My mother knows when I am hungry,' 'Thank God for my four-wheel-drive car, it can take me places I could never get by myself!' These statements indicate unoccupied sensory perception and can be worked with in practice by encouraging the creator of these sentences to imagine himself to be the person or object possessing his senses and to sense life through this person's or object's eyes, ears, etc.

At any given moment people identify themselves with particular channels, with their 'main' channels and tend to dissociate themselves from other channels. In the terms of

Jung, and in terms of the composite channels of consciousness, thinking types do not recognize their feelings, sensation types have little conscious intuition. In terms of the basic channels, visual types may have no proprioception, they do not occupy the proprioceptive channel. As a result phenomena happen in this channel as if they were occurring outside the personality of the visual type. He experiences body problems as occurring to him, as strokes of fate or as accidents. The proprioceptive type may be plagued by uncanny visions. The non-auditory type who does not focus on voices, may be plagued by paranoid experiences of voices following him. An occupied world channel is characterized by friendly relationships to the world, an unoccupied world channel is filled with fateful events and synchronicities.

The main and unoccupied channels are important for the process worker for if he can determine which channel is a primary one and which the unoccupied or secondary, then the main channel can be used to integrate irrational secondary processes. An unoccupied channel will bring the client the most powerful and uncontrolled experience. I will talk more about the main and unoccupied channels in the following chapters. Here, let me mention only that a visual type will need a language filled with visualizations in order to understand his body experiences, an auditory type will have to get the world to speak to him, a person suffering the wanton behavior of the world will need literal help in dealing with the transportation or job situation of a given city. A proprioceptor with little kinesthesia will suffer from broken limbs, an unoccupied relationship channel will be characterized by loving and hating processes originating outside the individual.

Total awareness and individuation or self-completion implies developing one's ability to pick up and deal with signals coming from all the channels. Processes often get blocked or stale-mated when people identify with only one or two of the above mentioned channels or with only their primary processes.

AMPLIFICATION

The most powerful tool of the process worker is his ability to determine the evolving structure of processes, i.e. their channels, primary and secondary characteristics. His second most useful tool is his ability to work with signals in their own various channels, to amplify these signals and bring them closer to awareness. The exact nature of amplification depends on the individual client, therapist and the channel. There is no one set of techniques which will fit every situation. Part of the creativity of process work is learning the methods of amplification implied by the signals themselves.

For example, one way of amplifying a visual signal is by encouraging the individual to see more exactly what is happening. Introverted proprioception may be amplified by encouraging the client not to listen, look or feel anything outside himself. Kinesthesis may be amplified by encouraging movement without looking or listening. Working with the extraverted relationship channel may be encouraged by telling the client not to pay attention to himself, etc.

EDGES AND CONGRUENCE

The point at which the client says, 'that I cannot do, or will not do', is the point where he has reached an edge. He may not be able to look at something, hear a certain voice or noise, make a certain movement, or feel a specific feeling like sex. He may not want to pay attention to a particular person in his environment, or deal with the world. The borders, the limits, the boundary of his personal ability tells you where his growing edge lies. Process work deals with the edge by staying near it, by switching channels and going around it, by letting it be, by jumping over it or by whatever means achieves positive feedback from the client.

The edge splits processes up into primary ones which the client identifies himself with and secondary ones which he feels are not directly associated with him. The edge contributes to making the individual congruent and incongruent or split. A visual person, for example, may not identify himself with his body feelings. Thus, when he gets a stomach ache, he refuses to realize his stomach is aching until it has become so severe that it incapacitates him. He says, his body is unimportant or that it cannot be felt and thus creates an edge which splits off his proprioception which then appears as a secondary phenomena which happens to him. He becomes incongruent insofar as he experiences two processes, one which he likes and is aware of, namely his visualization and another which he does not like, his stomach ache! Edges which continue for long periods of time develop into blocks and are associated with psychosomatic problems, apparently because information not consciously picked up is always rerouted through the body.

SECONDARY PROCESS AND DOUBLE SIGNALS

Recall that the signals of which you are barely aware are secondary processes. While thinking, scratching can be a secondary process. While talking, the tone and tempo of your voice are likely to be secondary. These secondary processes become double signals when they are incongruent with primary processes. If you tell me you agree with me but simultaneously shake your head indicating 'no', then your head is giving me a double signal, a second message which is not congruent with the verbal yes. If you were to say 'yes' and nod accordingly then the secondary process would be congruent with the primary one and there would be no double signal but one central message instead.

Double signals are natural, normal human phenomena which occur as disturbances in communication with yourself and with someone else as well. They are a combined product of your spontaneous creativity, of the existence of channels which are not at your disposal, of conscious inhibitions and of your inability to admit paradox. Some double signals occur at the perimeter of your awareness, some are further away. An accurate process scientist discovers these double signals and amplifies them or their relationship to primary processes; he then works with the edges involved in the split.

DREAMS AND PROCESSES

One of the most exciting discoveries of process science is that the evolution which results from amplifying primary and secondary processes is always mirrored in dreams. Thus, process work is living dreamwork in the sense that when we work with the total process of an individual, we are working with his dreams. This discovery gives rise to the concept of the dreambody,[3] namely the idea that your secondary body processes such as illnesses and symptoms appear in dreams. Moreover, since secondary processes can appear in the form of double signals we can see the dreaming process in others as well and even guess their dreams.[4]

An example

Let us say for example that you are a visual type of person with little body awareness and that proprioception is a weak and unoccupied channel for you. Thus your feeling and movement may be projected upon or occupied by your car, for example. In any case, you are comfortable with visualization and organize your life accordingly.

One night you dream that your car is worn out and that a cop arrests you for driving a car which is not in order. The morning after the dream you awake feeling a bit ill, you have a stomach ache which you neglect, you have an edge against proprioception and think that it is less important than your plans for the day. You see yourself going shopping and thus you make the plans to go and ask the kids to join you. While you are talking to them you barely notice the double signals you are sending out, the signals related to your stomach ache. The kids see the pained expression on your face of which you are not aware and decide not to come. You get angry at them and have a fight and leave. On route to the store your unconscious proprioception, that is your stomach ache, amplifies itself until you get so sick that you are forced to go home. Symbolically speaking, a cop caught you with a worn out car and sent you home. If you do not occupy your proprioception, he will!

If you were a process worker and had no edge against

your body, you would have realized that you were worn out and you would have realized the meaning of your dream. You would have amplified your secondary processes, your stomach signals, perhaps put them together with your primary process, your visual plan to shop, and communicated more congruently with the kids and had a better day.

SUMMARY OF CONCEPTS
The message of this tale is, be aware. These two words have been recommended by wise gurus since the beginning of time. Awareness could be a one-word book. Print it and send it around. The reason however why this wonderful recommendation has never quite succeeded is that people have edges against certain forms of awareness. Thus if you do not differentiate processes and signals into primary and secondary, and if you do not tell people about the channels and states they express they will 'forget' that such states exist!

Being a phenomenologist, a process scientist is a sort of a mystic and an empirical, rigorous scientist in one. He determines the existence of channels whose exact nature may never be completely understood and thus works with phenomena whose ultimate origins may even be unthinkable. Thus he discovers, without understanding why, that process flows like a river from one channel to another around edges, over objects, and ravines which only miracles could breach. He tries to follow the course of the river and adjust himself to its flow. He listens carefully to sentence structure, watches body signals, uses his hands to feel the dance of life and his imagination to explain his own responses.

When primary and secondary processes agree he speaks of congruence but when they are split off into double signals, body symptoms and communication problems he respects incongruity and satisfies himself with letting them be. In a world where the processes of nature such as sickness and health, death and life, love and hate remain outside his manipulation, he creates his own systems of belief, and leaves others to theirs. He lets nature show him the way and may even support unsolvable and painful situations without deluding himself with the naive superstition of the 'modern world' that personal and astronomical events are under his control.

Chapter 3
BODY CHANNELS

There are many processes which clients describe and experience which seem to have little or at least in the moment nothing to do with anyone else but themselves. Thus the world channels play a negligible role in these processes. Relationship channels and natural events are not essential parts of the work. In these situations we can talk about dreambody work by which we mean that the client's process remains in the visual, auditory, proprioceptive and kinesthetic channels. For study purposes then it is convenient to talk about these four channels together. In the following two chapters relationship and world channels are discussed.

When someone centers on a dream or body problem, then the process worker can assume that the relationship channel does not play a central role if there is no particular difficulty between process worker and client. When someone says that he wants to work on a dream then I make an attempt to notice just how the dreamer indicates that the dreamwork is to be done. I follow his primary process, that is his conscious problems and specific interests in a certain type of dreamwork, but I also pay strict attention to the method which the dreamer indicates while he is telling me the dream.

If he starts to speak with the dream figure while telling his dream then something like gestalt work or active imagination with that dream figure is likely to gain positive feedback on that part of the dream from the dreamer. If he stresses a certain word, uses a foreign term, stutters while saying a phrase or giggles while mentioning something, then I ask him to associate, fantasy about or amplify that particular work or phrase. If the dreamer is not able to do any of these things, or if he asks about the meaning of a certain situation or figure, then I might use Jung's idea of mythological amplification employing impersonal information to elucidate that specific part of the dream. If the dreamer unconsciously ~ts out certain parts of the dream, that is if he begins to ᵕ.ow me what happened in the dream while telling it, then I might begin by asking him to recreate those postures and start from there.

Frequently the dreamer will put his hand on a particular part of his body, or move closer or further from me during his dream reportage. Repeating these gestures and move-ments is often revealing. Often the dreamer is not even primarily interested in his dreamwork. Then he tells the dream while double signalling. This means he sends out facial expressions or body gestures which give me incon-gruent information unrelated to his reportage. Then I begin with this incongruence in such cases.

The point I am trying to make is that I attempt to pick up the signals of the total process, and encourage partial verbal statements, incomplete body motions, and inconsistencies to unfold and reveal their entire messages. In this way dreamwork becomes ritualistic respect of the total per-sonality's attempt to express and become itself.

Now I would like to give some specific examples of process work which focuses upon the flow of events happening in the moment. The reader who is looking for the more conventional type of case history should keep in mind that my focus here is not upon the client's entire life story or healing process. These aspects of psychology are important too and appear in process work when the client shows a spontaneous interest in telling his history or in asking me to help him recover from some illness or neurosis (of his definition). I neither encourage nor discourage such interest nor do I define my role in terms of healing or enlightenment.

As I have said before, I focus upon gaining positive verbal

and non-verbal feedback from the client and have discovered that this occurs most frequently when I let his
process and my momentary situation define the so called
'therapy situation'. Other forms of work seem to resist
nature, they exhaust the therapist and give the client the
experience of being misunderstood. Consider Ron.

RON'S MUSIC

Ron is middle aged and suffers from depression. I have not
seen Ron for a long time. As I enter my office he is already
sitting on the floor and comments to me that I seem to be
really happy. He claims that he is depressed. When he
begins to tell me about his depression I notice that his voice
is very melodious, in a way which I have not heard before.
He prefers not to pick up my comment on his voice, and
insists that we work on one of his dreams.

He tells his dream like a story. 'Once there was a flute
player who loved his flute. My connection to the flute was
like the connection between matter and psyche.' I noticed
that he enjoyed talking about the dream and I asked him to
go on talking, to tell me a story about this dream. Though
he was depressed he picked up my recommendation and
told me about the flute player and his instrument in such
detail that he even began to act out certain motions of the
playing during his recitation. As he repeated these kinesthetic motions several times I recommended that he play
more, and before long he became the flute player and began
singing a lovely but sad tune. He finished, saying that he
felt really well, that his life was meaningful and that he was
not depressed because he got in touch with his deepest
feelings.

PROCESS ANALYSIS

Ron's primary process was centered upon worrying about
his depression. His secondary process appeared in the
double signal of his voice (its melodiousness) and in the
figure of the flute player and the flute. By following his
interest in talking about his dreams, he began to do active
imagination with the dream figure by telling me a story

about this figure. Finally, by picking up on the musician's motions which Ron made while telling me the story it was possible for him to consciously connect to the musician in himself and with his own voice. This latter phenomena was gestalt-like in the sense of identifying with the motions of the dream figure. However, if I had asked him to do so in the beginning he could not have sung. Such a request would have skipped his interest in story telling. His process went through several channels according to an order which was characteristic of his particular situation, his and my psychology as well. In this process oriented dreambody work Ron's dream pictorialized the double signals in his voice. By following the channels of his process he was able to become more congruent, and then his depression lifted. By consciously occupying his own auditory channel, he had a strong experience, i.e. an awareness of his total self.

SAM'S INTROVERSION

Sam sat down and said that he was so tired that before he could speak he needed to close his eyes for a minute. Then I noticed that he moved his shoulders back and forth like people sometimes do when there is something frustrating them. I told him to amplify the motion until he said that something bothered him in (the pectoral muscles of) his chest. As he was moving his shoulders back and forth very gently I recommended that he do this with greater awareness. What happens, I said, when you move your shoulder a millimeter forward or a millimeter backwards? Immediately he said that moving forward was like being nice to people and moving backwards was moving into himself.

I let him make these motions spontaneously himself for a few moments until he suddenly made a discovery. He said, with excitement 'When I move backwards I can also be there for the other person, even though I am centered in myself.' This discovery was important to Sam who then told me how, as a therapist, he gets so tired by focusing upon others all the time. Before he left he told me a dream. In the dream a man was withdrawing from the sea into a house, and was throwing a tank of benzine back into the water. His two friends who stayed near the seaside saved the tank in the last minute.

In this work we see something which frequently happens in dreambody work. We can guess the dream from the body work. His dream tells us what we have already discovered. As a therapist, his introverted nature is fed up with extraverting and being open to others. Thus this part of him withdraws into his pectoral muscles and tends to make him introvert and meditate. From this comes a tank full of energy which is thrown into his work with others. That is why he gets so tired. The dream shows the possibility of saving this tank. In the work he learned to hold back his extraversion by introverting while extraverting, sitting back and then coming forward when he is ready.

In this work we see that Sam was interested primarily in talking to me but his proprioception stopped him. He had to sit back. His secondary process was withdrawing, his kinesthesis was unoccupied by his awareness. Working in a gentle way with movement, creating awareness through small motions, would be typical of the Feldenkrais method of body work. The important channels of this work were proprioceptive and kinesthesis. Through movement we investigated his 'housing' that is his withdrawing in order to be centered in his relationship to others.

In Sam's work we see that process work, follows the dreaming process. The dream itself can be used in Sam's work as a summary or a pictorialization of body processes. The dream, it seems, is a process trying to happen. Its symbols refer in part to body experiences which are trying to reach awareness.

ESTHER'S DEVIL

As Esther and I began to chat, she put her hand on the back of her head and told me that she had a hard time sleeping the previous night because she had 'pressing' pains in her neck shooting down to her lower back. She repeated her hand motions several times. Thus I decided to repeat them consciously with her. I said, 'Let me put my hand on your back or neck and you tell me where it belongs.' In doing so I was using her body wisdom, her proprioception to direct my hand to do things her hand was trying to do. Once my hand was on her back she told me to put it on her neck. I asked her how much I should press. She directed me to press more and more, until I was practically pressing her to the floor, exerting a lot of pressure on her neck.

Once her head was on the floor, she spontaneously told me that I was acting like one of her dream figures, a devil who was throwing her into a hole, in a dream. Once she had a clear visualization of the devil pressing her down, once her channels had switched from the pressure to the dream picture, we switched roles and she showed me how the devil pushed her to the floor. After a while the 'devil' said flatly, 'Either you take me with you when you go out or you will have to remain in a hole.' It turned out that she was learning to be more instinctive and honest in public. She was either too sweet or else absent. So I asked her to realize her dreambody work right there and then with me and to be devilishly honest with me about what she liked and disliked. This work then switched into the relationship channel.

In the work we see an interesting aspect of body behavior. Her backache and hand motions were angry reactions to herself because she was not honest, she was too sweet. Her backache was like a dream, a devil, trying to reach consciousness and tell her to be more direct. We could say that her body was dreaming through the medium of the backache. This dream appears in the proprioception of pain and in the double signal of the hand motion. All incompleted motions of the hands and feet are secondary unconscious signals, dream figures trying to express themselves more completely.

Esther's work is an example of working with incomplete hand motions, proprioceptive experience, dialogue and visualization. It is a work in which we see that the body itself creates pain as if it were a devil trying to get Esther to change.

In process work the dream is frequently explained by the

dreamer herself whose understanding is based upon having fully experienced the dreaming process. Interpretation is something which often forces itself upon the dreamer, it is not an intellectual exercise which must be struggled for mentally. Movement and proprioception are the business of the individual dreamer, and can not be organized according to the programs of the therapist. In many cases process work occurs simultaneously with physical healing. But even when this is not the case, body work reveals to the dreamer the meaning of the symptoms; and the experience of what they are trying to achieve.

RUTH'S GOD

Ruth came in complaining of severe headaches. She told me that the doctors wanted to operate on her brain because the computer scans indicated a growth in that area. Recently she has had epileptic seizures. There was a lot of fear expressed with her talk, her face looked like she was in a lot of pain. She told me a 'big dream' in which she met an angel who healed her. In the dream she went up to heaven in a sort of ascension.

The pain in her head got to be so severe while we talked that we switched from talking about the dream to her body experience. There was a great pain in her head, she said, or she put her hand on her head. I put my hand on her head and asked her to direct my hand to the exact place, and to indicate the exact pressure which her body needed.

As we began this 'body' work, I was pressing her head. She asked for more pressure. Then she started to put her own hand on her head again so we switched roles. I asked her to verbalize what she experienced as the 'pressure maker' making pressure on my head. He said, 'Go internal, be still.' After a moment, her pressure disappeared and she felt well. 'Light,' she said. 'I feel light.' Enjoy your ascension,' I said, 'and be quiet.'

In the next hour she began by being meditatively quiet. After a moment her eyes looked up. I asked her what she saw and she said that she saw a child. I told her to look. She moved her shoulders as she described the child, and I noticed this and told her to move like the child. After a moment the child looked upward. I asked her what she saw and she said she saw a loving god. Then, 'Oh, I remember a dream I had in which a child, full of belief, puts its head into the mouth of a threatening dog. Though she is afraid that the child will be eaten, the dog who is at first threatening, becomes loving. The child, dreamer and dog then play together and hug.' After she told me the dream she looked down. I asked her what she then felt. She said she felt like hugging. She said her dream meant that when she believed in God she knew she would not be killed by his rage against her.

The 'child' dream appeared in the midst of the process work and gave Ruth a feeling for the dreaming process and the experience of the dream which she had had. Thus, she understood it herself. The dream gives her a picture of what is trying to happen. In her is a child who naively believes in God and in spirits. This child is protected from the ravenous dog, which she said was a guardian of the gates. I asked her of what gates. 'The gates of God,' she said.

If the child would not believe in God, then the dog would become angry supposedly, and then the dreambody would eat her up. I often observed how death appears as a ravenous animal, in people with cancer, eating up its victims. In this dream, however, the death process had the potential of being reversed, apparently because the 'dog' is angry at her 'child' who believes in spirits. This healing potential was realized and Ruth's health improved.

Here healing, belief, dream and body work are integrated. Visualization was interchanged for proprioception, kinesthesis, then play, renewed memory of a dream and insight, etc. The dreamwork was completed in a way before we heard the dream.

Ruth's primary process was focused upon the life and death situations around her illness. The secondary processes, however, were concerned with the child and the experience of God's power. Process work combines both primary and secondary phenomena by focusing upon the fear of death but also upon the exact nature of the symptoms and their channels.

I make no reference to the explanation or examination of body chemistry or its relationship to dreams. Nor do I attempt to give a final account of what process 'really' is. This phenomenological attitude toward body work is derived from noticing that feedback is best, both in the moment of the work and at a later date, when staying very close to experience and awareness.

It was important to this client that her symptoms radically improved. Thus it was important for me to accept her primary process, her fear of these symptoms as a crucial part of her entire situation. However, it can also be important for the process worker to remember that health and illness are normally cultural concepts belonging mainly to collective definitions and rarely describe a client's secondary processes.

There are indications that a process-oriented approach to the body is beginning to take root in medicine as well as psychology. For example, the physician, Larry Dossey, uses the physicist, David Bohm's, holomovement theory of the universe to show that present concepts of health and disease belong to an outmoded Newtonian era.[1] According to Dossey, 'the body behaves more as a pattern and process than as an isolated and non interacting object. It cannot be localized in space and its boundary is essentially illusory.[2] And later, 'Connected as we are to all other bodies, comprised as we are of an unending flux of events themselves occurring in spacetime, we regard ourselves not as bodies fixed in time at particular points, but as eternally changing patterns for which precise descriptive terms seem utterly inappropriate.'[3] (pp. 142-9)

Dossey's concept of the body reflects the theory in physics that an 'implicate order' exists which manifests itself in 'explicate phenomena'[4] by 'enfolding' itself through the work of some perceiver. Thus process-oriented psychology is a concrete realization of the physicist's theory, one method of allowing dreaming or implicit order to unravel itself through the awareness, discipline and courageousness of the observer.

Practical reality, however, requires the process worker,

interested in perceiving and 'enfolding' 'implicate orders,' to have a wide range of experience and as much knowledge about 'subjective' human signals as possible. It is difficult to convey the precise nature of these signals on paper because many are non-verbal and because discipline is required to pick them up. Practical demonstration, personal experience, training seminars and the use of video equipment are useful aids in developing this discipline.[5] A very rough estimate of the amount of detailed knowledge required to pick up these signals predicts that knowledge of over five hundred commonly occurring body motions, gestures, facial expressions, hand motions, eye movements and breaths as well as an innumerable number of language constructions is required to achieve sufficient contact with a client's dream and body processes. And when these signals and methods of working with them are mastered, unknown channels and processes always seem to appear to humble the elation of first successes.

Chapter 4
RELATIONSHIP CHANNELS

One of the client's most complex and central channels is the therapist himself. The relationship between two people is called transference, which Freud originally meant to connote the projection of infantile problems onto the therapist. Jung took transference processes out of the Freudian, reductive setting and showed with the use of alchemical symbolism just how the transference implied not only the projection of family figures but also a host of other images such as the shaman, the wise old man or woman, the divine child and the great witch onto the therapist.[1] Jung indicated how relationship problems such as those which occurred during analysis took place in a collective 'bath', a milieu in which one could no longer divide the therapist's individuation process, his complexes and conscious problems from those of the so-called patient.

Relationship appears differently in different psychologies. Gestalt's Fritz Perls spoke of 'confluence', the flowing together of two individuals in such a way that the processes of the one became indistinguishable from the other.[2] For Perls relationship was a process of differentiating personal from collective events creating and destroying boundaries.[3]

Transactional analysis defines relationships in familiar terms such as parent-child, adult-adult and child-child.[4] Modern neuro-linguistic programmers practice Freudian theory in so far as personal relationships between the individual and therapist are avoided because they create dependence.[5] Behavioral therapists also avoid the trans-

ference as an unnecessary part of counseling.[6] Jung indicated some of the possible reasons why the therapists avoid
the transference.[7] He says that therapists crawl behind their
shields as doctor and healer when they have not worked
through certain problems and when they are therefore in
danger of falling into affects such as loving, hating and
getting turned on or off by the patient. Such therapists
develop methods partially in order to avoid their own
affects. Sitting behind a desk or method is essentially the
same; both shield one from the onslaught of projections,
and unpredictable processes.

DREAMED-UP PROCESSES
The transference is complicated by the confusing situation in
which there are two human beings interacting with one
another as two inextricably coupled systems which simultaneously behave as if they were one process. Every time a
dreamer tells a dream, the dream interpreter typically has
reactions to the dreamer, which dream figures have towards
the dreamer himself. These reactions occur before, during
and even after the dream is told. The reactions of the
therapist are 'dreamed up' so to speak by the dreamer.

For example, a dreamer who has difficulty appreciating
herself invariably dreams up real people to love her and
dream figures to care for her. A man who is blown up out of
proportions about his abilities, dreams up police to hold him
down and therapists who cut him down. A woman who is
unconscious of her own power gets into violent fights in her
dreams and manages to practically destroy a battery of
therapists. Yet she still feels weak.

Dreamers in need of body awareness dreaming of sex and
contact, dream up body therapists and massage techniques.
In other words, specific therapies can be dreamed up by the
dreamer without the therapist ever realizing that the reason
his method works is because it is the dreamer's process.
Most therapists rarely consider that their therapies and
reactions are subject to the dreamer's dream-field or that
they could be the creations of a collective unconsciousness.

I do not want to go into the mechanics of dreaming up

here as they are mentioned elsewhere.[8] Suffice it to say that the majority of dreamed-up reactions occur because the therapist has not consciously picked up the client's double signals and therefore reacts to them without even realizing what his reactions are due to. These double body signals are dreamlike, they are unconscious to the client and call forth communications and reactions in the therapist just as they call forth similar reactions in the client's dreams. However, there are some situations which are parapsychological in the sense that people can be dreamed up at such a distance that double signals cannot be spoken of. These dreamed-up phenomena have no simple causal explanations in terms of visual, auditory or proprioceptive communication based upon the speed of light, of sound waves, or of electro-magnetic fields.

The central point of the present discussion is that phenomenologically speaking we must conclude that many of the therapist's so-called counter-transference reactions to his client are dreamed up, that is they belong primarily to the dreamer's process and can be located there in terms of his dream figures. The therapist has unwittingly become an expression or channel of the client's process, a channel carrying signals and messages which the client is not aware of in himself and which he may not care to become aware of. The therapist becomes a part, so to speak, of the client's dreambody.

An example

Consider the situation of a client of one of my students. She had been complaining to him for months that she was plagued by feelings of self-hatred, without getting to the bottom of these feelings or changing them. It seemed as if her negative dream figures had been dreamed up in the environment and she now experienced unbearable hatred from her friends. My student admitted to me that he too was beginning to dislike her, without knowing why. He showed me a video-tape of a discussion with her and we soon found the problem. He began to dislike her when she sent out signals of inflation. In other words, his negative feelings were dreamed-up reactions to her signals of inflation. As soon as he realized this he understood himself to be a channel for her dreaming process, and could sympathize more completely with her negative dream figures. They came into being together with their dreamed-up counterparts in this woman's reality in order to balance her inflation.

PROJECTION AND DREAMING UP

As long as the therapist has a reaction which is short-lived and lasts only as long as he is in the vicinity of the client, we can speak of a purely dreamed-up reaction. If, however, this reaction lasts longer than the time of the interview, or if it was present even before the session, we must also consider the possibility that the therapist is unconsciously projecting something of himself onto his client in addition to being simultaneously dreamed up by the client.

Projection may be differentiated from dreaming up. If the therapist has a strong reaction to the dreamer which is long lasting and which cannot be found in the dreamer's dream or body work, then we must assume that the therapist has a projection onto the client, which belongs primarily to the therapist. We speak of dreaming up when the therapist has no affects before, after or as soon as the dreamer has integrated and understood his dream material.

Relationship processes are complicated by the fact that dreaming up and projecting often happen simultaneously in both parties. For example, a therapist may feel that his client should be developing more feeling while the client resists this change because he feels it is not right for him. The client dreams that he is plagued by a negative figure who is trying to make him into a feeling person while the therapist dreams about developing more feeling. Here, the therapist has become a negative figure for the client while the client has become a negative dream figure for the therapist who himself is in need of more feeling. Both are projecting and dreaming each other up!

WORKING WITH DREAMING UP

Process science thus empirically discovers that the therapist can be a channel for the client and vice versa. Since process work proceeds by amplifying the strongest signal occupying the foreground of awareness, if the therapist's reactions prevail, then these reactions must be amplified until processes begin. His reaction may then unleash something in the client who may then enter into his dream process more completely.

As soon as the therapist's process is incorporated into the work, therapy changes as roles such as doctor-patient, healer-healee disappear temporarily while process creates and annihilates, rebuilding the relationship on a firmer groundwork than before.

If relationship is not allowed to transform into a process, work becomes rigid and boring. The patient then frequently and correctly accuses the therapist of misunderstanding or authoritarianism while the therapist devises some sort of lame excuse for dismissing his client's reactions.

RESPONSIBILITY

The idea of projection places most psychological responsibility for affective processes upon the person making the projection and secondarily upon the individual who may and usually does have some sort of little 'hook' for this projection.[9] 'Dreaming up' places responsibility upon both parties. In the extreme case in which the therapist has nothing in his dreams reflecting the client's behavior and in which the client dreams of the therapist's affects, we must put responsibility for relationship problems upon the dreamer, even if he is a passive and apparent victim of the therapist's emotions.

I have been speaking of the client as if he is the dreamer. The reader should realize, however, that the therapist can also dream up strong love and hate reactions from the client, the so-called transference, simply because the therapist either loves himself insufficiently or because he possesses inadequate self-criticism.

CONTROLLED ABANDON

It takes courage to let yourself be a potential channel for someone else. Someone will always argue against 'letting things happen,' expressing reactions and abandoning the normal therapeutic framework in which a therapeutic program determines more or less what happens. For example, the argument goes that letting in the therapist's unconscious will swamp the dreamer or present him with a reaction he is not ready to receive.

CAUSALITY IN RELATIONSHIP

In a world where projection and dreaming up occur, we can say that every signal causes everything or that causality is insignificant. In other words people have not caused your problems but have rather become channels for your process—or vice versa.

In Diagram 3, pictures 1 and 2, we see how the dreamer may dream up the world of which the therapist is part, just as the therapist can dream up a client. Since, however, one person is not usually dreamed up by another without having some sort of unconsciousness, we have to consider two or more interacting dream fields as in picture 3. Since we cannot say to whom a dream belongs we can add the effect of two or more dream fields and arrive at picture 4. Here you see one field whose center is nowhere or rather at infinity. This implies that both dreamer and interpreter are part of a universal process, which uses both people as channels.

An example

An interesting demonstration of primary and secondary processes, projection, dreaming up and the universal field is reflected in Ruth's relationship with her husband David. David and Ruth have come to me because they are in the midst of a four- or five-month long battle. Ruth yells wildly that David has no respect for her interest in quietness and privacy. According to Ruth, David is a wild and exciting but insensitive person who in his profession as an entertainer and as a man at home is capable of waking up the dead.

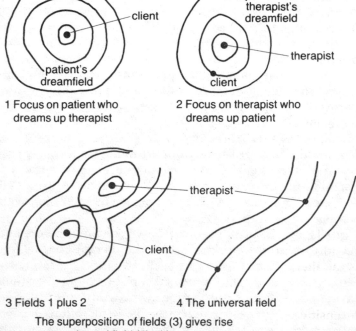

1 Focus on patient who
  dreams up therapist

2 Focus on therapist who
  dreams up patient

3 Fields 1 plus 2

4 The universal field

The superposition of fields (3) gives rise
to a universal field (4) without center.

Diagram 3

David, who doesn't notice her wild yelling, can hardly
understand what Ruth is talking about. He claims that he is
decent and quiet at home and has no interest in disturbing
anybody for any reason whatsoever. Ruth's primary process
and David's primary process are both being quiet and
decent. Ruth's secondary process is projected onto David.
Her secondary process is being wild, insensitive, noisy,
exciting and tense.

The reason that I say that she projects this upon him is
because when I asked her to play him she jumped up and
down, ran around, and was excited, noisy and insensitive,
naturally hoping while she was playing to provoke him and
to make fun of him. However, when I asked her to meditate

upon her behavior while she was doing it she said in fact that she herself was the way she had described David when she is without him in public. There she experiences herself as trying to get the center of attention, jumping around, being wild, exciting and full of tension. As the conversation between David and Ruth proceeded she acted extremely sensitively and quietly, sitting in her chair as prim and pretty as could be. The quieter and more decently she behaved in her conversation with David, the wilder and more impossible he seemed to become. David was being dreamed up to behave like her secondary process in part because she has too little relationship to this process. He is being provoked to compensate for her one-sidedness.

On the other hand, when David was alone, sitting and talking to me in another session, he tended himself to behave as he described himself, quietly, sensitively and related to what was happening. However, in one of the dreams he told me, Ruth was just as wild as could be. Naturally he was surprised by this dream because he does not see either her wild double signals or his own wildness. Thus we could say that he dreams her up to be wild and insensitive in part because he himself has little awareness of this side of himself, since he has more contact than she with wildness and he doesn't project it yet or have psychosomatic symptoms around it. So here's a case in which projection and dreaming up were happening in both partners simultaneously. I'm not going to say more about them right now, more about their history or how I worked with them, because I want to center simply upon the processes of dreaming up and projecting and the common field between them. This dream field is organized by the polarity between decency and wildness. Both David and Ruth are channels for a common dream-field process which is not caused by anyone!

THE UNIVERSAL DREAM FIELD
A process view of relationships gives us a noncausal, final perspective which sees them as aspects of a field of Jung's collective unconscious or as subjective impressions of a

universal Tao or archetypical process. A dream field is to psychology as Einstein's master field is to physics. Analogically speaking, each of us is an especially intense or condensed point in a field with dream dimensions. We are each channels for a universal Tao or process.

Actually this argument may be valid. It creates a powerful objection to group therapy, for example, in which people are encouraged to criticize others without reservation. Indeed, simply letting out a reaction can be potentially dangerous, for it can release a psychic avalanche or even a psychosis. The overly zealous therapist must realize that his reactions will usually be automatically integrated in time by his client even if these reactions are *not* expressed—if he is patient enough to wait for the dreamer to discover things on his own.

Therapists either liberally react to their clients or else repress their reactions. The theory of dreaming up, however, shows that both reactions are insufficient. Reactions released without any control whatsoever will be rejected even if they belong to the unconscious of the other person precisely because they are unconscious! Hence violent or uncontrolled reactions are met with equally violent and uncontrolled resistances.

However, repressing the therapist's reactions is no better because repression is an illusion. You can not repress dreaming up because it is not controllable. Repressed reactions only look repressed. The therapy scene under the domination of an even mildly repressive framework only looks orderly. Precise observation indicates that repressed reactions become somatized in the form of double signals and body problems, they make the therapist an incongruent, ill and unconvincing physician.

THE BODY IN THE THERAPEUTIC RELATIONSHIP

Each of us knows what it is like to be dreamed up physically. How 'uptight' or nervous we feel in certain people's neighborhood. How we get stomach cramps, headaches and other symptoms apparently in reaction to someone's behavior. These same reactions appear in thera-pists along with strong physical signals such as being exhausted by a dreamer, being turned on or off sexually by him, getting cramps, becoming nervous, suddenly becoming happy or sad, etc.

The average student therapist will, after some hesitation, bring in dreamed-up emotions such as anger, fear, hatred, love and boredom. But interacting physically out of a sudden need to touch, kiss, press, pull, hit, stab, kick, hug, love, sleep, walk, move, pinch or play is a different matter. We have culturally oriented inhibitions about body communication.

In addition to cultural inhibitions there are a host of personal reservations to body contact, some of which are a combination of psychic and physical resistances. Some people must resist close body contact because they are in danger of losing their own process. They feel obliged to focus only upon the needs of the other person during such contact and hence experience physical contact as a sort of death. For them contact *is* dangerous and must be avoided until they can bring their own physical needs to life.

There are other types of therapists who are so starved for body contact that they avoid it in order to save themselves from their exaggerated longings. These therapists have unworked-out problems and would be well advised to work more on themselves.

Some therapists do not touch people because they feel this would invade the other person's territory. Naturally there are moments when contact could truly be an invasion. However, consistent avoidance looks more like a symptom of someone who is projecting their own lack of boundaries than a true appreciation of the other's privacy. In other words the therapist fearful of invasion is too easily invaded by others himself. I should also mention that the therapist's hesitations may also be dreamed up and are part of a relationship process. If the therapist gets suddenly shy, it is possible that the client is hiding something!

SEX AS A DREAMED-UP REACTION

A therapist or anyone else whose physical functioning is limited dreams up the environment to become turned on or to enter directly into physical contact with them. Naturally getting sexually turned on to someone may be dreamed up by many other circumstances also. People who are hiding something turn you on in order to open them up. People who do not love themselves turn you on to love them. People who have cramps and diseases of the genital area turn you on to work out the problems there. Dying people can turn you on to bring them to life. People with beautiful bodies stimulate others if they do not have enough self-appreciation. Head trippers bait you to turn off their heads.

Being sexually dreamed up is often accompanied by physical and fantasiful resistances, the latter being projected onto partners or therapy systems. The typical fantasies are 'what will my partner think, how will the other person's partner feel? Is this therapy? Will someone see what I am doing?' These spontaneous fantasy invaders may appear at the moment of contact and do not belong to consciousness because they cannot be controlled. They are 'bona fide' unconscious processes seeking an amplification. Some of these contents turn out to be negative mothers and fathers, for example, who, like priests, are asking for enlightenment about sex. Other uninvited guests reveal themselves as protectors guarding against confluent invasion of personal territory.

I remember a student who got turned on by a woman and followed his body, pressing her with his back to the wall. Suddenly his excitement abated as she came out with the following story. Years ago she had been exposed to an exhibitionist who had paralyzed her with fear. At that time she could not move or defend herself. As soon as she realized what story she was telling she defended herself and told the student to move away. In other words she had dreamed up the past traumatic invasion of privacy and the present one because she herself needed to learn how to make boundaries.

SEXUAL CONTACT AND MALPRACTICE COMPLAINTS
The growing need for malpractice insurance especially among American physicians and psychotherapists seems also to be an aspect of dreaming up. The patient who is in need of or who is afraid of physical contact brings with him or herself an inner judge, a police court and a jury. As this client nears the therapist, the jury usually takes the foreground of the interaction and relationship is bound to be formal and social. As the two get to know each other, resistances are bound to take the background as the real needs come up. The beginning therapist often feels guilty and surprised about his own fear and social rigidity, and frequently jumps over this dreamed-up stiffness into physical contact with his patient. The typical client is at first pleased and then overcome by the unintegrated hesitation, the jury and court. The client is pressed from within to bring the therapist before an outer jury and his inner life is lived out in a courtroom.

This malpractice experience can be integrated as part of the relationship work. The therapist must bring in his uptight reactions saying, 'Sorry, I am interested, but not in you, I do not trust you, do not really know you, I do not feel your dream figures have all been brought in, your hesitations are still there, I am busy with someone else . . . etc.' The very attempt to discuss the situation takes the relationship phenomenon out of the somatic channels and allows what is happening to express itself verbally, the main channel for most western couples, and the one which can therefore be used to integrate what is happening into experiences of everyday life. When the jury and court are brought into the session, it seems as if very few relationship interactions have purely sexual characteristics.

RELIGIOUS ASPECTS OF CONTACT
If we wish to understand the dreamed-up nature of sexuality or the meaning of becoming a physical channel for someone we have to leave our cultural myths and look elsewhere to see how other people have attempted to integrate sexuality.

Indian practitioners of Tantra yoga[10] and Chinese Taoist alchemists[11] ritualized sexual contact, seeing it as the basic state from which religious experiences are derived. In Tantra, sexual contact is slowed down until it is almost stopped. Hatha yoga is then practiced in order to drive the sexual impulse out of the genital area, through the spine and into the entire body encouraging it to perform spontaneous postures which awaken somatic consciousness to the point of nirvanic experience. The Tantra yogi sees sex as one means for reaching a god experience and as a method for knowing this god as himself in contact with the goddess of the partner.

The Taoist uses the partner of the opposite sex as a stimulant for his 'mercury,' his 'prima materia,' the basic substance to be transformed into the 'panacea' for health and long life.[12] He captures his sexual stimulation and meditates upon it, 'circulating' its 'fire,' from the genitals into the stomach, heart and mind plexi and around through his back. The transformed and circulated substance becomes, through meditation, an immortal being or the so-called subtle body; the individual himself existing outside of normal consciousness.

A comparative study of these religious rituals gives us some idea of the possible archetypical pattern behind sexuality. Tantric and Taoist rituals 'work on' sex as if it were a basic condition leading to something else. They do not experience sexuality as a simple 'just-so-fact' or state but as a process which is trying to evolve. In the language of process theory, sex turns on proprioceptive channels which ritual then switches into vision and enlightenment. The transformation of sex into a 'higher energy' implies that what we call sex is only a presage of something which has relatively little to do with genital stimulation. Sex is one of many body states.

In so far as rituals transform sex into subtle body altered states of consciousness, sex is no different than any other body signal. All signals are signs of 'Shakti'[13] that is of god or of the the inner guides of the unconscious. All autonomous body signals create the sensation of an unpredictable spirit of life, requiring amplification in order to reveal its true nature.

ON THE SIGNIFICANCE OF DIFFERENT THEORIES
The concept of dreaming up makes it possible for us to appreciate very different kinds of therapists and therapy forms from a new angle. There is no one absolute theory that can be good for everyone, because a given person in a certain process dreams up a particular form of therapist. Thus therapists who are zealously involved in breaking through their clients' resistances are dreamed up by the fearful, mistrusting aspects of our culture. Overly conservative, head-oriented therapies are needed by people who are too loose, and in need of reflection. In one sense the power struggles between different schools of psychiatry, social work and psychology are irrelevant because different clients need different forms of therapy. Moreover, different cultures require different types of 'medicine men'. What we need is greater understanding of the common process and flexibility in different schools and therapists, not an annihilation of them.

RELATIONSHIP TO THE COLLECTIVE
One of the interesting conclusions of dreaming up is that you can become sick because of a given collective situation. Just as an acute symptom can be constellated in the neighborhood of someone who is not living his unconscious, a chronic disease may come from a culture which has rigidified. It is possible, for example, that much suffering related to presently intractable diseases such as cancer balances the personal, familial and cultural tendency of western people to avoid pain.

In primitive societies the relationship between collective and individual diseases appears in rituals where the shaman routinely requires the entire family or even tribes to partake in a given healing. I understand such rituals better after having been at body seminars. I never fail to be amazed at how physically relieving it is for everyone if one person lives a body or fantasy system. On the other hand, it is very stressful to be in a public situation which represses somatic channels and signals.

If you consider dreaming up then you can no longer innocently feel that a collective or individual has done something to you. Such causual thinking no longer holds. If you direct your attention with precision to your own dreams and to the dreams of your partners, you are bound to get a glimpse of the objective pattern behind what is happening. The important questions are no longer 'who is doing what?' but 'what is trying to happen?'

Causal attitudes towards dreaming up and towards relationship problems are natural, unconscious but almost always opposed by negative feedback from the environment. The very attempt at explaining to someone that they have dreamed you up or that you have dreamed them up always contains an element of blame because of the presence of the causal belief that the dreamer is 'doing' something. Dreaming up is a noncausal phenomenon, it is an aspect of a field whose localities are not connected through direct causal interchange alone.

Thus, though blaming and causal accusations are normal aspects of relationship phenomena, closer study of the secondary processes behind relationships indicates that an implicit or dream-like order is trying to enfold by means of individual lives.

Thus an individual can be considered as the unconscious or the split-off and dreamed-up part of another person or group just as the group can be understood as a part of the individual. If we switch our viewpoints and no longer consider the individual and his dream as the center of the universe, but the universe's process as the central phenomenon organizing the behavior of its individual parts, we enter that part of psychology which borders upon relativistic physics.

Chapter 5
WORLD CHANNELS

When objects and distant localities of spacetime behave as if they belonged to an individual's process as in *déjà vu*, telepathy and other forms of synchronicity, we can speak of the world as if it were a channel for the dreamer. Synchronicity is a generalization of dreaming up but differs from it insofar as we can not say empirically that the inorganic environment is dreaming up the individual in the same way as a dreamer might be understood as doing this. Though the empirical nature of the environment's 'dreaming' or implicate order may be different from that of a human being's, still the phenomenon of dreaming up gives us the feeling of how matter might 'feel' or experience itself as a part of our dream field.

The relationship between physics and psychology is nowhere as intimate as in the phenomena Jung called synchronicity though in principle the entire realm of psychology may be considered an aspect of physics and vice versa. One of the advantages of process science is its neutral basis. Since process work is based upon a phenomenological viewpoint, terms such as psyche and matter, inner and outer, psychology and physics, are replaced by the experiences, awareness and observations of a given observer. Thus the physicist's approach to 'purely material' events is, in principle, no different than the process worker's approach to body, dream, or relationship experiences.

It seems that the revolution now taking place in physics[1] is erasing the dividing line between that science and its reflections in psychology and mythology.[2] Physicists too have been testing the tyrannical nature of causal thinking and casting doubts upon the validity of our most commonplace notions of the world. After more than three thousand years of searching for the most elementary particles and principles of nature, scientists now consider the idea of atoms illusory. The most modern thinkers realize that physical theory is a reflection of the human personality.

Einstein's relativity theory, Bell's theorem and empirical investigations in physics force us to consider that objects and events can communicate with each other across great distances without apparent signal exchange.[3] The possibility of such communication disturbed physicists such as Einstein who held that a certain reasonableness about nature must be insisted upon. Even though Einstein upset our notions of space and time with his relativity theory, he rigidly held that a universe could not exist in which such events as telepathy and telekinesis could take place even though such events are permitted by the breakdown of the principle of local causes.[4] According to this principle events in a given locality are influenced only by that locality and not by signals from events at distances which would require signals to travel faster than the speed of light.

The breakdown of causality in the quantum world and the existence of signals traveling faster than the speed of light have shaken the conventional western logic and supplemented it with what the physicists call 'quantum logic.' This new way of thinking is close to process work and may be used in part to understand post-Einsteinian phenomena or processes occurring in world channels.

ONE-WORLD CONCEPTS

This new logic is based upon the experimentability of events in contrast to preconceived notions about them. The new logic implies, for physicists such as David Bohm, the existence of a 'one world.'[5] This one-world theory of the universe mirrors Buddhist concepts which rule out separate or independent localities. In the Buddhist's universe all events behave in conjunction with all other events, creating one larger universal process.

The one-world concept is occurring also to biologists such as Lewis Thomas.[6] Starting with the behavior of large groups of individual animals such as ants, he speculates that our entire planet behaves basically like a single cell in which each of us functions in a way which can be best understood by looking at the events of the entire world.

One-world concepts are found as well in analytical psychology. Jung theorized early in this century about the existence of a sort of field which he called the collective unconscious which can be seen reflected in the dreams of individuals at any given time. Already in the 1950s, Jung, together with the physicist Wolfgang Pauli, postulated something very close to quantum logic in order to explain telepathy and other parapsychological events. Jung said that events like telepathy which could not be entirely explained in terms of some sort of cause, could nevertheless be accounted for by a noncausal principle which he called synchronicity.[7] This principle has a strong Taoist flavor about it, and implies the existence of a meaningful order which pervades a given timespace.[8] For example the Tao, or prevailing meaning, would be a possible connecting factor between a dream, a hexagram of the *I Ching* pulled the same morning, and a real event mirroring the dream and *I Ching* occurring that afternoon.

We can guess that there is a common thread connecting physical concepts such as quantum logic, one-world theory, the principle of local causes and psychological ideas such as the collective unconscious and synchronicity. This thread leads us to suspect a meeting ground between the two sciences, physics and psychology. However, approaching this common ground is made difficult by the fact that physicists tend to be unfamiliar with psychological processes just as psychologists may be unaware of the theory and problems of physics. Nevertheless, attempts are being made to bridge the sciences.[9] In this present chapter I want to continue to investigate the common ground and in particular to show how the discoveries of process science give empirical weight to the notions of physics and how psychology is already living the one world of processes which physics is talking about.

DREAM AND BODY WORK

Let's turn to psychophysical processes in psychology in order to investigate post-Einsteinian signals. I recall one especially interesting synchronicity occurring during dream work. During one of my dream seminars a man began to tell a dream about a bear. Just as he was saying, 'and then the bear appeared,' in walked a man through the door of the seminar room, a man called Bear. Mr Bear told us that he was held up on his way to the seminar and could not maintain his normally punctual behavior.

The two events, namely the telling of the dream in which the bear appeared and the coming of Mr Bear have no simple causal connection, no ordinary electromagnetic signal connection which we can imagine (besides that is, some sort of magical causality). Of course we can consider the two counts as accidents, but the dreamer, his dream and seminar participants had strong emotional reactions to the events indicating that a theory of pure chance would deny or even repress the total reality of the observations. Ideas such as a theory of non-local causes, superluminal communications or synchronicity would be more appropriate here because the observers experienced the events as communicating with one another or as being connected by some sort of order.

Instead of analyzing this situation in detail, I would like to tell about a second synchronicity which took place during a body seminar. A participant was trying to lift up a very heavy object at one point during this seminar, allowing his body energy to express itself in the way it wanted. Falling backwards, exhausted by the impossibility of his task, the man exclaimed in an emotional tone that he felt that the object he was trying to lift was a god, something which he could not and was not meant to overcome.

As he was pronouncing his discovery there was a knock on the door of the seminar room. (It must be mentioned that this knock was surprising to us because the seminar was taking place in the high mountains where visitors were very rare.) We opened the door and in marched three children dressed up as the three kings of Bethlehem who, together with their great star were pointing the way towards god. They sang their songs (looking at the dreamer) turned and left. The atmosphere was so loaded that as soon as they disappeared people became very emotional, feeling that somehow god had been in the room. The day of the synchronicity was the 6th of January, the day in that Swiss mountain town when the children acted out the three kings' ritual. However, the children normally only acted out their rituals in the villages. Their very appearance high in the alps and at the exact moment of the man's enlightenment seemed to be non-chance events.

An interesting aspect of this synchronicity contrasts it to the bear story. In the bear synchronicity, everyone was shocked. In the god synchronicity everyone except the dreamer was shocked. In fact he said that he almost expected it to happen. He experienced the events as coherent and as agreements with his state partly because he had dreamed that he had lost a fight with god the night before and partly because he was in that special dream state because of the body work.

Why were the reactions of the dreamers in the bear and god synchronicities so different? What do these reactions say about the relationships between the observer and events? Can we imagine superluminal signals (i.e. faster than the speed of light) between events, or a post-Einsteinian universe where all is connected? What does process science tell us about the physicist's one world and psychologist's synchronicities?

We recall from the discussions in chapter 3 that proprioceptive experience is patterned visually by dreams and that the latter may be found in body symptoms when amplified. The invariance between dream and body processes gives rise to the dreambody concept.[10] In chapter 4 we discovered that the dreamer's environment behaves like specific dream activities, or that the world around him is 'dreamed up.' Dreaming up gave rise to the concept of the universal dream field which means that the body phenomena and exterior situations which one notices as disturbances are aspects of one's own dream process. Synchronicities indicate that the inorganic world as well as the human environment can also behave in dream-like fashion.

PROCESS LOGIC

The natural question which now arises is, of course, what the nature of the dream field is like. Phenomenological theory makes no attempt at answering this question unless empirical evidence arises, demonstrating either causally oriented signal-receiver phenomena or superluminal signals. Process science works with the facts of perception. These facts may be used to answer the following questions. Is there a sort of dream logic corresponding to a quantum logic? Are the dream field, the dreambody and the irrational aspect of quantum physics organized by some unknown pattern?

As we have previously seen, dream work indicates that outer events are not haphazard phenomena, but conform to patterns and have meanings. The course of inner and outer processes conforms to the patterns or archetypes found in the dreams of the observer. These patterns create the essence of process, 'process logic.' This logic gives coherence to all spontaneous perceptions. For example, apparently dissociated dream fragments are not independent pieces of some chaos, but cluster around a particular archetype. Jung called this archetype the 'architect' of dreams.[11]

For example, in the first story the man with the bear dream was living in a dream world architected by the archetypal image of the bear which organized his body processes, synchronicities and relationships. The second man who fought with god was living in a dream world structured by the archetypal fight with god, a dream term for the process which was drawing the dreamer towards religious experiences and enlightenment and organizing 'outer' synchronistic events.

ARCHETYPES AND WAVE FUNCTIONS

Now if we are exact, then we can not call archetypes by dream names such as the bear or god because these are too static. Archetypal patterns are processes or rather tendencies for these processes to happen. A dream report, for example, describes a certain tendency. For example, in the bear synchronicity, there was a tendency towards the process of meeting a great force. The dream report coinciding with the god synchronicity described a tendency towards conflict, humility and enlightenment.

Process-oriented dream and body work shows that dream images and symptoms are the beginning of tendencies towards particular psycho-physical processes. One can outline these tendencies by using entire dreams or body experiences mirroring these dreams.[12] In process work one sees these tendencies amplify and actualize themselves, creating body expressions, fantasies, understanding and synchronicities.

Now we have seen that the empirical universe which the process worker observes may be called a dream universe, described and oriented not only by the reasonable and commonplace logic of ordinary consciousness, but also by archetypal tendencies towards processes. They may appear in body problems, relationship conflicts, dream and synchronicities, in proprioceptive channels or referred channels such as people or outer objects.

Now it is just these tendencies which connect psychology to physics. The physicist has described the world since the early part of this century in terms of quantum mechanical tendencies. Physics had to drop normal ways of describing events in terms of elementary images such as atoms, time and space. It was discovered that what happens in the sub-atomic realm of being could only be accounted for by certain probabilistic equations, which, because they also describe wave phenomena in the real world, were called wave equations. The probabilistic interpretation of these wave equations caused physicists great problems. At first they were upset and baffled by the idea that a mathematical probability function described reality more accurately than a one-to-one cause and effect connection between events and theories. Quantum mechanics created religious conflicts for Einstein judging by his famous statement to Bohr that the god of the physical universe could not be probabilistic and 'play with dice.'[13]

After debates which are still going on today, the majority of physicists finally settled upon the so-called Copenhagen interpretation of the wave equation which says that it tells us about the probabilities and tendencies for things to happen. In the words of Werner Heisenberg who was greatly responsible for formulating the 'new' physics, the wave equation was

> . . . a tendency for something. It was a quantitative version of the old concept of 'potentia' in Aristotelian philosophy. It introduced something standing in the middle between the idea of an event and the actual event, a strange kind of physical reality just in the middle between possibility and reality.[14]

The lack of clarity about this 'strange kind of physical reality,' has led some scientists to project Buddhist thought into the formulation of physics. The one-world experiences of meditation and the pervading reality of the 'atman' fill the intellectual gaps created by the post-Einsteinian world of non-local causes. According to some, language itself can no longer be used in describing this world because the world can only be experienced.[15]

If, however, we compare the Copenhagen interpretation of the wave functions as 'a tendency for something' or of Heisenberg's 'potentia' with the idea of the archetype as a tendency towards certain processes, we are forced to a conclusion. The physicist's wave function is a mathematical aspect of the tendencies the psychologist calls archetypes. The physicist's one world then corresponds to dream world, and other terms used to describe the world of tendencies.

Jung used medieval expressions to describe this one world. He said with the alchemists that the 'Unus Mundus,'[16] was the one world which existed before the first day of creation. Jung meant that this world can be experienced but not grasped, that it is the vessel of preconscious contents, a world which he later termed the 'psychoid unconscious.'[17] The Unus Mundus is the world of archetypes in contrast to the world of archetypal manifestations such as dream processes and synchronicities.

Von Franz has extended Jung's idea of the Unus Mundus into the world of mathematics. She defined the substratum from which ordinary integers arise as the 'one continuum.'[18] Each number is an elementary unit which carries the quality of the one continuum with it as well as a differentiable aspect which makes it an individual number. The one continuum or Unus Mundus reflects a level of existence from which the manifest world is created, a level physicists such as David Finkelstein would define as 'a primitive concept of process' which comes before space and time.[19] As far as I can see, in our culture this level of existence refers to nonvisual proprioceptive awareness.

DETACHED OBSERVATION VS EXPERIENCE

The various one-world formulations of the dream universe are based upon a standard reference frame, our ordinary chronological reality. As long as we sit in this framework we experience the dream universe in terms of this framework, namely in terms of static states and differentiated descriptions such as tendencies towards specific processes. From this framework we can speak of process logic and of the patterns which are trying to occur in the form of processes.

Process differs from the other one-world descriptions of the dream-world universe in that process implies the experience of dreams and body phenomena. Process describes the observer's experience of the flow of events in which he is now taking part after having temporarily left his static rigid framework while process logic refers to observations of an observer standing with a chronological frame of reference. Wave functions, 'strange physical realities,' post-Einsteinian signals, the Unus Mundus psychoid unconscious, are important aspects of process logic which describe observation as a classical observer in consensus reality.

Process, however, implies detachment and involvement in these archetypal tendencies, which manifest in specific channels.

THE OBSERVER'S PSYCHOLOGY

We have seen how the one world of physics described by wave functions is similar to the dream world and its archetypal tendencies. We saw how the descriptions of this world in terms of tendencies is organized by process logic and depends upon the observer's frame of reference. This frame of reference defines his psychology.

For example, if at a given time and place an observer genuinely feels no emotional involvement with whatever he may be experiencing then the world he is observing is one in which chance, probability and non-sense may be ruling. Of course, the fact that he is observing anything at all may require some minimal emotional involvement. But just now I am describing a limiting case, an extreme situation of minimal emotional participation.

If, however, the observer finds himself emotionally touched by whatever he is seeing, hearing or feeling, he becomes involved in a totally new situation which is oriented by emotions, projections, dreams and archetypal tendencies. The universe becomes a dream world governed by the patterns of processes.

We may differentiate several typical ways which observers use to relate to the dream world determining to some extent the way in which subsequent processes evolve.[20] For example, there is the chronological observer who talks about processes as tendencies. He may look at manifestations of these processes in dreams and body problems, he may intellectualize about them, but he does not get into them. He maintains his normal intellectual consciousness, keeps his distance from the tendencies he subtly experiences and does not let go of his normal consciousness or give himself even in part to the tendencies which he feels are around.

The chronological observer therefore tells us that the dream world is a 'strange world,' a foreign universe. Personally he may be overcome by this world in a dream or by an emotion. He may feel it pressing upon him as an enemy in the form of a difficult disease or feel spooked by this world. He maintains the position of a Newtonian scientist in a classical space and time framework. He may be a rational person who appreciates and supports the conventions and doings of his reality, finding the other world 'a separate reality,' a 'para' phenomena, a body with a disease, a dream from out of the blue, a person giving him trouble, but not as an aspect of himself. Dreams are dreams, diseases are diseases, and reality is reality for him. He himself is whoever he standardly identifies himself to be. The world is a staccato series of movements between static states.

We can define another observer's relationship to processes, the fluid ego. When this person feels a tendency trying to happen in his body, in a conversation, or a fantasy, he lets himself change, moving into the body experience, mood, or fantasy. The fluid ego is more flexible than the chronological observer who relates everything to his time and space, seeing the world in a solid, frozen static state. The fluid ego lets go of his identification with time, space and cultural tradition, with his conscious intent and primary processes. He temporarily lets his definition of himself and the world stop and experiences its tendencies and strangeness as part of himself. He steps over his edges, follows his secondary processes, guided by momentary experiences and not by a prearranged reality program. When this person gets sick or has trouble with his world he experiences his body and world as a dreambody or dream-world process, not as a disease or outer problem but as something which he is trying to express. Conflicts in relationships are battles he is having with himself, moods are gradients and paths along which he may temporarily choose to move. He becomes an unpredictable and mercurial person who lives in one world, participating in it as if it were him and as if he were one of its vital parts. He does not observe synchronicities but feels processes occurring in outer channels and experiences events as 'agreements,' of his path.[21]

A chronological observer however, is located in his space and time and observes strangely coupled events and paranormal facts in weirdly connected channels which he cannot fit into his normal logic and which are divorced from himself. He theorizes that events follow the pattern of dreams and tendencies while the fluid ego lives these processes. The dream world of the chronological observer is composed of separate localities, as static states with weird post-Einsteinian noncausal connections, while the fluid ego experiences only processes. The chronological observer is like the classical physicist. The fluid observer is a new type of psychologist-physicist who participates in the world he observes.

Still another type of observer can be discovered who is a mixture of the first two! A process scientist. He is able to both participate and hold his distance from events. He identifies himself with his primary processes in time and space, and also with the stream of events, those secondary perceptions. He maintains his normal sober intellectual consciousness while simultaneously participating in processes. He sees that all is his process but, because he is also in space and time, realizes the existence of static outer world order. For him, the world is a dream-world reality, a constantly changing mixture of real things and dream-like phenomena.

The dream world is a process which he describes in terms of channels, tendencies or chance occurrences according to his own reactions. He realizes the existence of stable states and process logic, but sees that they are momentary phases of a dream-world process. For him observing events and experiencing processes, thinking and feeling are all momentary states of his own evolving. His relationship to processes is fluid. He may be as analytical in one moment as he may be process oriented in another. He would correspond to a psychological ideal, the integrated or whole individual, someone who is simultaneously involved and clear about his involvement.

UNIFYING PSYCHOLOGY AND PHYSICS
At present the average physicist and psychologist are chronological observers who participate only minimally in their observations. The physicist sits in time and space and

wonders at the mysteriousness of a natural universe in which signals travel in unknown ways. The average psychologist either analyzes states or tries to program change. Their bondage to chronological reference frames creates as many theoretical problems as it solves.

The Newtonian concepts such as the conscious and the unconscious prove inapplicable, for example, to psychotic states, deep body experiences and parapsychological or out-of-the-body experiences, where the very idea of the ego is difficult to define. Likewise the concepts or channels called matter and psyche are too vague to be practical to enable us to work efficiently with psychosomatic problems. Jung would say that the sciences are still in the 'mother', in a state of potential which has not yet touched concrete reality.

There are several notable attempts in physics to change this situation around, and to redevelop theory more closely with the changing aspect of our world.[22] According to Finkelstein, 'classical quantum mechanics is a hybrid of classical concepts (space, time) and quantum concepts (states, tests). A more consistently quantum mechanics is proposed, with space, time and matter replaced by one primitive concept of process.'[23] Bohm, in his *Wholeness and the Implicate Order*, tells us that 'flow is, in some sense, prior to that of the "things" that can be seen to form and dissolve in this flow.' He has also said that 'various patterns that can be abstracted from it have a certain relative autonomy and stability, which is indeed provided for by the universal law of the flowing movement.'[24]

Psychologists and physicists have believed in process structures for centuries. But belief is not enough. Process science is a study of perception, and until we realize that the way we observe is strongly determined by our primary process identity of remaining cool, objective and whole, we shall lack the necessary awareness required to translate dreams of the 'new age' into reality. The changes implied by process science can not happen over night because they are based upon a highly refined awareness only dreamed about until now at least by Buddhists, Taoists and modern physicists.

It is difficult to know what sort of theory will develop to deal with psychotic, parapsychological and political events but it will have to explain the apparent consciousness of the field we live in and be more closely related to our experience of ourselves. Perhaps the world will turn out to be an anthropos figure after all, a mythological structure mirroring the nature of its perceiver, man himself.

In any case in a post-Einsteinian universe, where telepathy, synchronicity, dreams and somatic body trips occur, the concept of process unifies events which move from psyche to matter, imaginations into the body. This concept allows psychology and physics to come together and allows the process worker to deal with post-Einsteinian signals and channels, regardless of their inner mechanisms or superluminal nature.

According to process concepts we can look at any event such as synchronicity from the viewpoint of the individual or from the viewpoint of the collective, depending upon which dreamer or observer we are dealing with. Thus, for example, from the individual's point of view, the bear or god synchronicity were dreamed up in the environment in part to show the individual in a differentiated fashion, more about his own bear-like nature. A bear-like tendency or archetype, an implicate order or probabilistic pattern, was present in his personality trying to enfold and express itself.

From the viewpoint of the collective, the individual dreamer was part of a group process whose pattern dealt with the bear archetype or its amplifications in terms of the wild and ecstatic and berserker behavior found, for example, in early Germanic mythology. The individual dreamer was then part of the collective unconscious, he represented an aspect of the group process which was not yet in the foreground of common awareness. Therefore, this group witnessed his process. In this moment, he became a channel for the world just as it had been a channel for his process.

The process scientist sees the individual as a world unto himself or understands the universe as a unity with parts such as people and objects. These parts think they are independent beings and sometimes forget that themselves are channels for a greater process happening right now.

Part II
THE ROOTS OF
PROCESS CONCEPTS

Chapter 6
PROCESS MYTHOLOGY

Process concepts are becoming increasingly popular with advances in psychology and physics. However, like these sciences, process work itself is a process whose roots turn endlessly backward through alchemy, primitive religion, Taoism and mythology. Since tracing these roots gives us a fuller understanding of the implications of process concepts, I have chosen to devote the second part of this work to discussing the origins of process concepts found in the energy and time symbols appearing in mythology and religion.

Mythological and religious concepts appear cyclically like threads in historical patterns. Thus, early Greek analytical thinking is now being replaced by something like Taoistic thought in modern physics. The different forms of modern psychology also have religious patterns behind them. This fact explains why the followers of different schools are so fervently involved in their propagation. For example, something like wotanic and violent Yawehistic deities appear in modern gestalt practices which recommend 'losing the mind' in order to 'gain the senses.' There is definitely something light and fun-loving, something Dionysian, about humanistic psychology's stress upon the reduction of suffering and the enjoyment of life. The confessional, serious and abreactive aspects of classical psychoanalysis are vaguely reminiscent of a primitive's penitence after having broken a religious law or taboo set up by the gods. Process work, too, has something like theology in its background. It tends to be a nature religion, embracing all the divinities. Thus, in any given session, the unfolding of a given process is likely to encompass shy confessions, ecstatic explosions, berserk expression of fury or thoughtful analytical reflection.

In the first part of this book I have chosen to discuss process in terms of its modern formulations by using concepts such as information, signals, channels, awareness, primary and secondary phenomena, dreambody events, relationships and physics. In the second part I wish to go back to the roots of process concepts found in mythology, Taoism and alchemy because these ancient traditions, rituals and beliefs contain the seeds of modern ideas. Discussion of these ancient process systems will give us more understanding of where modern concepts come from and what they may be missing. Hopefully the study of mythology will lend us some objectivity upon the development and state of modern psychology and physics. Let us look at process ideas as if we were anthropologists!

Anthropologically speaking process science is that sort of tribal religion which believes in nature divinities. Other tribes place their gods above those of other peoples and create a hierarchical mythology and animosity towards the divinities of their neighbors. Process science, however, does not place one god over another, matter over psyche, body over mind, sex above power, the here and now over the past.

According to Joseph Cambell;

> In cultures dominated by nature deities you could go from one locality to another and say, 'The deity whom you call Neptune we call Poseidon, and so we have the same gods.' without getting into trouble.[1]

Western science, however, has tended to be hierarchical, until now at least. When Freud came across the archetype of sex, he expected others to feel that this was the most important god. Campbell points out that the Freudian ego tried to control the 'id' or instinct and thus mirrored Yahweh's animosity towards nature goddesses. Freud inadvertently created a sort of hierarchical theology which characterized western culture's fear of nature, of process. 'But nature,' Campbell argues, 'is not so chaotic. Energy comes to us already inflected, specified and organized . . .'[2] We would say process appears in exact channels with specific types of signals.

Jung's definition of psychic energy placed psychology in the realm of process science. Jung saw many gods in the psyche's pantheon, which he called the collective unconscious instead of sexual libido. Jung realized a nature mythology in which all gods were equal in the sense of sharing the same energy and potential significance for a given individual.

Einstein also relativized the gods Time, Space, and Matter. He realized that these latter divinities may transform into one another and called their basic stuff energy. Einstein implied in the general theory of relativity that matter, space and time are equivalent in the sense of transforming into numerical fields of energy. Thus, theoretical physics says essentially, 'the god you call matter we call energy and so we have the same god.'

Thus, even though our western tribe has had its prejudices, animosities and fears of process, this nature divinity has slipped into our sciences in the form of physic's energy and psychology's concept of the collective unconscious. Nevertheless our western fear of nature creates controls over process which must be kept under the domination of a sort of police force because, if it is not, we suspect process will create chaos. Einstein and Jung would agree with Campbell, however, and say that this fear or control is not quite justified for empirical nature appears to the observer in terms of inflected, quantized and organized energies, as quantum phenomena, numbers or, as I have pointed out in the preceding chapters, channels.

Since process is a nature divinity, it should not surprise us that it appears in terms of mythical time deities or that these figures carried with them divisions and organizations which quantized process in terms of channels!

TIME

Though the very idea of process is very very old, process consciousness will be a new form of thinking for many people because prevailing western consciousness is chronological and state oriented. Our consciousness and religious systems divide events up into predetermined categories such as life is good and bad, moral and immoral, healthy and sick.

However, we have not always possessed a polarizing, chronological consciousness which divides events into opposites. Christian thinking characterized by differentiated concepts such as good and evil was already beginning to wane in the medieval period. Von Franz points out that the seeds of change were sown in legendary figures such as Merlin the Magician who was good, evil and more.[3] He was mercurial, unpredictable and tricksterlike. Merlin prefigured the coming Aquarian age which is symbolized in astrology by the waterbearer who feeds the fish. Von Franz speculates that selfhood and individuation will become more important than the opposites in the coming perod of western consciousness.[4] If figures such as Merlin and the Aquarian waterbearer relativize the absoluteness of the opposites, then the Aquarian age might be typified by living with the flow of events in contrast to concepts about them, by the fluid not the chronological observer.

In order to imagine a process oriented consciousness we might look at our own early Greek psychology or at the mythology of modern non-technical peoples such as the American Indians. The Hopi Indians, for example, are process oriented. Their time concept does not include past or future but only that which 'is beginning to manifest' and 'that which is manifest', like rocks and objects.[5] We would call these 'secondary and primary processes!' They do not use future or past verb tenses but live close to phenomena themselves. For them the moment to do something is not predetermined, but an unpredictable creation requiring process awareness to know when 'something' is beginning to manifest. In contrast to the Hopi Indians a state-oriented consciousness watches the clock in order to know when to begin. The Hopi would in principle, watch events themselves.

I am neither predicting nor recommending that we transform our mentality into that of the Indians. We could not do so even if we wanted to because we are different from our less technical relatives. If à western, state-oriented individual becomes process oriented then part of his process is bound to be characterized by state-oriented thinking! In other words, he will be a total observer. There will be times when he follows his mental, divisive frameworks and other times when he allows his behavior to be governed by the flow of events themselves. There will be moments when he creates frameworks for existence and other moments when events create these frameworks.

From experience, I know that there are moments when it is easier to apply a given program to someone's process, and watch the results. When these programs make me uncomfortable or begin to block the client's growth and change I awaken and attempt to discover the structure of my client's process which is implicit in events. Only then do I look for primary and secondary phenomena, channels, double signals, etc. or ask the client to help me discover the structure in what is happening.

OCEANOS

At the dawn of western history our concept of time was symbolized by the Greek figure of Oceanos.[6] Imagine him. He is pictured as an immense serpent encircling the world and sometimes carries the zodiac on his back. He has several interesting characteristics. First of all, his name shows us that he stands for water. He is god of the oceans. As a water demon he symbolizes flow and process. Early Greeks, like the Hopi Indians of today, were process or 'water' oriented.

Let us now consider Oceanos' serpent nature. Serpents, because of their undulating nature, point to the periodic nature of processes. Everyone who has studied himself over long periods of time will have noticed how typical problems and states are forever returning. One is periodically happy, then sad, free, then imprisoned, etc. In fact, processes are so periodic that we often predict that the opposite of the present state will soon occur even though we can not predict the speed or exact nature of the coming state. Thus serpents point to the periodicity of processes.

But serpents can be venomous too. The poisonous nature of processes occurs primarily when we are unconscious of them. Process work often shows us that criticism which has not been made conscious turns against us in the form of aggressive cramps. Dreams picture how an animal can become furious and bite us if we have neglected our instincts too long. The venomous aspects of processes often appears when one first begins to feel the way into dreams or body processes. A woman who refused to accept her fantasies, for example, was bitten in a dream by a bird (a fantasy symbol) which turned into a vicious snake.

2 *Double-headed serpent in turquoise mosaic, Mixtec workmanship, Mexico, 13th-14th century (British Museum)*

Ancient time concepts were process oriented and hence filled with unpredictable, lucky but also vicious powers. Such process concepts are vastly different from our modern mechanical idea of time. For example, in India, time is symbolized by the god Shiva or goddess Shakti or her sister Kali who represents the violent brutal nature of time.[7] Kali or a variation of her often appears in the processes of sick people who have been naive about their own reality. In their dreams, vicious ugly things often happen, prefiguring the catastrophic experiences which are awaiting them. Their processes have become deadly in part because they have not accepted the brutal aspects of their natures.

One of Oceanos' most interesting characteristics is that he is wrapped around the world. The snake wound around the world could picture human experience imprisoned by time. What does this mean? If we think in modern terms, then we

3   *Shiva with the River Ganges flowing from his head (Crown copyright, Victoria and Albert Museum)*

4   *Kali in her rage on the battlefield, overcoming Shiva, c. 1880 (Crown copyright, Victoria and Albert Museum)*

know right away what it means to be in a 'time cramp.' All of us at one time or another feel pressured to do things on time. We sometimes call this state of affairs a 'reality cramp.' It is partially caused by the way we organize life, preprogramming routines instead of letting things develop as they want to.

However, this interpretation of reality cramping is weak because the serpent is an unconscious animal, not a human being. To more fully understand our reality compulsion we have to consider the possibility that our processes are cramping us. Imagine for a moment that you are not part of the human world, but that instead you are a snake wound around the planet earth. Then you might have any one of a number of experiences. You might discover that you are cramping the world and yourself because you (as the world) are lazy and need a cramp in order to get something done. You might discover that you are cramping yourself because you need boundaries and homelife, security and warmth. You might be cramping yourself in order to discover your own strength. In any case, as soon as you identify with the reality cramp, you discover the snake and your own process. Immediately you experience your own psycho-physical nature and withdraw your projections onto the surrounding world. 'Time' does not stress us, our own process wants to create boundaries, cramps, challenges, edges.

People who consciously experience their processes in dream body work with symptoms and projections frequently find themselves suddenly at the limits of reality. They are at their edge between primary and secondary processes. This experience is symbolized by Oceanos who forms the outer limits of the world, the boundary to the unknown. Process work brings one to one's edge, which may be described variously in such terms as 'far out,' disoriented, swimming, lost, 'spaced out' or 'not knowing where one is.' Oceanos is a process which rescues those who are insufficiently organized by creating structure and boundaries but disorients others who have been too controlling, too limiting. In other words, the way one approaches the edge determines Oceanos' behavior.

One way of approaching the edge of one's world is to refuse to admit that it is there and to go back to safe thinking and believing. Such a person is then usually flipped by Oceanos, the unwanted edge. I am thinking in the moment of a woman who entered a mental hospital saying that she was the great goddess Kali. I asked her why she wanted to cut off men's heads and she said because they were not nice to her. Apparently this woman could not face earlier realizations that her boyfriend did not like her. When he left her she flipped. Such an idea was an 'edge' for her and therefore flipped her identity. Another kind of person would have come to this information edge, and let the negative thoughts structure her changing relationship.

THE KUNDALINI

One of the eastern equivalents of Oceanos who encircles the world would be the great serpent goddess Kundalini who is wound three and a half times around the base 'chakra' or center of the body, the 'muladhara,' the root or earth of the human being.[8] However there is an important difference between the Kundalini and Oceanos. He is wound around the world while 'she' is coiled up within the human body.

Thus while the western mind experiences stress mainly from outer world sources the Indian tends to be aware of imprisonment within the body. The Kundalini's winding about the base of the 'muladhara' is thus a symbol of body cramps, tensions, desires, armouring and potential energy.

The yogi in principle goes about releasing the Kundalini in a very different manner than a western therapist. The western body therapist tends to fight the cramps in the body trying to overcome them. Body symptoms for the yogi, however, are godlike, they are manifestations of Shakti or Kundalini which must, in principle, be worshipped, not repressed. The way of liberation in yoga is thus to meditate upon the Kundalini's windings, to focus breath and concentration on her until she spontaneously arises, shooting through the body and awakening it with streaming energy flow.

The yogi's method of liberation conforms to a process oriented psychology in which body phenomena are focused upon and amplified. Sometimes body processes ask for repression but most appear as the beginnings of new processes. The process oriented psychologist discovers that body problems can be the beginnings of an enlightening energy whose messages were somatized. In other words, the body is not necessarily full of pathological problems which must be overcome but of messages from coiled up or potential energy sources which must be tapped.

Consider a Kundalini experience I recently witnessed while working with an elderly man. He felt that there was a 'coil' in the center of his head, creating headaches. He amplified and meditated upon this coil by shaking his head to feel the pain more. Then he said, 'Oh, I want to be a coil and jump!' He moved his hands up and down, and so I recommended that he jump with his whole body. His immediate insight was, 'I have given up on life but I am actually still full of excitement and want to have more fun!' Here, a potential energy or process in his body was awakened, and led to an enlightening and insightful experience.

AION

Before leaving the serpentine aspect of processes we must discuss Oceanos' later developments. Later Greeks conceived of him in terms of Chronos, Zeus and Aion.[9] Aion was a more complex development of Oceanos. Apparently Aion was originally a vital fluid in human beings which lived on after death of the individual in the form of a snake. Aion was also considered to be the creator and destroyer of all things and a sort of 'world soul.'[10] Aion was connected also to Mithras who appeared as a monster with a lion's head holding a staff around which a snake was coiled.[11] The signs of the Zodiac, Sol and Luna, together with the seasons also appear around this monster. Ogawa goes on to say that the snake was considered to represent the heavenly course of the seven planets while the staff was the tool or thunderbolt of the gods.

If we conceive of Aion as a development of Oceanos we can see how process concepts developed. Aion represents a more differentiated picture of processes than Oceanos. Aion includes subtle body or 'out-of-the body' experiences since

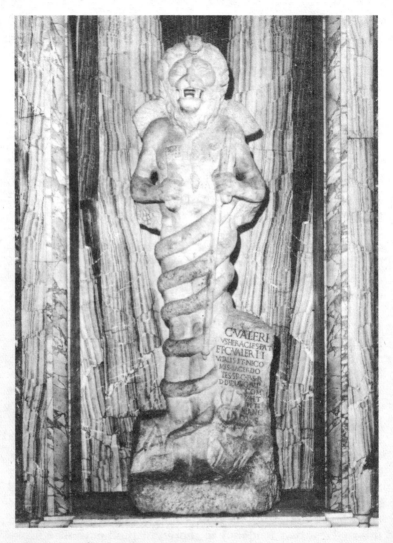

5   *Aion (Biblioteca Apostica Vaticana)*

he is a fluid transcending death. Aion's association to the universal course of the stars shows that individual processes also have collective and inorganic characteristics. Aion thus points to dreambody processes which transcend the life-death and personal-collective differentiations. Aion is a symbol of a world or universal consciousness, and thus of the collective unconscious, the universal dream field of which we are all parts.

In other words, our individual human process is not simply individual but has collective and universal aspects. This is why, when we identify ourselves at least partially with our processes, apparently personal difficulties and experiences frequently lead to cosmic feelings. Such feeling is considered enlightenment in many religions. The 'Kings' process discussed on page 59 of the last chapter is an example of such a cosmic experience. In her discussion of Ogawa's work, von Franz points out that Aion's lion nature symbolizes fiery spiritual power, while the snake corresponds to the monster's earthy, watery side.[12] She also points out that Aion as well as other supreme deities which are connected with time, such as the Dakota 'wakanda,' the Algonquin 'manitou,' the Australian Yao 'mulungu,' and the Melanesian 'mana,' are primitive energy concepts which are related to later Greek and modern quantitative concepts of energy. She traces the energy concepts into mathematical physics and also to Freud's libido and Jung's psychic energy.

Modern biologists relate energy to the concept of life as well. Asimov, for example, shows how the physicist's concept of energy (related to mechanical work) may be used as a measure for life and applied to the entire spectrum of inorganic and organic material events.[13]

Returning to Aion we notice first of all that two aspects of processes appear in him, the lion head and snake wound around the staff. The mythological amplifications indicate that the lion would represent the fiery spiritual aspect of processes, their tendency to manifest in dreams. The snake wound around the staff in the lion's hand implies that the original energetic dream impulses persevere in the sense of repeating themselves again and again. In other words, processes have dream-like beginnings which then periodically repeat themselves.

The differentiation of energy, time and process by Aion's

symbolism of dream impulses and perseverations bridges
the gap between what we today define as body and mind.
Modern energy concepts are less holistic. The physicists'
definition of energy is quantitative, and measurable.

CONSERVATION PRINCIPLES

If we take a closer look at the sciences of psychology and
physics we notice that the energy concept is really not as
split as it looks at first sight. Physicists separate imagination
from matter, enclose it in a box and notice that in a closed
system measurable quantitative energy is neither created nor
destroyed. This discovery, called the conservation of energy,
also appeared to psychologists such as Jung, to fit psychic
processes. In an article on psychic energy, he states that
psychic energy tends to be conserved too.[14] When one is
depressed, for example, energy flows out of consciousness
into the unconscious, often into body symptoms. Energy
never disappears but transforms and may reappear in
dreams, inner or outer life. Or, in other words, energy or
process is always present in one or more channels. If it is
not in dreams or visualizations, it is often found proprioceptively. If it is neither in the dream nor in the body, it is
found in relationship phenomena.

One way of putting psychology, biology and physics back
together again is by leaving the modern energy concept for
the moment and focusing on its archaic predecessor, Aion,
i.e. process. One of the advantages of talking about
processes instead of energies is that we are no longer bound
by the latter's modern implications, its quantitative and
qualitative definitions. Process is related to the occurrence of
events and not to any one of their particular qualitative or
quantitative characteristics. Process is a psycho-physical or
neutral description of events and accords with symbols such
as Oceanos and Aion who were simultaneously inner body
experiences, outer organic life, universal and spiritual
phenomena. The concept of process and information thus
bridges modern terms such as matter, psyche, life and even
energy.

CONSERVATION AND TRANSFORMATION

One of the widespread beliefs found in world religions is life after death. If we formulate this belief in terms of process theory then we come upon a conservation pattern. Of course we do not know for certain whether processes are really conserved or whether people really go on existing after death. We can only take this motif as a speculation. But the speculation is so ancient and so persistent that we must also ask if there is not a natural law, a pattern or an archetype involved.

The analogous concept in modern science to the religious belief of life after death would be the conservation of energy in physics and psychology. The process description of the conservation of energy would be the idea that *process is constant*. Process may manifest or transform in different ways, but yet, it is a potential constant for a given observer. The belief of surviving death thus implies a natural law such as the conservation of process. Human observers are processes which transform but are basically conserved over time and space. Process awareness is then equivalent to the experience of immortality, liberation or freedom from time and death which the yogis call being dead in life.[15]

The evidence of the conservation of processes extending beyond death occurs frequently in dying people and has been discussed in the last chapter of my *Working With the Dreaming Body*. The conservation of processes is a different problem in the living, however. Here the question for the empirically oriented psychologist or process worker is not, does awareness go on after death, but where does information go now? The answer from the foregoing work is that process is constant and appears in one of the channels of perception. If it is not in dreams, it is in the body, the outside world or another person!

ZODIACS AND CHANNELS

Channels appear in connection with process symbols such as the Kundalini, Oceanos and Aion. Oceanos and Aion were pictured with the zodiac. The Kundalini appeared with a chakra system. The zodiac was, in early Greek times, considered to be a map of the stars, a description of how the universe evolved. Each stage of its process corresponded to a particular constellation, and each constellation was described, like star groupings today, in terms of dramatic constellations. Thus the zodiac is a symbol of a process's possible channels or modes of manifestation.

Today time is no longer divided up into phases governed by the deities but is measured mechanically. Thus we scarcely realize the divine qualities behind our dimensions of reality. The divine nature of our channels appears whenever they are called into question. Then we realize they were parts of our personal theologies. Many people today, for example, still try to repress the existence of parapsychological phenomena and get emotional about inconsistencies in their dearly prized concepts of time and spaces. Body therapists feel body channels are all powerful, dreamers feel dreams are god. Physicists believe only in the measurable, psychologists think physicists are rationalists, etc.! Channels themselves are like gods corresponding to people's psychology and beliefs.

FRAMING

Oceanus did not flow into a prescribed maze set up for him. He carried the zodiac on his back! Since the zodiac is a symbol of process channels we can understand the zodiac being carried on the back as a picture of processes carrying their own channels.

If we try to organize events as if we were chronological observers then we frame processes before they occur. If we watch events themselves and see what sort of frameworks they carry with them (on their backs!) then we are no longer state-oriented 'framers' but process-oriented scientists.

Framing often mirrors people's worst problem: deciding what to do ahead of time, pressing themselves to do things whether or not they feel like it and regardless of the direction of events. Framing life instead of letting it determine its own process is, psychologically speaking, an inflation. One has inadvertently identified oneself with the governor of nature, the gods. Framing nature is so common that most of us do not notice a most dangerous inflation, in attempting to rule life.

Reference to other cultures is humbling and relativizing. One notices in the Aztec myths, for example, how the framework of reality is created by the process itself and not by human consciousness. In their creation myth the Aztecs imagine a god called Omtéotl, the original and supreme deity (like Aion) who was mother and father of all.[16] They tell us that he was 'a mirror that illumines all things.'

In our terms, this god would be the process, the creator of existence who illuminates by mirroring. Everyone knows this mirroring in the phenomena of perseverating, doubling and repeating. We become conscious of our process because it constantly repeats itself, dreaming up the world around us reflecting until we see what is happening. If we do not see it, the process continues to repeat, it goes into a cycling activity which we experience as feeling 'stuck' or going around in circles.

CREATING CHANNELS

However, I am not telling the Aztec myth in order to reflect upon process but upon the channels it creates. The myth continues and tells us that Omtéotl created four more gods, the so-called Tezcatlipocas, who in turn created the world. These four gods were identified with the directions of the compass with specific animals and colors. These directions, animals and colors symbolize the channels in which human processes of growth can manifest themselves and are the dimensions of Aztec reality.

If we translate this myth into process terms then we see that the process itself, Omtéotl, the mother and the father of all things, also creates its own dimensions. This myth compensates 'common sense.' We tend to think that if we do not structure nature that it will create chaos. We feel that *we* are responsible for holding nature together. If we do not plan and define everything in advance the world is going to fall apart. Naturally there are moments when it is important to use ordinary consciousness and to define what is going to happen and to hold to this program. But frequently the opposite is true.

RELATIVITY AND CHANNEL SYSTEMS

The Aztec myth tells us that Omtéotl creates the gods, that processes manifest new and unpredictable channels. Thus, sticking to one set of channels can be unnecessarily limiting to growth and change.

Let me give an example from India. Myths tell us, for example, that the Kundalini created the world and then settled down in the base of the 'muladhara' to rest.[17] Part of the world she created was the chakra system, the seven body 'channels' located in specific parts in the body. Routinely using only this system can be inhibiting to body work, however, because each person's process develops their body channels in specific and not altogether predictable ways. Thus body centers may appear in places which do not correspond to the Indian chakra system. *Any place* a symptom manifests itself is a potential channel for processes to occur! Thus the chakra system is only one possible frequently occurring system of channels but not the only one.

Jung's discovery of dream imagery he called the anima, animus, shadow and self would correspond to the Indian chakra system insofar as these dream figures are centers or channels through which the unconscious manifests itself in imagery. An uncreative dream worker will not pick up the individual dream language but frame dreams in this known system just as an uncreative body therapist works according to given programs instead of the phenomena themselves.

STOPPING THE WORLD

A chronological observer who frames processes into states instead of letting them create their own dimensions, dreams up life to become unpredictable and worn out. Frequently fate impinges from outside upon such a person from dreams, body problems, relationships and accidents threatening to upset or even stop the world one is living in. Castaneda's shaman-tutor Don Juan would say that such fate is a moment when one should 'stop the world.' He should consciously follow the disturbances and stop perceiving reality in the old channels, let new modes of awareness arise.

Naturally, one cannot change channels simply because one chooses to do so. Real change happens when the world is stopped as processes themselves recreate channels. When such changes take place, the world as we experience it, together with some of our gods and belief systems, loses its former validity. The loss of these systems always coincides with temporary feelings of disorientation. Xenophobia, fear of new and unexperienced life occurs together with death of the old gods and confrontation with the ineluctable flow of nature, the Tao. This fear frequently maintains the old channels, while threats of destruction impinge from the universe.

According to the newspapers, the threat of nuclear war can be understood as one unconscious and unnecessary way of stopping the world. The alternative to this negative and destructive aspect of Oceanos, Omtéotl, Aion and Kali would be a transformation in the way we perceive and process the world. Either we participate in channel changes and relativize our control over events, or we will become overly fascinated with really stopping the world. The violence of ancient process gods is a warning to us as individuals and nations to restructure life as much as possible from day to day instead of from lifetime to lifetime.

Chapter 7
CHANNELS IN TAOISM

Process science appears spontaneously wherever people follow the flow of events as distinct from preconceived notions about how they should go. I pointed out in the last chapter that process and channel concepts are not really new ideas, but are found in old Greek and Aztec Indian time theories, in ancient myths.

The most complete process theory which I have come across until now is expressed in the main oracles of Taoism, the *Tao Te Ching* and the *I Ching*. I show in this chapter how these ancient texts offer us a philosophical and numerical basis for developing process theory.

I strongly recommend to the reader who is unfamiliar with Taoism to study the *Tao Te Ching* and experiment with the *I Ching* if he wants to know more about process work. Introducing these texts here in a complete way is beyond my resources. Their philosophy is difficult to translate and their methods of ascertaining the Tao must be experienced. I can only hint here at the phenomenological psychology I feel lies hidden in their messages.

The Taoists were first-class process scientists. They observed events, noted their spontaneous arrangements and did not doubt or attempt to explain them. I would call them religious scientists but the term 'religious' is misleading because they had no special gods. In fact our pantheon of deities finds no analogy in Taoism. There the single and most important principle is simply process, that is, following the Tao.

THE TAOIST AS PROCESS WORKER

In fact, *Tao Te Ching* and *I Ching* can almost be directly translated to mean process science. According to Raymond van Over, Tao is usually taken to mean the way or the path along which all things move.[1] Te refers to activity in the world. Thus Tao Te would mean, 'the way of activity' which is very similar to one of the Oxford Dictionary's definitions of process as the 'course of action'. Richard Wilhelm reports in his *Eight Lectures on the I Ching*, that 'I' means changes as shown, for example, in the symbol of a salamander or snake which changes its skin periodically. 'Ching' refers to a text or pattern as one finds in weaving and cloth. Hence, 'I Ching' means process as perceived in terms of the changes occurring in given patterns.

Let us focus for the moment on the Chinese word for the Tao itself. The word for Tao was originally derived from the same root as the words for sage, king and priest.[2] Priest and king then connoted the maximum human achievements, divining, communicating and following natural forces. Thus, the word Tao implies following nature as a guide.

The root word connecting priest, Tao and sage was composed of three horizontal lines standing for heaven, earth and man. This trigram was connected by a vertical line which completed the word for Tao. (≢) Heaven, earth and man were designations for the way in which nature manifests itself. That is they are channels roughly equivalent to what we call psychic stuff or dreams, conscious situations and material events such as body problems. Using process language we can say that the Tao is the flow of events in and between channels. Tao signifies a process which simultaneously manifests in a number of different channels. Since the word for sage has the same root as Tao, a sage would be a process worker; a person who congruently mirrors processes manifesting in dreams, body and environmental phenomena.

Helmut Wilhelm warns us:

It is in constant change and growth that life can be grasped. . . . If it is interrupted, the result is not death, which is really only an aspect of life, but life's reversal, its perversion. . . . The opposite of change in Chinese thought is growth of what ought to decrease, the downfall of what ought to rule.[3]

If the Tao ought to rule, then the opposite to the Tao would be a tyrant, a 'framer' who insists on determining how things should go. The opposite to the sage or the Tao is an 'anti-process,' a state-oriented attitude which preprograms behavior and frames events before they occur. Thus the opposite to process is a predetermined standardization, a therapy, rule or goal.

TAO AND WHOLENESS
According to Granet, the concept of Tao underwent many changes in the evolution of Chinese thought. Early Taoists saw the Tao as a mysterious and unfathomable process. Later Taoists, however, understood the Tao as a static balance between opposites such as yin and yang and pictured this balance in the famous yin-yang symbol.

According to the *I Ching* the yin-yang symbol was originally meant to represent the 'primal beginning' as including the two polar forces of the universe. Tao, an invisible way, serves to maintain the interplay of these forces so that they are constantly regenerated, constantly in tension, a constant potential creating the world anew in every moment, but without ever becoming manifest. There is always a state of tension between these primal powers, which keeps the 'world' constantly regenerating itself. In process terms there is always a state of tension between primary processes of which we are aware and secondary ones of which we are less aware. This state of tension is maintained by the edge. The total world or Tao thus rarely manifests because, as our awareness grows, the edge which separates processes continually moves just one step beyond our reach, and we must create new awareness and channels to reach it. Thus the yin-yang symbol did not originally represent a static concept, but rather a renewal of tension.

This later and more static concept of the Tao sharply contrasts its earlier conception. The earlier Tao is a process which creates the world and its channels. The later static concept of the Tao mirrors present state-oriented psychological concepts of human totality. These concepts picture wholeness as a balance of already existing opposites such as good and bad.

This state of 'wholeness' then becomes a fixed goal in most cases which the growing person much achieve through effort. He tries to mechanically create balances and harmonies within himself. Theoretically such a person could not suffer from strong emotional conflicts.

The earlier concept of the Tao, however, implies that a sage or an individuated person is one who is aware of processes and who adjusts himself according to this awareness. He does not attempt to create balance with his will but instead tries to know and then follow what is happening.

The state-oriented person perceives such a 'sage' as unpredictable. It is unlikely that the process-oriented Taoist would debate later Taoist ideas. However, if he did he might argue that organization and wisdom must be continuously discovered anew in the flow of events themselves.

THE EVOLUTION OF PROCESS CONCEPTS

Apparently the early idea of the Tao as a creative flow lies behind Taoism's main oracles, the *Tao Te Ching* and the *I Ching*. Lao Tsu says in the former: 'The Tao which can be expressed in words is not the Tao.'[4] He is saying that our descriptions of events in terms of predetermined ideas and vocabulary does not accord with the reality of events themselves. I see the practicality of Lao Tsu's viewpoint in process work. There I observe how process students tend to use their preconceived systems of understanding in explaining the body processes of their student colleagues in supervision seminars. The student observer uses *his* channels to frame processes and not the spontaneous vocabulary and actions of events themselves.

Lao Tsu is suggesting that a 'beginner's mind'[5] is necessary in understanding the Tao. One has to keep one's perception open and see things as they are. However, if we examine the evolution of Taoism, we see that Lao Tsu's recommendation was not followed!

This evolution can be expressed approximately as follows. At first some scientist with a beginner's mind sees reality as it is and describes some of the channels it spontaneously produces. Students of this 'beginner's mind' then standardize the channels he saw and ignore the Tao which 'cannot be expressed with words.' As time passes events occur which no longer conform to the logic of the older channels and someone with a 'beginner's mind' appears again and rediscovers Lao Tsu's Taoism.

And so it goes. First there is a unitarian theory of nature accompanied by a fresh description of life in terms of new channels of growth. This description is dogmatized and soon becomes inappropriate as events overlap old channels, relativizing their absoluteness. These events create or recreate holistic theories which relegate the significance of channels to second-order principles with respect to process.

Many examples of such an evolution will come to the reader's mind. Every change of religious order is a manifestation of changing channels. The Jewish god Yahweh could be heard but not visualized. Jesus could also be seen! Physics and psychology are channels which replaced the earlier concepts of alchemy. Time and space were overcome by relativistic events. Divisibility and causality have been seriously shaken by quantum physics. Psychosomatic phenomena and parapsychological events are loosening the rigid border still separating psychics from psychology. As psyche and matter flow together, physiological categories such as the five senses will disappear and new descriptions of matter will arise out of the inapplicability of the old ones.

AMPLIFICATION

If process science is itself a process then how can we catch it long enough to formulate it? Fortunately, people have been asking themselves this question for at least four thousand years in China and have summed up their conclusions in what we now know as the *I Ching*. Here we find an unprecedented integration of centuries of thought about the mysterious Tao and its channel creations. For example the *I Ching* explains the Tao as that: 'which completes the primal images (and) is called the creative. (The Tao) which imitates them is called the receptive.'[6] Here process is divided into 'creative' and 'receptive.' According to the *I Ching*, the creative phase of processes energizes or creates the 'primal images,' the channels. The receptive phase of a process 'imitates' or repeats the original impulses in the channels.

The *I Ching*'s Tao reminds us of the Aztec deity Omtéotl who created the four channel gods, the Tezcatlipocas, who in turn imitated their creater by then creating the world. Omtéotl was the 'creative' while Tezcatlipocas would be the 'receptive.' Aion, the Greek process god, also had a creative phase or lion phase and a repetitive phase symbolized by the coiled snake on his staff.[7]

The *I Ching*'s ancient saying has practical consequences for process work. The text tells us that processes manifest themselves energetically by creating specific channels, the so-called primal images. Processes repeat or perseverate in these channels in the receptive phase.

If process work follows the Tao, then its first job is to recognize energetic manifestations in terms of channels, and to accurately observe their perseverations. Examples illustrate amplification.

If a patient resists a certain therapy process or has a negative projection upon the therapist, then amplifying resistance might mean encouraging the client to consciously assist his aggressiveness.

If someone sees powerful visions and searches for their meaning, then the search for meaning requires amplification through mythology, fairy tales or personal associations. If someone is fascinated by the colors and figures of a dream, then the colors may be amplified by visual (imaginary) intensification. The figures may be talked to or acted out. If someone cannot stop scratching his skin, the itch might be mechanically amplified in order to see what it wants. If there is pain in the stomach, then a proprioceptive message asks for conscious reception. In any case, the specific methods of amplification are derived exactly from processes themselves.

The novice student of process work generally faces two basic problems. Firstly, he may feel responsible for something happening and feel he should play creator. Then he 'pushes', that is he tries to recommend new ideas and therapies so that processes will occur. Or, he becomes impatient when things finally do happen and does not give them a chance to perseverate. If he ignores perseverations he will not learn from events themselves what and how to amplify. In this case he compensates for insufficient observation and lack of patience by applying standard procedures which are not tailored to the individual situation. Then his work becomes erratic and exhausting. In either case the student therapist suffers from feeling too important.

ANALYZING AND EXPERIENCING

The *I Ching* continues to explain process science to us by further differentiating the Tao: 'In that it (the Tao) serves for exploring number and knowing the future, it is regulation. In that it makes for organic coherence in change, this is the work.'[8] Here we find a description of how the *I Ching* works. The Tao unfolds itself in the hexagrams through expressing itself in terms of the binary system, the yin-yang code, and a combination of this code, in six different channels (e.g. ☰). Insofar as events manifest themselves spontaneously in images such as binary codes, hexagrams, or in terms of dream pictures, acoustical tones, pains and proprioceptive sensations, the Tao creates and lets us 'explore' patterns or 'numbers.'

These patterns in turn give us 'regulation.' In other words, we can see the overall map of what has happened and what is likely to occur next by examining the hexagrams, dreams, body phenomena, etc. 'Knowing the future' and 'exploring number' are basic process analysis activities. We examine processes and try to understand their implicit patterns.

However, the very same Tao which unfolds the images, associations and representations also creates 'organic coherence in change.' According to the I Ching this 'organic coherence' is 'the work.' The I Ching thus defines process work in terms of analytically 'exploring number' or the patterns behind things and then experimentally following processes organically.

'The work,' like the alchemist's 'opus,' is transformation. No amount of knowledge can replace the experiential aspect of the Tao because without involvement in the evolution of visions, noises, body sensations, extrasensory perceptions, transference phenomena, or synchronicities, processes remain empty patterns without life.

The value of experiencing cannot be overestimated, especially since psychologists early in this century placed much importance upon insight and understanding as a cure for all things. The one-sided aspect of insight was naturally soon compensated for by another one-sidedness, experiencing. The existentialists in contrast to the psychoanalysts tend to see events as they are and require experiencing without critical analysis. Taoism or its modern correlate, process work, combine analyzing and experiencing according to the I Ching. In one phase of a given person's process exploring number or analyzing is the Tao while in another time experiencing the unpredictable flow of things is the Tao. Analysis and experience do not conflict, each has its own time.

PROCESS UNCERTAINTY PRINCIPLE

The I Ching continues its discussion: 'That aspect (of the Tao) which can not be fathomed in terms of the light and dark is called the spirit.'[9] In order to define this 'spirit' we must find out just how much of the Tao or of processes can actually be fathomed by the process in these channels. I can guess in which channels new experiences will occur but I cannot tell exactly what form the new experiences are going to have or when they will happen. Only process can reveal this information. For example, a woman who suffers from stomach trouble experiences her stomach as full of feeling. She dreams that a feelingless man dies. Her situation implies that she is moving out of feelinglessness and into the world of emotions and feelings, into stomach and gut reactions, into body or proprioceptive sensations. However I cannot tell her exactly *what* feelings are going to arise nor can I tell her *when* these are going to take place. Only living will reveal this.

The maximum amount of information which we can give someone about their process involves the channel in which they are functioning, the probable new channels which may open up, and the patterns of their present behavior in terms of primary and secondary phenomena. Jung formulated some of this information in terms of opposites. He discovered years ago that dreams are compensations for conscious behavior.[10] In process terms we would say that the secondary moves in a direction which is likely to be the opposite of momentary behavior. If one identifies with being weak we can guess that they will eventually become stronger and that their secondary processes are full of power signals. If they are having trouble in one channel such as seeing, or if they are plagued by a negative father who is determining and programming reality, we can guess that they are going to move into an unprogrammed life-style and let their eyes focus freely and randomly.

That which cannot be fathomed in terms of light and dark, in terms of the channels or their opposites is, according to the *I Ching*, the 'spirit.' In terms of the above, the 'spirit' is the unfathomable aspect of process work. It is the speed and exact form of future processes, the moment when channel changes occur, or when total awareness of the Tao will happen.

Thus processes contain an uncertainty principle which implies that their predictability is limited. We cannot guess when or exactly how things will manifest.

ARCHETYPES IN THE I CHING

Jung's definition of the archetypes sounds very much like process structures or hexagrams.[11] According to Jung,

> archetypes are not determined as regards their content, but only as regards their form, and even then to a very limited degree. . . . Its form, however, might perhaps be compared to the axial system of a crystal, which performs the crystaline structure in the mother liquid although it has no material existence of its own. The first appears according to the specific way in which the ions and molecules aggregate. The archetype in itself is empty and purely formal, nothing but a possibility of representation which is given a priori. . . our comparison with the crystal is illuminating in as much as the axial system determines only the stereometric structure but not the concrete form of the individual crystal. This may be either large or small, and it may vary endlessly by reason of the different size of its planes or by the growing together of two crystals. The only thing that remains constant is the axial system, or rather the invariable geometric proportions underlying it. . .[12]

Jung's definition of the archetypes describes them as process structures with a common mathematical basis. Certain aspects of this basis, such as Jung's 'axial systems', refer to the dimensions of the archetypes, or the channels of their expression. The tendency of one archetype to run into another (the tree may be related to the sun which is connected to the father, etc.[13]) is explainable by reference to this common structure.

It is not the least bit surprising that other process-oriented systems such as the I Ching have very similar concepts to the archetypes. In what follows, I am going to relate the archetypes to the hexagrams, and attempt to derive aspects of the former from the latter. According to the I Ching itself, these hexagrams were constructed originally as follows:

> The holy sages determined the Tao of heaven and called it dark and light. They determined the Tao of the earth and called it the yielding and the firm. They determined the Tao

of man and called it love and rectitude. They combined these
fundamental powers and doubled them. . .[14]

and in this way developed the hexagrams. Those who are
familiar with the *I Ching* will recognize in this ancient
formulation not only a description of the archetypes but a
description of how the oracle is used. The diviner first
formulates and contemplates a basic question in as simple a
manner as possible. When he is clear about this question
and has achieved an open mind to the ways of fate through
the use of incense or meditation he then enters into a ritual
procedure in which he allows fate to unfold itself.[15]

The *I Ching* employs one of two numerical rituals for this
procedure. One is called the yarrow stalk method in which
the questioner randomly divides forty-nine yarrow stalks
and computes the result so that one of two outcomes must
occur, yin or yang represented respectively by a divided
line, a ——— , or – –. The second method is a coin-throw
procedure in which three coins are flipped. Their outcomes
again are calculated in terms of the same binary system. The
result of repeating any one of the two procedures, (that is
the yarrow stalk or the coin throw) six times is the so-called
hexagram, a picture with six lines such as ≡≡o≡≡ The
possible sixty-four permutations and combinations of these
six lines have particular names and are described and
commented on by the *I Ching*.

A psychological commentary on the *I Ching*'s hexagrams
would be a work unto itself, and certainly worth perform-
ing. Here, however, I am going to examine only the
numerical properties of the hexagrams.

THE CHANCE ASPECT OF ARCHETYPAL IMAGES
One of the most fundamental properties of the hexagrams is
their chance-like nature. The hexagrams are created in such
a way as to cancel out ego manipulation. The questioner is
requested from the beginning to empty his mind of any
desire for a particular outcome. Then he enters into a
procedure which he cannot influence in any known causal

way. In the coin throw, for example, he is not able to influence the movement of the coins unless we speculate some form of magical or parapsychological causality. Such speculative theories are basically foreign to the *I Ching* which merely assumes that a chance event is a measure of the Tao. If we translate the chance aspect of the hexagrams into practical process work, then we arrive at a useful consideration. Namely, the archetype appears spontaneously in a multitude of channels through non-ego action.

ARCHETYPES AND CHANNELS

The archetype is the connecting pattern organizing spontaneous events. Thus dreams would be a channel of the archetype since one has minimal control over them. Body problems which cannot be influenced in a causal manner would be another channel of the archetype. Spontaneous acts of fate also belong to the description of the archetype. We see that the archetype is a total picture of the spontaneous phenomena occurring in all possible channels.

Notice that the hexagrams are a composition of *six* lines, or (according to the *I Ching* itself) a doubling of three lines. What are these three lines? The ancient sages determined the Tao of heaven, earth and man and then doubled these Taos, thereby creating the hexagrams.

What is the meaning of heaven, earth and man? The reader will recall from the previous chapter that the manner in which processes appear was discussed in terms of their individual characteristics or channel modes of communication. Heaven, man and earth would thus correspond to the channels in which the old Chinese experienced the workings of processes.

A careful reading of the *I Ching* might allow us to approximately translate heaven, man and earth in terms of what we today consider to be the world of dreams (heaven), the world of ordinary life (man), and the realm of inorganic and organic existence such as the body (earth). I cannot give an exact translation of the Chinese channels in terms of ours because their concepts overlap our modern ones and make a one-to-one correspondence impossible. My translation merely emphasizes the idea that the Tao expresses itself in terms of channels.

The *I Ching*'s use of three basic channels seems to be more a description of the human being's message-receiving capacity rather than an absolute quality of nature itself. The reader will recall, for example, that when Omtéotl created the world, he first created four Tezcatlipocas who were the dimensions or channels of reality. The *I Ching* uses three such channels, the fourth is the movement or change implicit in the three. Modern people still tend to organize nature in terms of the three spatial coordinates and one of time which is the movement implicit within the three, or in terms of space and three time dimensions (past, present and future).

Modern psychology too has channel-like dimensions. Freud's channel to the unconscious, which he called the 'royal road,' was dreams. The existentialists say that the 'here and now', the foreground or behavior of things, is everything, the 'royal road,' so to speak. Wilhelm Reich and his followers used the body as another 'royal road.' So today, we understand the human personality to be a (not yet unified) combination of dreams, here and now consciousness, and body life.

In any case, a practical consideration arises from the manifold channel composition of hexagrams. Namely, an archetype is a doubling or repetitive pattern appearing spontaneously in three or four relatively independent channels.

Hence, a total picture or hexagram, an archetype or pattern of a given situation is one which includes repetitive body problems, dreams, here and now pictures or other individual channels which process work evolves. The process definition of an archetype is the interrelationship between various channels.

BINARY CHARACTERISTICS OF ARCHETYPES
An important aspect of the hexagrams is that they are composed of binary information: yin and yang, or 0 and 1. The reasons for using a binary system are not discussed by

the ancient sages. For them, things are simply the way they are and that is that. I accept the fact that the binary code is a basic method of communication between the non-ego and the ego, however, and I would also like to share my ideas about this binary code.

My theory about the binary code is based upon our innate ability to perceive things. Human beings are special types of receivers. Either we notice something or we do not. We are stimulated and pick up information, or we are not stimulated and perceive nothing. My theory does not involve the quality of information or its implicit message or meaning, but simply the process of our perception. The hexagrams are based upon the binary system of our reception apparatus, not upon the 'absolute' nature of the unconscious. The individual lines or channels are filled with binary signals yin or yang, without particular meaning attached to them! The significance of the binary code of any given channel appears only in terms of the total hexagram.

In process work, the binary system appears as the most primitive way a verbally oriented consciousness communicates with a non-verbal source of information. Let me give you an example. Let us say that you have a pain in your stomach. The most primitive communication between you and your stomach consists basically of a signal such as 'yes,' there is pain or 'no,' there is no pain. You could, if you wanted to, verbally communicate with your stomach without disturbing the authenticity of its proprioceptive communication potential by employing this system. For example, you could do a verbal proprioceptively oriented active imagination with your stomach if you determine for example that increased stomach pain means 'no,' decreased means 'yes.' Then you could ask the stomach anything you wanted to and get a yes or no answer. For example you might ask, 'Will you speak with me?' If pain increases (meaning 'no') you are too aggressive, passive, etc.

Let us say that a visual channel sends you a signal. A primitive verbal communication with the visual process asks it binary questions. You might say, 'Well, will you talk to me?' Increased intensity of light means 'yes,' etc. We should credit the neurolinguistic programmers for developing binary communication with auditory, visual and proprioceptive channels.

BINARY FLICKERING

However, credit must be given to the *I Ching* for having developed binary communication with extrasensory sources. In fact the binary system of the *I Ching* is more differentiated than a simple 'yes-no' code. Studying this differentation leads to an extension of the simple binary system which then appears to be a special case of a more general method of communicating with the unconscious.

The *I Ching* manifests process in terms of a 'yes' and 'no' but also two other possible signals, thus enabling the non-verbal source to answer in a total of four signals: namely, yin, yin moving, yang and yang moving, corresponding to the numbers 6, 8, 7, and 9[16] (and the results of throwing three coins whose 'heads' are valued three and 'tails,' two).

The 'moving' lines have extreme values (6 and 9) and are referred to as being especially 'charged.' These lines are used by the questioner to determine which line (or channel) of the overall hexagram (or archetype) is most applicable to his question. Change occurs in the overall hexagram because of these extremes or moving lines. If for example one gets a 9 in the fifth place and a 6 in the third in the following hexagram (as well as a 7 in the first place, a 7 in the second, a 7 in the fourth and an 8 in the sixth) then only the 6 and 9 lines change. These lines change to their opposites thereby transforming the entire hexagram. Thus we have,

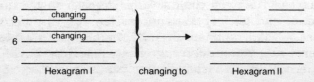

Hexagram I   changing to   Hexagram II

An example

This representation of change in the archetypes gives rise to

special methods of communication with secondary processes. An example comes to mind. Imagine a man with a stomach tumor. He is a simple man without particular psychological interests and comes to me because he is afraid of his tumor. He has no background in any of the techniques of modern psychology which would help him to contact his unconscious. He speaks about a pain in his stomach and only about this pain. Amplifying and following his process thus means staying in a verbally described proprioceptive channel. He says, 'Sometimes the pain is there and sometimes it is not. Why does it hurt me?' His communication system is thus basically binary. 'What question would you like to ask your stomach?' I say to him. He repeats, 'Why do you hurt me so much?' Then I say, 'Try to ask it something simpler which it can answer in yes and no.' 'Will you tell me why you hurt me?' he asks. He focuses on the pain which disappears and this means yes to him. 'Do you not like me?' The pain goes away again implying, yes, it does not like him. 'Do you want to kill me?' Again a yes. 'Will you tell me why?' Again a yes. 'Why?'

This time the pain goes away but flickers back again indicating a yes but basically no. The secondary process says it will tell him but that it does not want to. The flickering answer indicates among other things that the unconscious has an evolving and not a static answer. In other words the answer is more than a simple 'yes' or 'no.' At this point the receiver has one of two choices. He can reformulate his question implicit in the flickering 'yes moving to no.' Following the latter would mean momentarily dropping his verbal framework and realizing that the unconscious is speaking in terms of a proprioceptive process in contrast to a static answer. Staying with a verbal receiver system limits the expressiveness of the unconscious. If the receiver chooses to examine this expressiveness then he must focus his attention on proprioceptive channels and 'feel' with his inner receptors and follow the pain's evolution. Such following may require experience and practice.

In the present case, the man let his inner feeling evolve at its own pace. After a while he 'felt' something and said that his basic problem was that he had never had a relationship to himself. Then he felt better. Thus the answer to his question, 'why do you hurt me so much?' and also the solution to his pain occurred simultaneously.

The advantage of a simple binary system of communication is that it allows non-verbal sources to communicate in a verbal language framework without disturbing consciousness and without seriously perturbing the authenticity of the non-verbal source. Such a system can be especially useful to people who are novices in process work.

On the other hand the disadvantage of this system is that it limits a non-verbal source to a restricted communication potential. The 'moving lines' of the *I Ching* which correspond to binary flickering phenomena in a particular channel thus extend the static binary system. A binary flicker indicates the existence of a process. Following this process coming from a flickering channel or moving line, however, depends to some extent upon the individual's ability to temporarily abandon his normal communication framework and to enter another type of communication. This latter type may be experienced as a scary adventure. The choice about entering into this new communication can be determined only by the ego. If the fear is great, the fear is a process indicating that one must remain in one's own framework and press the unconscious to express itself there. A more adventurous situation would be indicated by less fear. Let us look at such a situation.

Another example
A man with a neck tumor complains about the fear and pain of the symptoms and repeatedly puts his hand on his neck. The flickering signal in the foreground which I shall amplify will be proprioceptive sensations in the neck. The dreams (visual channel) and relationship problems (relationship channel) may interest me but the proprioceptive experience in the neck is emphasized by the patient. The overall situation may be described by the case of an elderly man who has never been able to stand up for himself as a professional. He often suffers from inferiority feelings and

tends to be placating to others.

In this example amplification consists in introvertedly experiencing the tumor. After a few quiet moments the client says to me that he experienced his neck as if it were being strangled. Since he showed me with his hand what it was like to be strangled, I followed his motion and asked him to use that hand to strangle himself with. The 'strangler' promptly said, 'I shall kill you, you weak fish.' After more dialogue associated to the strangling activity, the neck muscles finally resisted saying that 'No one, not even fate is going to kill me.' This statement brought about an overall change in the man. He said that he was stronger than he had been aware of and that he now had to live his life without wondering 'how' to be strong but by simply 'being' strong. He said he felt better.

A process analysis of change based upon the numerical patterns of the I Ching would go something like this. The archetype or overall situation consists of an elderly man suffering from inferiority problems with one channel manifesting extreme flickering phenomena in the neck. The work focused on the neck and amplified the proprioceptive sensations there. The neck was the battleground between the weak and the strong. By amplifying the foreground experience of the strangler, the weak changed from weak to strong through the challenge. As soon as change happened in one channel an overall transformation occurred in which the neck felt better (there was a temporary relief from coughing caused by the tumor), insight into the personality spontaneously occurs and a program for future change was created.

Only the beginning and end phase of the processes can be described clearly. Amplification of the channel manifesting intense proprioceptive activity in the foreground, however, produced a moment in which there was no clarity, no governing picture or archetypal image. In terms used by the I Ching that aspect of the work which can be 'fathomed' in terms of the dark and the light (i.e. the opposites) would be the hexagram, i.e. the archetypal patterns of the beginning and end states. That aspect of the work which is 'unfathomable' in terms of the opposites (or their channels) is the 'spirit,' i.e. the speed and moment of change. In short the 'work' consists in letting the 'spirit' create 'organic coherence in change.'

The similarity in structure between the archetypes and hexagrams, lines and channels, moving lines and foreground channels, Tao and process are so striking that it seems certain that the same motivation which created the *I Ching* is trying to regenerate itself in modern times. This might be why the *I Ching* seemed to be ready to appear to western audiences.[17]

Chapter 8
PATTERNS IN THE I CHING

Now we move to a study of the hexagram or archetypal image as a whole and leave the investigation of its parts. The archetype is apparently more than the sum of its parts. It is the implication derived from individual channel characteristics.

According to Wilhelm,

> The situation represented by the hexagrams as a whole is called the Time. This term comprises several entirely different meanings according to the characteristics of the various hexagrams.[1]

The Time is further delineated by a very old Chinese mantic procedure in which a wheel with one set of trigrams is spun relative to another stationary wheel with another set of trigrams.[2] The resulting combination of the so-called earlier and later heaven arrangements is thus a combination of two times, an earlier and a later, or inner and outer, dream and reality. According to the *I Ching* the earlier heaven is composed of opposing forces which do not combat one another but rather hold each other in equilibrium. The later

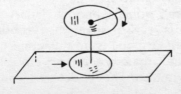

heaven is constructed according to the periodic changes in the day or the year. This later heaven arrangement comes out of the Lo River according to legend.

The view of the archetype as Time means that the archetype itself is a process, not a stationary condition. Helmut Wilhelm stresses process in his introduction to the *I Ching*:

> The eight trigrams are images not so much of objects as of states of change. This view is associated with the concept expressed in the teachings of Lao-Tse, as also in those of Confucius, that every event in the visible world is the effect of an 'image,' that is, of an idea in the unseen world.[3]

Wilhelm significantly reminds us that the hexagrams are not objects but processes, not static states but active in motion. The archetype is not the static momentary dream image or body problem but the 'process maker' so to speak, the repetitive impulse which amplifies itself in all channels of awareness.

THE ARCHETYPE AS A DOUBLE PROCESS

If we return for a moment to the quote on page 99 of the foregoing chapter we recall that the sages created the hexagrams by determining the Tao in three channels and then doubling the resulting trigram to form a hexagram. We also remember from page 109 how the old Taoists divided the Tao by using two spinning wheels, the earlier and later heavenly arrangements. Why were the trigrams doubled and why were they called earlier and later?

The double, 'earlier' and 'later' quality of process structures are crucial aspects of the hexagrams. These qualities remind me of the Hopi Indian categories of 'that which is manifest' and 'that which is beginning to be manifest' and refer to what I call primary and secondary processes. The primary process is 'earlier' than the secondary one in the sense that the primary one is now 'manifest,' it is closer to present awareness than secondary processes which are beginning to manifest. They exist now on the fringe of awareness and will become focal interests in the near future.

Moreover, the primary or earlier processes have the quality of the earlier heaven arrangement (see page 109), which is composed of patterns which are relatively stable. Secondary processes are like the 'later heaven' which is constructed according to the periodic changes in the days and seasons.

An example

Consider a woman who is so busy that she barely has time to sleep. She is in an existential panic about life, and arrives in my office out of breath, late for our appointment. After telling me about how she was held up by traffic and about all that she has to do, she begins to support her head with a hand while resting her elbow on the arm of the chair. Her primary process, the one she is aware of and the one which is relatively stable is her identity with her busy life. Her secondary process appears first in the form of the traffic jam which held her up and in the form of the arm-head signal which lies at the fringe of her awareness and which is now beginning to manifest. I recommend to her to let me hold her head and to experience more exactly what her head was doing. She says, 'Oh, what a pleasure just to let go and to be supported!' Then I recommended that she use her supporting arm to hold my head. She said, 'Yes, I can support the need to let go' and then she did and began to meditate. This quiet meditation was the secondary process implicit in the recurring traffic jam and arm–head signal.

Her overall pattern was composed of a primary process connected to rushing and a secondary one consisting of double body signals and outer world phenomena which were attempting to transform the primary one by doing things in a more centered way.

COUPLING WITHIN THE ARCHETYPE

Thus what Jung called archetypes and what the *I Ching* refers to as hexagrams appear to be very differentiated process structures. These structures are self-creating, they arise spontaneously, express themselves in a multitude of channels, have primary and secondary time characteristics which appear earlier and later in awareness, and have secondary processes with a repetitive nature. The *I Ching* continues to differentiate process structures by referring to the coupled nature of the 'lines,' or channels of expression.

The book refers to 'holding together,' and to 'correspondence' between the lines of the individual trigrams which themselves are connected as 'heaven' and 'earth.' The overall significance of the lines is derived according to their 'place' and their coupling to other lines.[4] The relationship between the lines is further differentiated as 'members of a family.'

The coupling between the individual lines of a hexagram corresponds in process science to the coupled connections between the phenomena occurring in different channels. We know from preceding work that these connections lead to concepts such as the dreambody and dream universe and that the invariant aspect of the coupling is called process logic. In other words, the streams of our perception comprise a sort of family of observations connected by the meaning of the overall pattern.

The *I Ching* does not reduce and separate the hexagram into its parts but understands the coupling of the lines in terms of the meaning of the whole. This means that a given 'mysterious' coupling between channels can be understood not simply in terms of the causal connections between them but in terms of the overall pattern. For example, psychosomatic medical processes, parapsychological phenomena such as psychokinesis or levitation, synaesthesia and sychronicity can be comprehended in terms of the relationship between the individual channels of these phenomena and the overall situation of the observer.

Synaesthesia occurs frequently in process-oriented body work where channels overlap and intermingle. In synaesthesia, one might hear with the skin, see with the bones, sense pressure with the eyes and thus mix auditory, visual and proprioceptive channels. Such experiences look very strange at first inspection because we expect seeing, hearing and feeling to operate in association with eyes, ears and proprioceptive receivers, respectively. Our expectations standardize the way in which our perception normally functions and lead to confusion when they do not function in a standard way!

Process logic reduces much of synaesthesia's mystery by looking at the overall picture of a person who experiences an intermingling in the channels. In this picture the individual might appear too organized, too predetermining, and too logical in the way he has been living. We can almost predict that such an individual will experience mixing or overlapping of channels in order to relativize his state-oriented consciousness and introduce him to the fact that nature is more than he expected.

Psychokinesis, or moving objects at a distance, also antagonizes our normal expectations of matter and psyche. However, every therapist has experienced at one time or another what it is like to be physically moved by a patient to do something as if under the influence of that patient. Voodooers and black magicians have been busy with psychokinesis since the beginning of time. If, however, one looks at the dreams of the therapist or those of the patient, then one sees that a given archetype may be constellated which dreams up the environment.

The *I Ching*'s logic may be used to unravel the significance of a group Tao by understanding each member of the group as a specific channel just as a given person's archetypal situation is composed of his individual channels. Thus the group's members are its channels.

For example, family life may be understood as if the family were an individual composed of the events happening within each of its members. Process science then predicts that each member and his relationship to other members of the family are coupled processes whose meaning is finally unraveled only by examining the overall process of the family at any given time. Analogically speaking troubled members of a family or couples of a community forced to undergo unusual processes become the 'moving lines' of a group archetype so to speak, the charged channels whose development is dreamed up and belongs to the evolution of the entire community.

LIBERATION

Thus, the *I Ching* indicates that the phenomena occurring in a given individual or group channel are coupled together through the overall pattern created by the composition of channels. The implication of the ancient book is that liberation or enlightenment occurs through divining this pattern and adjusting oneself to the overall flow. The process formulation of this implication is that individuation means perceiving and following the structure behind the body phenomena, dreams, relationships and worldly difficulties.

The problem with the *I Ching*'s philosophy is that it is almost impossible to follow!

In practical everyday life processes often occur in exactly those areas which are most antagonistic to consciousness.[5] The saint represses his sexuality, the adult refuses his jealousy and anger. The simplest, human, natural phenomena are often too much for most of us to accept. Nature is complete but we are one-sided and filter out what we perceive.

Thus freedom and liberation are fraught with frustration because following secondary processes takes us to the very edge of our abilities and philosophies. We need time, patience and often help from our friends in becoming aware of our totality. Often we fall backwards in fright and tiredness in the face of our total reality. Liberation from a cyclical rut, a symptom or complex is no simple matter and does not usually occur without a very courageous consciousness or unless a life and death struggle which shoves us over our edges, our conscious reservations. The *I Ching* realized these difficulties centuries ago and warned us that:

> the changes have no consciousness, no action; they are quiescent and do not move. But if they are stimulated, they penetrate all situations under heaven. If they were not the most divine thing on earth, how could they do this.[6]

Here our ancient divinator guide to process work reminds us that the process or present situation in which you live will not change by itself. It needs 'stimulation' and awareness. It needs amplification, we would say. And then process moves, it changes and the worst rut, impasse, symptom and complex can be 'penetrated.' The *I Ching* tells us that this is the 'most divine thing', which means that there is some sort of god experience, a type of religious and wondrous thing, in processes which we cannot grasp without experiencing it. But people have an edge against such experience!

It seems to me as if the weakest point in Taoism is that it does not deal with the edge. The legendary Lao Tsu, author of the *Tao Te Ching*, wrote down his wisdom, for example after most of his edges were crossed, just at the point when he was about to resign from life irritated at the lack of awareness typical of the human condition.[7] Some gate keeper in western China apparently stopped him from leaving the city and dying in the desert for long enough to get him to write his concept of the Tao. He says in chapter 21 of his work *Tao Te Ching* that:

> The greatest virtue is to follow the Tao and Tao alone.
> The Tao is elusive and intangible.
> Oh, it is intangible and elusive and yet within is image.
> Oh, it is elusive and intangible yet within is form.
> Oh, it is dim and dark, and yet within is essence.
> This essence is very real, and therein lies faith.
> From the very beginning until now its name has been forgotten, Thus I perceive the creation.[8]

Lao Tsu reminds us that it is very difficult to discover the Tao; he says it is very real and very tangible, but does not tell us 'how' to discover the Tao. It is important to note that the answer to this 'how' may lie in this story of his writing. Taoist philosophy appears at the point of death!!

The Zen master, Wu Tzu, balances Lao Tsu by stressing that extreme and dangerous circumstances teach the existence of the Tao. He tells a tale which goes something like this.[9] Once there was a boy who earnestly wanted to learn how to be a burglar like his father. The latter, interested in the boy's development, took him on his first 'job' to a rich man's house in the neighborhood. The father-son team broke stealthily in by night, found the treasure chest and opened it. But as the boy stood in front of the the box marveling at its contents, the father quickly shoved him in and locked the chest. Then the old man ran from the house, slamming the door behind him purposely awakening all of its sleeping members. The boy, lacking air and fearing death, scratched like a mouse at the walls of the chest until a curious maid heard the noise and fearfully opened its cover.

Lo and behold! The boy sprang forth like the wind, put out the maid's candle and ran for the door. As he passed the well in the garden he paused for a moment, picked up a stone from the ground and threw it into the water. The family, pursuing the thief, heard the splash and assumed that the thief had drowned.

When the boy got home he asked the father why he locked him in the chest. Instead of answering, the father only inquired about how the boy got away. After hearing the tale he complimented his son on having learned the thief's art.

Wu Tzu implies that tension between life and death is required to learn how to follow the Tao, or to become an enlightened person. This implication is very familiar to me from my practice. Years of training, belief or psychotherapy are not sufficient to help one overcome one's fears of or blocks to perception.

Consider the middle-aged man who had a lung tumor. I had been working with him regularly for some time in a most undramatic fashion. Now the fear of death impelled him, he explained, to get over his 'reservations'. We had touched upon breathing problems earlier, but for some reason the moment did not impel us to really get down to the root of his difficulty.

He began by telling me the following story. He had had a non-malignant tumor removed from his lungs some years ago. Now it had returned to the same spot. This time, his question was, should he operate on it again or not. 'Perhaps it is malignant?' he giggled. We worked with the giggle and he admitted that he felt as if he had regressed. He felt he should not need help even though he did! While he spoke he put his hand on his chest and said that when he felt his impeded breathing experience he saw someone pressing him. I switched channels with him and recommended that he look more closely at his vision. Then his arms moved slightly imitating a sort of hug as he described his vision. I switched to movement and amplified his arm motion by strongly hugging him. As I pressed another memory suddenly reappeared. 'When I was a kid, two friends squeezed me until I fainted! But when I awoke, the world was completely in order!!' He thought a moment and then cried. He admitted for the first time that he was an alcoholic, secretly drinking every day. He spoke of the way he loved 'passing out' and how useful drinking was to him. It enabled him to deal with painful situations. I heard what I guessed must be his passing out in his low tone of voice, and suggested he listen to his voice, leave the words out, and then hum the tone he heard in himself. He began humming and immediately fell into a trance. A moment later he came out of it and slowly said, 'Why operate? Now I am well! Wow, did I need a tumor and chronic breathing problem to get to this state?'

The enlightened Taoist, it seems to me, can be any person who is not only fascinated by the idea of following the processes but who also has the great luck to have a father who sets up the prerequisites for learning or a life with enough trouble, danger and fear to force even a stubborn person to become flexible and aware.

Chapter 9
THE ALCHEMICAL OPUS

The alchemist, like the Taoist, also believed that process contained its own solution. He discovered and defined processes in his laboratory, amplified them and marveled at the transformations which miraculously occurred. Like the Taoist, he also got stoned on his work and claimed that it cured everything and healed all problems. He exclaimed that it helped him to transcend death and even spoke of channels which overlapped and amalgamated. Such labora-

6   *An Alchemist and his laborant at work, c. 1530 (Mary Evans Picture Library)*

tory workers existed and even exist today. Their work is referred to as the 'Opus.'

Their science, alchemy, is probably the oldest science in the world. It has been practiced universally wherever advanced civilizations existed, and mixed in with prevailing religious beliefs. For example, the Chinese Taoists practiced alchemy. They coupled alchemy together with meditation procedures and tried to transform material objects as well as their own physiology.[1] They were interested in becoming subtle bodies which lived forever. The Taoist alchemist saw his own person as the 'prima materia' and cooked it under the controlled fires of his breathing.

We find alchemy also in India intermixed with hatha yoga, tantra and shamanism.[2] Alchemy in Egypt centered on creating immortality.[3] Here, body work was intimately connected with preserving the dead body. Most Arab nations were interested in gold making.[4] The Greeks borrowed laboratory techniques from Egyptian alchemy, added religious philosophy and were the forerunners of the European traditions which I shall focus on in this chapter.

Alchemy reached its peak in medieval Europe but fell upon hard times with the rise of natural science. Jung rediscovered alchemy in the twentieth century and showed that it was the forgotten mother of modern medicine, psychology and physics. He applied the alchemist's laboratory or 'shoptalk' to the transformations of the personality and showed that the *prima materia* was a symbol for the unconscious and that the process of creating gold mirrored individuation.[5]

THE OPUS
Now, like the alchemist, I want to drop my theories and talk about practice. I want to speak to the experimental process worker in this chapter. I want to make him feel at home in the 'shoptalk' of alchemy. I am going to use this ancient science in order to help the process worker express his psychotherapeutic psycho-physical labors more completely. In what follows I am going to speak directly to you, dear reader, as though you were a process worker and show you

that what you are practicing is a modern version of the most ancient science known to us. If Taoism is your theory, alchemy is your art.

What do you do when you go to your laboratory? Sometimes you feel like playing but mostly you are bound to be gripped by something more serious. Your work may be on yourself, or it may be concerned with someone else, with a couple, a group, a punching bag or a piece of unmolded clay. But whatever it is, a work presents itself to you.

7   The opus (Biblioteca Apostica Vaticana)

The alchemist experienced his work similarly and called it the 'opus.'[6] He had various ideas about what it must be but never formulated this work exactly because, like the process worker, the method interested him more than the result most of the time.

SOLVE ET COAGULA
He had his own shoptalk of course. As he sat in front of his flasks and bottles, his fires and vapors, he heard his unconscious whispering into his ear the famous alchemical

secrets, 'Solve et Coagula,' and 'Solvite corpora et coagulate spiritum.'[7]

Dissolve the body and coagulate the spirit. 'Switch channels,' he must have thought. See if a body problem can bring insight or if a dream can be expressed kinesthetically! The alchemist apparently was interested in volatilizing the concrete and concretizing fantasy.

He imagined his 'opus' to be a stone. In fact he called the goal of his work the 'philosopher's stone.' If you are a process worker, you will understand him when he tells you that his goal was the philosopher's stone and that his method was (watch out for the switch here!) the 'stone of the philosophers.'[8] I do not think that he meant to be confusing, for only a theorist would be confused here at the reversal of method and goal.

The alchemist's goal was his method! The alchemist was like you, dear process worker. He was not primarily interested in creating the cure-all like modern psychotherapists striving for the panacea. The true alchemist was someone who was his destination, so to speak. You will understand him, I am sure. He tried to follow processes and realized that when he succeeded in following nature nothing more was required. His opus was his method, the attitude of religiously following nature.

The paradox is that the way is the goal. This paradox conforms to your experience. You have noticed, I am sure, that people repeatedly meet with old problems regardless of what sort of psychotherapy they use. The happiest of them are not the ones who have made birch trees out of maple trees, who have solved their problems or changed themselves but the ones who got birch saplings to grow respectfully into birch trees. Their goal was the never ending process of unfolding.

THE *PRIMA MATERIA*

Don't you sometimes get embarrassed when your neighbor asks you what you do? What can you tell them? If you are a process worker, you never know what you are going to do before you get into your laboratory. Other professions can

8   An alchemist at work 1544 (Mary Evans Picture Library)

be clear. But if you are too exact you are not a process worker! Sometimes you help kids learn to read better, sometimes you work on a back tumor, at other times you spend an hour crying yourself, then there are periods of nervous embrace, deep breathing, dream work, lecturing like a minister, recommending diets, being silent for the day. One hour you work like a poet; the next like an auto mechanic. Who is going to understand all this? To begin with you can tell the neighbors that you work with people or problems and hopefully this explanation will suffice.

The alchemist would blandly say when your neighbor asks what he does, that he is doing his 'opus,' working on the *'prima materia.'* If the neighbor were impertinent enough to ask what this was, then the alchemist would uninhi-bitedly speak chemical poetry. He did not live in the latter part of the twentieth century.!

The *'prima materia,'* he would say, is a 'constant soul' and also an 'imperfect body' which may be found buried underground in a mine.[9] The time to dig for it depends upon the horoscope. This statement will quiet the neighbor, I am sure.

But you understand the alchemist immediately. The *'prima materia'* is another word for the beginning of a process. Why did the alchemist not call his process the Tao or the Time? Well, he almost did when he said that you could find the *'prima materia'* only when the horoscope indicated the moment had arrived to begin an opus. The alchemist, however, stressed the *'materia'* aspect of processes, while the ordinary Taoist was concerned with the structure of events around him. The European alchemist experienced processes mainly in his pots and pans. The Taoist was a proprioceptive visual type, a philosopher, the alchemist basically a visual kinesthetic person. He would have loved body work and certainly have been fascinated by experimental physics!

However, the alchemist was not materialistic. He did say after all that the *prima materia* had a 'constant soul.'[10] You know what he meant? He implied that the processes he worked with were perseverating (i.e. constant) events. He would not simply have attacked the first itch he saw, but would have waited to see if the itch perseverated, if it had continuity. He waited to see which processes repeated and these he worked on.

He said quite clearly that the *'prima materia'* was an 'imperfect body' by which he meant that it had to be perfected. It began by being impure, incomplete and in need of transformation. Any ordinary tumor, itch, anxiety, headache or stroke of fate is an 'imperfect body' asking to be cooked and transformed. Fantasies and tics are 'imperfect' because they are not congruent with the rest of the personality. The *prima materia* transforms to perfection by unifying all of its separate, incongruent and disharmonious parts, by focusing simultaneously on primary and secondary processes.

THE *IGNIS NONNATURALIS*

I am sure that your neighbor will have stopped the conversation by this time. But if you get together with other process workers, and talk 'shop,' one of them is bound to mention that 'things happen by themselves.' An alchemist would help you express yourself more exactly by saying that there is an *'ignis nonnaturalis,'*[11] a natural spark in processes which makes them evolve.

You get excited at this point because you too have seen this *'ignis.'* You often observed that you need not put much energy into the work because the energy is already there. Each incongruent process has its own *'ignis.'* Here is a 'new' term for your shoptalk!

Recall the man who began his work by rubbing his brow. Recall how you amplified his rubbing and how the rubbing energy transformed into visions and active imaginations. The amplified *ignis* transformed the kinesthetic channel into vision. Remember the woman who complained about always being turned on? You encouraged her to experience her *'ignis'* and she felt immediately whole. You were afraid she would attack you sexually and were surprised when her excitement became her life dance. Proprioceptive energy turned into movement! Thank god!

The alchemist described his *'ignis nonnaturalis'* as a 'dry water which does not wet the hands,' and also as a 'fire which does not burn'[12] and you know just why he said this. He had to because he was so amazed that the processes he observed, the wild fires he experienced, did not harm anyone. You too have seen many sexual impulses go the way of tantric yoga in the sense of switching channels or becoming integrated as whole experiences without burning anyone. How many fits have you seen in which people banged on your punching bag, screamed at their parents and teachers without ever having even scratched themselves in the process? How much water have you seen which did not wet, how many tears which did not drown the person but brought him to a state of enlightenment? Amazing, but in the many hundreds of hours you have watched the *prima materia* doing its own opus with the help of the '*ignis nonnaturalis*,' you have never once seen an injury—to date at least—which exceeded a scratched elbow or bruised fist. Apparently people are less dangerous to themselves when they are doing process work than when they are letting out their affects without awareness.

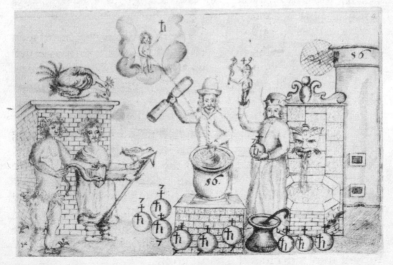

9 *The oven and the egg (Biblioteca Apostica Vaticana)*

THE EGG

Once you find the *prima materia* and discover that it has its own energy, say in a tense back, a moving finger, a stroke of fate or a vision, you put the *prima materia* into an egg, a 'philosopher's egg.'[13] 'Philosopher' meant for the alchemist a 'lover of wisdom', and egg meant literally a place to grow.

Even if you may not have loved your academic background, you may still be a philosopher if you are a lover of wisdom. In fact, if you are a process worker, you have to be a philosopher because you guide your own life by a form of wisdom which is greater than any you may have learned; the process itself.

This is why you undertake the opus in the first place. You need to discover and know. If you knew how to lead your life you would not have anything to do with this form of work, unless of course you were simply a mad experimentalist. But such madness is foreign to you. You are not interested in science for science's sake but for your own human use. That is why you focus on the *prima materia* in a loving way and thereby create an egg in which it can develop. The egg encircles the *prima materia* and singles it out as the work. First you define the *prima materia* as a process buried underground at quite a distance from consciousness in one of the double or triple non-congruent signals of the personality. Then you wait until the process perseverates demonstrating its own '*ignis nonnaturalis*,' and then, bang! You hermetically seal this inside an egg by intensely focusing on it with all your heart, waiting for the process to transform. Your egg is your commitment to the process, your conscious attitude which says, 'I trust whatever is in my focus, I believe it will bring me whatever it is I am supposed to discover about this life.'

But since the philosopher's egg is also just a simple egg, it is a piece of nature not created by man, and is thus not a product of the will. The egg symbolizes a property which most people have, a natural focus, attention or interest which brings creative sparks to birth, which unfolds the essence of your person.

The essence of this spark is known to everyone. Something put you on this earth in the first place, something is keeping you alive, and something is unfolding this spark into the evolution of your life. People forget about the origins of life, however, and do not feel, see or hear it in themselves.

Process work brings one back into contact with this spark because it depends upon your dreams, body and outer situation. The Taoists focused on that crazy little spark which puts dreams into your head, which makes you aware of fantasies, which moves your body in this direction or that, and which creates internal dialogue with the unfathomable spirit.

Thus the egg is the capacity to pick up this spark and carry it to its conclusion, to listen to internal dialogue, to care for fantasies, to notice your body motions and follow them. The alchemist as a philosopher or lover of wisdom differentiated himself from others. 'Having a process' in a conscious way is a very unusual thing. Most people are not very interested in becoming lovers of their process wisdom. Others might be interested but are led away from their processes. The horde of teachers, psychologists and physicians tell these people that their processes are wrong and try to get them to change themselves, to get rid of their problems and their symptoms.

Thus we learn other people's wisdom, fit ourselves into eggs which do not belong to us and do not arrive at the point where we have our own process. We may find temporary solutions to our griefs and symptoms but do not get around to solving the larger, and central human problem: learning how to have a process, mother the inner spark of life which put us on this planet and which sends us back to wherever we came from.

THE OVEN
Following alchemical tradition, you put the egg in 'Athanor,' the oven which is devised to keep the process at constant temperature over long periods of time.[14] Until now, your work has been mainly observation. You had to find the *prima materia*, single it out, seal it off and divide it from all

other things in a loving way.

Now, the work changes. You must begin cooking. By studying amplification and practicing it on body processes, dream images, strokes of fate, and relationship problems you have in fact created a man-made object, an oven. You know just how important this oven can be. If you heat things up too much with amplification, if you push something more than its nature allows, you can split the opus in the egg to pieces and may even get hit by the parts. You can lose your commitment!

Have you not heard stories from your colleagues about therapists who were too ambitious and who did not follow the process of their clients? Remember the therapist who broke a client's resistance, opened her up too early with body work and did not respect her character armour? He left her defenseless and she was subsequently attacked on a New York street and almost killed. A good story to remember when you think it is your job to push things farther than they want to go.

On the other hand, how many times has your oven functioned without enough heat? You were too shy to step in on something, and things went cold and died. Your client went to another therapist who was more real and direct than you. Indeed, keeping things at a constant temperature which is neither too hot nor too cold is difficult. You have to constantly check the process by looking through the little window in your oven to get the necessary information to see if things are too hot or too cold. You need to listen to the client's voice, watch his posture, observe his eyes to see how things are going.

THE PUFFERS
When you have a bad day you turn into a 'puffer' and blow like hell through your bellows, impatient that the oven will not bring the *prima materia* in the philosopher's egg quickly enough to completion. You should throw in your towel, go home and rest. Otherwise you will turn into your shadow, the puffer:

He knows, he claims the means to accrue within one's own home the mother lode of all treasures, without any other riches than that of a part of those one possesses. On the strength of his words . . . one succumbs, one sows one's gold to reap but smoke. . . . There are few artists who are true alchemists. . . . True alchemists do not glory in their science; they do not seek to swindle or cheat other people out of their money because . . . he that has everything, needs nothing . . .[15]

The puffer, in short, is the power shadow of psychology, the one who claims to achieve wondrous effects and who identifies himself with creation itself. Beware. Process work is so much fun and creates so much numen that if you are not careful you will either think too much of yourself or else suffer from inferiority when you lose your ability to follow and respect the process. You push. Watch out! The *prima materia* is full of poisons. Remember that you can be dreamed up by blocked clients to puff too much. Let people do their own work. But alas, few people are prepared—in the beginning at least—to discover their own process. And many have little *'ignis.'*

STAGES OF TRANSFORMATION
Now the work begins. The alchemist peeks into his oven and what does he see? CONFLICT!!

I am sure he did not always see a fiery conflict. But he saw it so many times that he assumed that conflict was the beginning of transformation of the *prima materia*. The solar, hot and male principle (sulphur) attacked the lunar cold female essence (mercury) and all hell broke loose.[16]

How many times have you seen process work begin with a conflict? Sometimes people tell you they are in conflict with others. At other times they tell you they do not like even you. (Then the two of you are in the pot.) Sometimes their bodies are in tension and their conflicts are somatized. Remember the case of the neck tumor? (last chapter) There, the male principle was the strangler the 'sun', and the lunar principle was the weak ego. When you work on headaches you often find a powerful solar force straining against a lethargic lunar mercuriality which needs awakening. How many cramps turned out to be arousers in which solar power was trying to awaken an easy-going, quiet, lunar personality? Any incongruent signal is in conflict with awareness. Primary and secondary double signals do not get along in part because no one paid the double signals much respect before.

THE *AQUA PERMANENS*

As long as things are in conflict, everything is tense. But after focusing on this conflict, processes move out of the realm of opposites. They literally kill or exhaust one another. The alchemist looking into his pots imagined the solar and the lunar principles fighting to extinction.

You know what this is like. You begin with one extreme, one polarity in process work, let it move or speak for itself, and then another extreme becomes activated and begins to fight. After a while, they begin to amalgamate or flip into one another so that they become indistinguishable. The angry father sounds like the little boy, the helpless child turns into a powerful god. The aggressive fists of the puncher turn into the fluttering chest of wailing depression. The opposites annihilate each other or become indistinguishable as flow takes the place of polarity.

The alchemists called this flow the '*aqua permanens*', or permanent water.[17] *Aqua permanens* is the fluid process, the energy or life which was locked up in the tension of conflict which has now been freed through the flow between the opposites. Fluidity comes from conflict. Whereas before there was a boundary between conflicting opposites, between intent and reality, streaming energy now transforms therapy into natural science.

THE NIGREDO

That moment in which the opposites disappear and in which the liquid of life arises is called the *nigredo*, 'the darkness darker than dark,' the 'black of blacks.'[18] Strangely enough the alchemist claims that this is the 'first sign that (he) is on the right path.' He said that there is 'no generation without corruption.'[19]

You as a process worker will be surprised about the alchemists' positive attitude towards the *nigredo*, because you know how many hours you have sat wondering about the loss of consciousness which takes place when people leave their known primary process! The 'black of blacks' is *exactly* that, and anyone who has followed processes through the *nigredo* will know that this darkening is something which requires the deepest respect and also fear.

Don't puff! You often wonder why many people in practical work stop their processes at the solution to the opposites. In fact, this is where state-oriented psychology, which created therapies in order to create solutions, came from in the first place. Conflicts arise, and then solutions and then goodbye—see you next week. The same conflicts arise again—and new solutions appear and so forth. Not everyone must go on beyond the opposites, beyond revealing the existence of a conflict.

I am impressed with Jung, who, in the year 1913, so painfully deliberated over his first active imagination and finally let himself fall into that imaginary visual in his fantasy world.[20] I recall the warning of Don Juan to deliberate well before entering the nagual. First the apprentice must become a hunter, then learn the exact and controlled methods of the warrior before letting go and controlling his abandon.[21] I have read many Zen texts about teachers who recommended to their pupils to stay with the opposites, to hold on to given moral rules and disciplines, to refrain from sex, eat vegetables and go to bed early after meditating.[22] These mores are something different from ordinary dogmatic religious principles. They are channels and opposites meant to hold the apprentice together until the moment arrives when he can leave the channels which consciousness has identified itself with and move on into other worlds.

The approach to the *nigredo* is thus not a matter of the will but a process which is lengthy and sometimes life-long. Some reach it only at the moment of death itself and indeed, there have been many dying processes which I have witnessed which seemed to center around the need to annihilate the opposites, enter the *nigredo* and become fluid.

In any case, there is no sense in puffing towards the *nigredo*. I say this because many therapies are developing today which feel that their job consists in bringing people to the point of the nagual and then returning them again. They have many 'good' recommendations like bang on the floor or beat on a rug with a rubber hose! Each to his own.

The process worker knows how many people go to the stage of opposites and stop. That is the end, for the moment, at least. But there is also another type of process which continues. This process phase frequently is presaged by comments such as, 'I am losing my orientation,' or 'I do not know where I am.' Sometimes process returns to the land of the opposites in order to gather more control. A wild trip without a pilot usually brings nothing but a lot of excitement. An uncontrolled journey leaves one feeling empty afterwards.

However, there are others who, after long studies, because of fateful stress or because of inner need, are pressed to abandon themselves in a controlled way to their own inner rulership of their process. I have seen many such processes occur, some can be described, others are unmentionable. Some spin through space without knowing where they will land, others make weird noises, hum strange tunes and enact unthinkable body postures. A few look like trance shamans learning to develop awareness in new spaces and to contact foreign beings. Others suffer untold misery and uncertainty, mistaking their wandering for insanity.

People who have prepared themselves typically relive well-known archetypal processes experienced for thousands of years by alchemists, shamans and medicine men. If you know about these processes, you are able to sit back and let nature happen. If you are not informed about these ancient processes, have not read about shamanism, studied yoga, gone on vision quests or simply lived enough yourself, then you will block such processes from happening because you are afraid of the unknown.

An example

I remember one very strong confrontation with the *nigredo*. A client came to me because of periodic psychotic episodes which began during some workshop she had attended in which breathing exercises had been used. My client was a visual type and therefore focusing upon her unoccupied proprioception in breathing flipped her. Even as she told me about how terrible her previous psychotic states were, she began to access past memories and breathe deeply with loud gasps punctuated by distressed facial signals asking for help. She whispered 'and then I lost all sense of my movement on this planet and fell unconscious.' As she said this, her body began to vibrate so violently from head to foot that I told her (using her main channel and last statement about movement) 'Look at your body, and move the movements, follow the movements you see there!' This recommendation helped her. She jittered and vibrated with awareness and said, after two or three moments, 'You know, I am shaking because my body gets cold when I leave this planet.' 'Settle the problems you have here, work on the warmth-coldness issue before leaving,' I suggested and she immediately began talking about relationship problems.

My client fell into the *nigredo* because she began occupying a channel in which she had little awareness. She needed to learn more about body feeling, about love and hate before dropping her intellect and drowning in the *nigredo*.

Switching channels is a violent act. It is as therapeutic as it may be dangerous. When it happens spontaneously, time can be a devil, or else the only therapist. However, how long one remains in the *nigredo* and how one fares there also depends, in my experience, upon the therapist's ability and the client's awareness in unoccupied channels.

There is no doubt, however, that deep transformative experiences usually pass through the *nigredo* because in this state, in the unoccupied channel, lies the weak link holding up the personality, the inferior function, the treasure in the mine, and the missing information in consciousness. I suspect that learning how to deal with the altered states of consciousness, with the experience of secondary processes and the temporary darkening of the primary process will be the task for psychology for a long time to come.

MERCURY OF THE WISE

Look! Something is happening in the egg! The *nigredo*, like the night sky, is suddenly punctuated and illuminated by a 'starry aspect,' a constellation referred to as 'Mercury of the Wise.'[23] The stars were considered by the alchemist to be directions from within the *prima materia* itself. The star indicated to him that a new child was born, signifying a sense of guidance from a distant source of wisdom.

But, you, dear process worker, have seen this too. The black of blacks only seems like a starless night in the first moment. As you become accustomed to wandering outside the lighted area a new director variously called 'personal power,' or the ally, the self or dreambody wisdom directs one as a star in the night.

In practical work, the stars appear as sudden visions or as the impulse to perform certain body postures. In the previous example, the body's shaking was the star in the night. At other times, the stars may appear as a form of extrasensory perception, or even as a synchronicity.

In any case, the stars in the alchemist's symbolism refer to a birth or rebirth of their 'divine child.' The new thing which is born or discovered is wisdom implicit in processes themselves. Until now one has had to govern life according to learned and conscious principles. And now, one knows that one can let go because a 'personal power,' or a special ally is at hand. One can afford to let go because awareness of the 'star' inhibits one from falling into oblivion. The ground principle of life itself is the inner directness of one's own process, a new earth, the alchemists would say which supports one in the darkness. Perhaps this was the *nigredo*'s purpose in the first place. One had to die in order to discover a new life principle.

THE PEACOCK'S TAIL

The advent of the starry stuff on the surface of the liquid *nigredo* signals that the dark of darks is coming to an end and that a new phase is beginning. Out of the destruction of the opposites comes a new volatile principle which is strikingly like the old one. The alchemists fantasized that from the earth a bird arises like a flash, trying to free itself from the gravitational pull of the earth. Failing, it falls again and again onto the 'new earth' and is amalgamated by it. During the flying up and plummeting down, many colors appear which the alchemist called the 'peacock's tail.'[24]

The image of the bird flying away from and landing on the 'new earth' symbolizes the process immediately following the *nigredo*. Many people coming out of the *nigredo* feel that their work is finished. They will even say, 'well, thank you,' try to get up from the floor, rise out of their 'samahdi' and return to the place they came from. But their eyelids seem unwilling to open, their body only rises halfheartedly, their limbs no longer obey the commands from the chakra between the eyes because a new earth, a new power, has pulled the spirit back where it came from.

Like a metal filing unable to leave its magnetic field the regenerated primary process is drawn into the field of the secondary one. In fact, the opus is just beginning a second and even further stage of process work. At this point different types of exclamations appear, such as, 'Wow, I have not even experienced this on an LSD trip and I seem to be going on yet for more,' or 'I want to get up but I get dizzy if I move. Something pulls me back.'

These exclamations are the colorful reactions occurring as one tries to fly back to where one came from but is caught by the tenacity of the process itself. The process has become so strong that it attracts and involves ego focus. The ego for its part has been transformed, and now, relieved of its command, feels secure in the existence of another power. Happy, it returns to the new earth. Ordinary life was anyhow not so interesting.

THE *ALBEDO*
Sometimes the peacock's tail goes on for a long time during which integrating experiences of the unconscious are taking place. Often quiet periods ensue in which nothing seems to

be happening from the outside. But inside a gradual whitening is occurring which the alchemist calls the '*albedo*.'[25] He said that at this stage of the work, the *prima materia* was strong enough to withstand destruction.

Empirical observations of individuals who have proceeded beyond the *nigredo* show that the eyes both figuratively and literally open by themselves. The individual might say (when asked later) that he awakened as if from a dream, as if the dawn were coming.

Eye phenomena are useful process signs. The eyes close when there is too much light. Often other channels are trying to open up when the eyes close. Proprioceptive experiences or even visions which have not been allowed to exist can now happen. The eyes close in part to decrease relationship contact with the outer world, to hear what is happening within or to experience breathing, heart rate, energy variations and fatigue. The eyes close in order to become inner directed. Children will often shut their eyes when they feel danger is coming because reality for them is visual-outward. Adults look away when they are in danger of losing their own processes to the outer world.

In the *albedo* however, the eyes gradually open and actually give rise to the visual experience of whitening. Coincident with the opening of the eyes and focusing on the people and places where one is, are a nod of the head and insights such as 'so this is what has been missing in my life,' or 'that is what was wrong before.' Along with these insights the noise of the world is heard again replacing the sound of inner tones. Real objects appear to melt with inner visions as one moves over a dreaming threshold. Sensations move from proprioceptive and visceral experiences to the large muscles and movement.

These signals tell us that the first stage of the deep-sea journey in process work is drawing to a close. Awakening is an autonomous power. Altered states of consciousness and unused channels fluidly switch into the world as one knew it before.

CONJUNCTIO

At this point, process scientist, you probably pack up your supplies, clean your office, and prepare to go home. You say goodbye to your starry-eyed companion with whom you shared a secret drama and with whom you now feel at home.

State-oriented reality meets you once again and with it a not altogether surprising insight occurs. The process is still unfinished. Even though you may have hoped that the *albedo* had prepared the individual to withstand the tension of time, in fact, you learn that this is not the case. Processes are replaced once again by insensitivity and unconsciousness. Insight, experience, special promises to oneself and feelings which occurred during the *albedo* do not remain. They drift away as if they were a dream.

But, alas, this too is part of the process. Your office was but a flask, a measure of reality but no substitute for the world. Completion happens only during the last phase of the work, the *'conjunctio'* which is described by the alchemists as the 'king uniting with the queen in the fire of love.'[26] From this union only does completion occur in which the stone is born.

The king, according to Jung, symbolizes the alchemical process itself while the queen stands for the servant of the process. She is the loving attitude which supports that which is trying to happen.[27] She is that regal attitude which gives up one's own way in order to amplify the supraordination of fate.

Until now, the process worker and not the client has been the queen. Hence, method and process, receptive and creative or king and queen have not been quite married. True, there may have been isolated moments when method and process were one in your laboratory flask, singular and meaningful times when the client supported his own process. But now, near the end of the opus, method and process are married. As the client grows to appreciate the impossible nature of process, he approaches its spirit of transformation and joins this spirit upon its restless journey. Until now he could afford to examine processes and actually flirt with their energy and wisdom. But now, he finds that he himself has found a relationship to the world of nature and its happenings and can follow them even when their direction seems foreign.

UNIO MENTALIS

Alchemists like Dorn differentiated the last stage of the alchemical process. He divided the *conjunctio* into three phases and called the first, the *'unio mentalis.'*[28] Jung compares this phase to mental solutions which change one's attitude towards reality. In this state of the work, one realizes the meaning of process, and has insight into its nature. One understands one's dreams but cannot yet live them.

THE CAELUM

Jung identifies Dorn's second *conjunctio* stage, the *'caelum,'*[29] as mental solutions which are brought together with the physical body. One not only understands process and has an 'ah ha' reaction to it, but simultaneously feels the meaning of things in the body. The *'caelum'* symbolizes that stage of the end of the work in which insight simultaneously occurs with body experience, one dances and has a *'satori'*, an enlightenment, one feels pain and understands the meaning of one's fate.

UNUS MUNDUS

Dorn differentiated a final state of the *conjunctio* which he called the *'unus mundus,'* the one world in which the *caelum* or mind-body solution was joined with the universe.[30] In the *unus mundus*, all that happened in the flask, in your private office or room happens out here on the city street, in the midst of real, everydaylife.

You know, dear process scientist, just how many mental solutions to problems you have seen and how many mind-body relaxations and congruencies you have witnessed in the confines of your laboratory which fell asunder under the impact of daily life. Surprisingly little of the *unio mentalis* or *caelum* held up under the stress of the social pressure outside your laboratory. The occupation of the world channel seems always to come last.

The stage just preceding the '*unus mundus*' is known to all. One works successfully on dreams and body problems but nevertheless melts confluently and unconsciously with the routine streaming of the collective world, adapting to whatever is expected. The body reacts with pain while nightmares shake the night. Personal incongruence is the heavy price paid for following linear time and social pressure. Dreams of walking lonely paths in nature filled the philosophical egg before one dared birth. Now as the final stage of the *conjunctio* nears, old and familiar opponents from the inner world are dreamed up to be the judges at the edge of the land you are leaving. You would like to return to womb-like and familiar territory but something like death pushes you beyond the aging visage of fear.

No one should be naive because total congruence between mind, body and nature does not mean only joy and relaxation. In fact, the opposite may be the case. Since congruence requires relating primary and secondary processes and since secondary processes become double signals when they conflict with consciousness, the more congruent you become the more you transform your own identity and the more you conflict with ruling deities of order which no longer nourish your soul.

Thus, the individual growing towards wholeness dreams up his peers to be misoneistic primitives who reject unpredictable fluidity. Luckily the pain generated by the conflict between secondary processes and common sense is ameliorated by contact with the Tao, the feeling of truth which remains after the old gods have died.

Until now, this truth has been projected onto the wave equations of physics, the potential world of the archetypes, the alchemists, *unus mundus*, mythology's Oceanos, Aion and Kundalini. Now Tao is an experience. It is your ally, an inner certainty related to the overall state of the world which detaches you from the opinions of your group.

Talmudic literature, American Indian tradition and Taoist stories remind you of the powerful and ameliorating effect of this ally.[31] They predict that if one person gets himself together while being in this real world, that the whole world will fall into order. Process theory agrees, for we know that if one channel, one person changes, then the pattern for the rest of us changes as well. If one person is real and honest everyone is relieved! Inversely, it takes one person to be out of himself to disturb a group or one sick group to disturb an individual. Being your total self in the world is an important and difficult task.

GOLD

Apparently the alchemist's gold, imagined as the finale of his culinary labors, is a complex thing which consists of more than sunshine. This opus was supposed to produce the panacea from the dung heap of human mystery. But no one said much about the difficulties of bearing the tension and pressure, the loneliness and darkness which arise when the individual conflicts with collective patterns. True, process awareness relieves the body of much suffering and even sometimes creates the experience of liberation. But symptoms and problems do not simply disappear, they continue until one is able, for the moment at least, to experience all channels.

Thus the gold turns out to be something different from the yogic super powers, the ability to walk on air, ingest fire or heal wounds. Of course there were mind-boggling channel changes, overlappings, levitations, healings and immortality. But unlike the alchemical puffer who sweated in vain for some sort of LSD trip which would free him from this world, a person in the *unus mundus* loses interest in the original dreams of gold and immortality. Empirical work with the living and dying indicate that increased process awareness obviates future expectations. Such awareness may be the gold. This point is where Taoists, Buddhists, Yogis and modern psychologists meet. The closer you get to the end, the more you realize there is none, unless you are able to consider openness to new challenges as the last step.

RIVER'S WAY

And so it seems as if the goal of alchemy was in part to find the river's way, that is the process of perception. This makes practical sense because once a person's awareness has been increased to the point where he is able to pick up his own signals alone, his own body feelings, movements, visions, words and vocal tones, he has all that one can give him to go on alone, with or without the love and help of someone else. There seems to be no objective real world 'out there,' no gold for the seeker, no object for the physicist, no dream for the analyst to gain mastery over, to possess, own or manipulate.

However this eastern-sounding conclusion, together with its western counterparts in theoretical physics, does not mean that objective reality does not exist. It means that the discipline, effort and accuracy applied to creating health, peace or wealth can be equally well applied to discovering more about the nature of perception. It implies that when a person complains that he has a stomach ache, you need to find out exactly how he perceives this ache. Is it like a fist, fire, movement or what? When you work with his perception, it changes. Though the sufferer may tell you he feels better, you still do not know what his stomach ache really was. Such questions may be unanswerable. We can only be certain about your and his perceptions.

Much more needs to be understood about this process. In this book I have contented myself with noting that perception is organized according to its channels and distance from consciousness. The flow of the river, the Tao or evolution of our world, is structured according to the patterns of this perception. I was amazed to find process concepts hidden in ancient time and energy deities. Even more thrilling was to find channels and primary and secondary processes in the *I Ching*. I almost expected to find amplification methods and process stages predicted in the alchemist's dreams.

My studies have given me greater respect for history and, at the same time, increased insight into the limitations of alchemy and Taoism. It seems likely that one of the reasons why Taoism has remained more of a theory than a practice is because most of the events Taoism deals with are accidental. They are secondary processes which, like dreams, are hindered by edges from reaching our conscious attention. Questions about what to do next would be alleviated if we could perceive what we are doing now. Until we can perceive this the mystery of Taoism and the magic of alchemy will remain essentially theories without direct applications.

But what will future scientists have to say about the present state of psychology? How close are we to bringing even modern theories of the unfolding universe to earth? I myself wonder what a detailed study of psychotic states is going to do for process work. What will we learn from synchronicity? Until psychology deals with world problems as well as it does with individual ones, the *unus mundus*, Taoist sage and alchemist's gold will remain unrealized dreams of a bygone age.

But most important of all, what will happen to the individual when his ability to perceive increases? If experience is an indicator, increasing ability at picking up signals and courage in working with their implications will liberate the individual from false teachers and healers. Neither knowledge, luck nor intelligence but expanded sensitivity to the wisdom of one's own process creates the independence of a congruent personality.

NOTES

CHAPTER 1   INTRODUCTION

1 C.J. Jung, 'Principles of Practical Psychotherapy', *Collected Works* vol. 16, pp. 3, 4.
2 B.K.S. Iyengar, *Light on Yoga, Yoga Dipika* (New York: Schocken Books, 1979); Alexander Lowen, *Bioenergetics* (New York: Coward, McCann & Geoghegan, 1975).
3 Wilhelm Reich, *Character Analysis* (New York: Farrar, Straus & Giroux, 1968).
4 Moshe Feldenkrais, *Body and Mature Behavior* (New York: International Universities Press, 1973).
5 Ida Rolf, 'Structural Integration,' *Confinaia Psychiatrica* XVI (1973), pp. 69-79.
6 Ilsa Weith (translator), *The Yellow Emperor's Classic of Internal Medicine* (Berkeley, California: University of California Press, 1966).
7 John Niehardt, *Black Elk Speaks: Being the Life Story of a Holy Man of the Ogalala Sioux* (Nebraska: University of Nebraska Press, 1961).
8 J.L. Moreno, *Who Shall Survive?* (New York: Beacon Press, 1952); Lewis Yablonsky, *Psychodrama* (New York: Basic Books, 1976).
9 Barbara Hannah, *Active Imagination* (Los Angeles: Sigo Press, 1980).
10 Lu K'uan Yu, *Taoist Yoga: Alchemy and Immortality* (London: Rider & Company, 1972).
11 Fritz Perls, *Gestalt Therapy Verbatim* (Lafayette, California: Real People Press, 1969).
12 Eric Berne, *Beyond Games and Scripts* (New York: Grove Press, 1977).
13 Richard Bandler, and John Grinder, *Frogs into Princes, Neuro-Linguistic Programming*, ed. by John O. Stevens (Moab, Utah: Real People Press, 1979).

14 Adelaide Bry, *A Primer of Behavioral Psychology* (New York: New American Library, 1975).
15 Virginia Satir, *Helping Families to Change* (Hays, Kansas: The High Plains Comprehensive Community Mental Health Center, 1972).
16 C.G. Jung, *Man and His Symbols*, together with M.L. von Franz, Joseph L. Henderson, Jolande Jacobe, Aniela Jaffe (New York: Dell, 1971).
17 C.G. Jung, 'Synchronicity,' *Collected Works*, vol. 8 (London: Routledge & Kegan Paul).

CHAPTER 2   ELEMENTS OF PROCESS SCIENCE

1 See C.G. Jung, 'Psychological Types,' *Collected Works*, vol. 6; and M.L. von Franz, 'The Inferior Function' in von Franz and Hillman, *Lectures on Jung's Typology* (New York: Spring Publications, 1971).
2 *Ibid.*
3 Mindell, *Dreambody* (Boston: Sigo Press, 1981; London: Routledge & Kegan Paul, 1984) and *Working with the Dreaming Body* (London and Boston: Routledge & Kegan Paul, 1985).
4 In the *Dreambody* I concentrate on the connection between visualized dreams and proprioceptive experiences. In *Working with the Dreambody* I integrate dream and body work with practical examples of process theory. *The Global Dreambody* focuses upon channels in family and couple's processes.

CHAPTER 3   DREAM AND BODY CHANNELS

1 Larry Dossey, *Time, Space and Medicine* (Boulder, Col.: Shambhala, 1982).
2 *Ibid.*, pp. 139-41.
3 *Ibid.*, pp. 142-9.
4 D. Bohm, *Wholeness and the Implicate Order* (London: Routledge & Kegan Paul, 1980).
5 A. Mindell, *Working with the Dreaming Body*.

CHAPTER 4   RELATIONSHIP CHANNELS

1 C.G. Jung, 'The Transference,' *Collected Works*, vol. 16.
2 Fritz Perls, *Gestalt Therapy Verbatim* (Lafayette, California: Real People Press, 1969).
3 *Ibid.*
4 Eric Berne, *Beyond Games and Scripts* and Claude Steiner, *Scripts People Live By* (New York: Bantam, 1975).
5 R. Bandler and J. Grinder, *Frogs into Princes* (Moab, Utah: Real

People Press, 1979).

6 A. Bry, *A Primer in Behavioral Psychology* (New York: New American Library, 1975).

7 C.G. Jung, 'The Transference,' *op. cit.*

8 Arnold Mindell, *Working with the Dreaming Body* (London: Routledge & Kegan Paul, 1985). I should also mention here the work of the now Freudian, Thomas Ogden, who in *Projective Identification* refers to projective mechanisms which evoke congruent feelings in others.

9 Jung defines projection in 'Psychological Types', *Collected Works*, vol. 6 (Princeton, New Jersey: Princeton University Press, Bollingen Series XX, 1971); Von Franz, Marie-Louise, *Projection and Reflection in Jungian Psychology* (La Salle, Ill.: Open Court, 1980).

10 Philip Rawson, *Tantra: The Indian Cult of Ecstasy* (London: Thames & Hudson, 1973).

11 Lu K'uan Yu, *Taoist Yoga: Alchemy and Immortality* (London: Rider, 1972).

12 *Ibid.*

13 Rawson, *op. cit.*

CHAPTER 5   WORLD CHANNELS

1 Some of the original papers of these physicists are:
John von Neuman, *The Mathematical Foundations of Quantum Mechanics*, trans. R. Beyer (Princeton, New Jersey: Princeton University Press, 1955); Albert Einstein and L. Infeld, *The Evolution of Physics* (Cambridge, Mass.: Cambridge University Press, 1971); H. Stapp, 'Theory of Reality,' *Foundations of Physics*, 7 (1977); David Finkelstein, 'Quantum Physics and Process Metaphysics,' in *Physical Reality and Mathematical Description*, ed. by Enz and Mehra (Durecht, Holland: D. Reidel, 1974).

2 See Gary Zukav, *The Dancing Wu Li Masters* (London: Rider, 1979); Fritjof Capra, *The Tao of Physics* (London: Wildwood House, 1975); Bob Toben, *Space-Time and Beyond* (New York: Dutton, 1975).

3 See the popular discussion of these events in Zukav, *The Dancing Wu Li Masters* (London: Rider, 1979), pp. 308f.

4 *Ibid.*, pp. 317f.

5 David Bohm, 'Quantum Theory as an Indication of a New Order in Physics,' *Quantum Theory and Beyond*, ed. by Ted Bastin (New York: Cambridge University Press, 1971).

6 Lewis Thomas, *The Lives of a Cell* (New York: Bantam, 1975).

7 C.G. Jung, 'Synchronicity, An Acausal Connecting Principle,' *Collected Works*, vol. 8 (Princeton, New Jersey: Princeton

University Press, Bollingen Series XX, 1960).

8 Richard Wilhelm, *The I Ching or Book of Changes* (London: Routledge & Kegan Paul, 1973). Here he interprets the Tao as meaning.

9 The most notable attempt to connect physics, mathematics and analytical psychology is made by Marie-Louise von Franz in her *Number and Time* (Evanston, Illinois: Northwestern University Press, 1974).
See also Arnold Mindell, 'Synchronizität,' in *Behandlungsmethoden in der Analytischen Psychologie*, ed. by U. Eschenbach, Fellbach-Oeffingen (Bonz Verlag, 1979). 'Synchronicity: An Investigation of the Unitary Background Patterning Synchronous Phenomena. (A Psychoid Approach to the Unconscious),' *Dissertation Abstracts International*, vol. 37, no. 2 (1976).

10 Arnold Mindell, *Dreambody* (Boston: Sigo Press, 1981; London: Routledge & Kegan Paul, 1984).

11 C.G. Jung, 'Review of the Complex Theory,' *Collected Works*, vol. 8.

12 *Dreambody*, op. cit., chapter 10.

13 J. Holten, 'The Roots of Complementarity,' *Eranos Jahrbuch*, 37 (1970), p. 50.

14 Werner Heisenberg, *Physics and Philosophy* (New York: Harper & Row, 1958), p. 41.

15 Zukav, *The Dancing Wu Li Masters*, op. cit., pp. 284ff.

16 In C.G. Jung's *Collected Works*, vol. 14, he expands upon the relationship of psychology to physics in terms of the 'Unus Mundus.' See, for example, para. 765ff.

17 C.G. Jung, *Collected Works*, vol. 8, para. 368ff.

18 Marie-Louise von Franz, *Number and Time*, op. cit., pp. 64-77.

19 David Finkelstein, 'Quantum Physics and Process Metaphysics,' *Physical Reality and Mathematical Description*, op. cit.

20 The discussion of this section was originally developed in my 'Synchronizität,' op. cit.

21 Don Juan, the shaman hero of Carlos Castaneda's *Journey to Ixtlan* (New York: Simon & Schuster, 1972), speaks in the first chapter of that book of events which match the mood and situation of a sorcerer who has adjusted himself to what we might call the Tao. These 'agreements form the world around us,' as he calls them are positive experiences which cluster about one's actions like variations on a musical theme.

22 David Finkelstein, 'Primitive Concept of Process,' (*Physical Reality and Mathematical Description*, op. cit.) formulates processes in physics as a new basis replacing time and space.

23 *Ibid.*

24 David Bohm, *Wholeness and the Implicate Order*, (London: Routledge & Kegan Paul, 1980), p. 11.

CHAPTER 6 PROCESS MYTHOLOGY

1 Joseph Campbell, 'Man and Myth,' in *Voices and Visions* (New York: Harper & Row, 1976).
2 *Ibid.*
3 Marie-Louise von Franz, 'The Anti-Christ,' unpublished lecture.
4 *Ibid.*
5 Marie-Louise von Franz, *Time, Rhythm and Repose* (London: Thames & Hudson, 1978).
6 *Ibid.*
7 *Ibid.*
8 Arthur Avalon, *Serpent Power* (New York: Dover Publications, 1974).
9 Von Franz, *Time, Rhythm and Repose, op. cit.*
10 *Ibid.*
11 H. Ogawa, 'The Concept of Time in the Mithraic Mysteries,' *The Study of Time III*, ed. by J.T. Fraser, N. Lawrence and D. Park (New York: Springer Verlag, 1971).
12 Marie-Louise von Franz, 'Discussion and Comment,' in *The Study of Time III*, ed. by J.T. Fraser, N. Lawrence and D. Park (New York: Springer Verlag, 1971).
13 Isaac Asimov, *Energy and Life, An Exploration of the Physical and Chemical Basis of Modern Biology* (New York: Avon, 1972).
14 C.G. Jung, 'On Psychic Energy,' *Collected Works*, vol. 8 (Princeton, New Jersey: Princeton University Press, Bollingen Series XX, 1960).
15 Mircea Eliade, *Yoga: Immortality and Freedom* (Princeton, New Jersey: Princeton University Press, 1977), p. 272 (quote on dead men in life).
16 Von Franz, *Time Rhythm and Repose, op. cit.*, p. 8.
17 Werner Bohm, *Chakras, Lebenskrafte und Bewusstseinzentren im Menschen* (Weilheim Obb.: Otto Wilhelm Barth, 1966).

CHAPTER 7 CHANNELS IN TAOISM

1 Raymond van Over, *Taoist Tales*.
2 Marcel Granet, *Das Chinesische Denken* (München: Piper Verlag, 1963), pp. 89, 246.
3 Helmut Wilhelm, *Eight Lectures on the I Ching* (New York: Harper Torchbooks, 1964), p. 18.
4 Lao Tsu, *The Tao Te Ching* (New York: Vintage Books, 1st Edition, 1972).
5 Shunryu Suzuki, *Zen Mind, Beginners Mind* (New York & Tokyo: Weatherhill, 1976).
6 Wilhelm, *The I Ching, Book of Changes, The Richard Wilhelm Translation*, rendered into English by Carl Baynes (London:

Routledge & Kegan Paul, 1973), p. 300.

7 See previous chapter.

8 *The I Ching, op. cit.*, p. 300.

9 *Ibid.*, p. 300.

10 C.G. Jung, 'Practical Use of Dream Analysis,' *Collected Works*, vol. 16 (Princeton, New Jersey: Princeton University Press, Bollingen Series XX, 1960).

11 C.G. Jung, 'Review of the Complex Theory,' *Collected Works*, vol. 8.

12 C.G. Jung, 'Psychological Aspects of a Mother Archetype,' *Collected Works*, vol. 9, para. 155.

13 Marie-Louise von Franz, *An Introduction to the Psychology of Fairy Tales* (Zürich, Switzerland: Spring Publications, 1973), pp. 9, 10. She puts it this way. 'In the unconscious all archetypes are contaminated with one another. It is as if several photographs were printed one over the other. They cannot be disentangled. This has probably to do with the relative timelessness and spacelessness of the unconscious. It is like a package of representations which are simultaneously present. Only when the conscious mind looks at it, is one motif selected. Thus for one scientist the mother is everything, for another everything is vegetation, and for another everything is solar myth. . .'

14 *The I Ching, op. cit.*, p. 264.

15 John Blofeld, *The I Ching, The Book of Changes* (New York: Dutton), pp. 61f. The introduction explains the use of incense and meditation in great detail.

16 *The I Ching, op. cit.*, p. L1

17 *Ibid.*, see Jung's introduction to the *I Ching*.

CHAPTER 8 PATTERNS IN THE *I CHING*

1 *The I Ching, The Book of Changes*, translated by John Blofeld (New York: Dutton, 1965).

2 *Ibid.*, pp. 266 and 269.

3 *Ibid.*, p. xxxvii.

4 *The I Ching, op. cit.*, pp. 359f.

5 *Ibid.*, p. 315.

6 Lao Tsu, *Tao Te Ching* (New York: Vintage Books, 1st Edition, 1972).

7 *Ibid.*, chapter 21.

8 R.G.H. Siu, *The Portable Dragon, The Western Man's Guide to the I Ching* (Cambridge, Mass.: M.I.T. Press, 1979), p. 405.

CHAPTER 9 THE ALCHEMICAL OPUS

1 Lu K'uan Yu, *Taoist Yoga: Alchemy and Immortality* (London: Rider, 1972).

2 Mircea Eliade, *Yoga: Immortality and Freedom* (Princeton, New Jersey: Princeton University Press, 1972), pp. 274-92.

3 Marie-Louise von Franz, *Alchemical Active Imagination*, p. 1f. Here von Franz gives a brief, singularly clear introduction to the psychology and history of alchemy.

4 Stanislas Klossowski de Rola, *The Secret Art of Alchemy* (London: Thames & Hudson, 1973). Here a short version of alchemy is expressed with minimum interpretation.

5 C.G. Jung, 'Alchemical Studies,' *Collected Works*, vol. 13, and *Mysterium Coniunctionis, Collected Works*, vol. 14. (Princeton, New Jersey: Princeton University Press, Bollingen Series XX, 1960).

6 Klossowski de Rola, *op. cit.*

7 *Ibid.*

8 *Ibid.*

9 *Ibid.*

10 *Ibid.*

11 *Ibid.*

12 *Ibid.*

13 *Ibid.*

14 *Ibid.*

15 *Ibid.*, Klossowski quoting Don Pernety's *Dictionnaire Mytho-Hermetique*.

16 *Ibid.*

17 *Ibid.*

18 *Ibid.*

19 *Ibid.*

20 C.G. Jung, *Memories, Dreams and Reflection*, recorded and edited by Aniela Jaffe (New York: Vintage Books, Random House, 1965), p. 179.

21 Carlos Castaneda, *Journey to Ixtlan* (New York: Simon & Schuster, 1972).

22 John Blofeld, *The I Ching, The Book of Changes* (New York, N.Y.: Dutton and Co., Inc.), pp. 36, 37.

23 Klossowski de Rola, *op. cit.*

24 *Ibid.*

25 *Ibid.*

26 *Ibid.*

27 C.G. Jung, *Mysterium Coniunctionis, op. cit.*, p. 473.

28 *Ibid.*, para. 663f.

29 *Ibid.*

30 *Ibid.*

31 See Brad Steiger, *Medicine Power, The American Indian's Revival*

of his Spiritual Heritage and Its Relevance for Modern Man (New York: Doubleday, 1974); C.G. Jung, *Mysterium Coniunctionis*, *op. cit.*, para. 604.

BIBLIOGRAPHY

Asimov, Isaac, *Energy and Life, An Exploration of the Physical and Chemical Basis of Modern Biology*, New York: Avon, 1972.

Avalon, Arthur, *The Serpent Power*, New York: Dover Publications, 1974.

Bandler, Richard and Grinder, John, *Frogs into Princes, Neuro-Linguistic Programming*, Moab, Utah: Real People Press, 1979.

——, *The Structure of Magic, A Book About Language and Therapy*, Palo Alto, Cal.: Science and Behavior Books, 1975.

Bateson, G., *Steps to an Ecology of Mind*, New York: Ballantine, 1972.

Berne, Eric, *Beyond Games and Scripts*, New York: Grove Press, 1977.

Blofeld, John, *The I Ching, The Book of Changes*, New York: Dutton, 1968.

Bohm, David, 'Quantum Theory As An Indication of a New Order in Physics,' in: *Quantum Theory and Beyond*, New York: Cambridge University Press, 1971.

——, *Wholeness and the Implicate Order*, London: Routledge & Kegan Paul, 1980.

Bohm, Werner, *Chakras, Lebenskrafte und Bewusstseinzentren im Menschen*, Weilhelm Obb.: Otto Wilhelm Barth, 1966.

Bry, Adelaide, *A Primer of Behavioral Psychology*, New York: New American Library, 1975.

Campbell, Joseph, 'Man and Myth,' in: *Voices and Visions*, New York: Harper & Row, 1976.

Capra, Fritjof, *The Tao of Physics*, Boulder, Col.: Shambhala, 1976.

Castaneda, Carlos, *Journey to Ixtlan*, New York: Simon & Schuster, 1972.

The Concise Oxford Dictionary, revised by E. McIntosh, London: Oxford University, 1964.

Dossey, Larry, *Space, Time and Medicine*, Boulder, Col: Shambhala, 1982.

Downing, George, *The Massage Book*, New York: Random House, 1972.

Dusen, Wilson van, 'The Phenomenology of a Schizophrenic Existence,' in: *Gestalt Is*, New York: Bantam Books, 1977.

Dychtwald, Ken, *Bodymind*, New York: Jove, 1978.

Ebin, Victoria, *The Body Decorated*, London: Thames & Hudson, 1979.

Einstein, Albert and Infeld, L., *The Evolution of Physics*, Cambridge: Cambridge University Press, 1971.

Eliade, Mircea, *Shamanism: Archaic Techniques of Ecstasy*, London: Routledge & Kegan Paul, 1970.

——, *Yoga: Immortality and Freedom*, Princeton, N.J.: Princeton University Press, 1977.

Ellis, Albert, *Humanistic Psychotherapy*, New York: McGraw-Hill, 1974.

Fabredga, H. and Manning, P.K., 'An Integrated Theory of Disease: Ladino-Mestizo Views of Disease in the Chiapas Highlands,' in: *Rediscovery of the Body*, New York: Dell, 1977.

Feldenkrais, Moshe, *Body and Mature Behavior*, New York: International Universities Press, 1973.

Feynman, R.P., 'The Theory of Positrons,' in: *Physical Review*, vol. 76, no. 6 (1949).

Finkelstein, David, 'Quantum Physics and Process Metaphysics,' in: *Physical Reality and Mathematical Description*, Holland: E. Reidel, 1974.

——, 'Primitive Concept of Process,' in: *Physical Reality and Mathematical Description*, Holland: E. Reidel, 1974.

Franz, Marie-Louis von, *Number and Time*, Evanston, Ill.: Northwestern University Press, 1974.

——, *Projection and Reflection in Jungian Psychology*, La Salle, Ill.: Open Court, 1980.

——, *Time, Rhythm and Repose*, London: Thames & Hudson, 1978.

——, 'The Anti-Christ,' unpublished lecture.

——, *Alchemical Active Imagination*, Dallas, Texas: Spring Publications, 1979.

——, *Patterns of Creativity Mirrored in Creation Myths*, Zürich, Switzerland: Spring Publications, 1972.

——, *Introduction to the Psychology of Fairy Tales*, Zürich, Switzerland: Spring Publications, 1973.

Franz, Marie-Louise von and Hillman, James, *Lectures on Jung's Typology*, New York: Spring Publications, 1971.

Granet, Marcel, *Das Chinesische Denken*, Münich, Germany: Piper-Verlag, 1963.

Grinder, John, see Bandler, Richard.

Hannah, Barbara, *Active Imagination*, Los Angeles: Sigo Press, 1981.

Heisenberg, Werner, *Physics and Philosophy*, New York: Harper & Row, 1958.

Herink, R., see *The Psychotherapy Handbook*.

Hillman, James and Franz, Marie-Louise von, *Lectures on Jung's*

Typology, New York: Spring Publications, 1971.

Holten, J., 'The Roots of Complementarity,' in: *Eranos Jahrbuch*, vol. 37 (1970).

Infeld, L., see Einstein, Albert.

Iyengar, B.K.S., *Light on Yoga, Yoga Dipika*, New York: Schocken Books, 1979.

Judge, A.S.N., *Development Through Alternation*, Brussels: Union of Interiation Associations, 1982.

Jung, C.G. (with M.L. von Franz, Joseph L. Henderson, Jolande Jacobi, Aniela Jaffe), *Man and His Symbols*, New York: Doubleday, 1965.

The Collected Works of C.G. Jung. Edited by Sir Herbert Read, Michael Fordham and Gerhard Adler. Translated by R.F.C. Hull (except for vol. 2). Princeton, New Jersey: Princeton University Press, (Bollingen Series XX) and London: Routledge & Kegan Paul, 1953-   . Cited throughout as *CW*. Volumes cited in this publication:

Vol. 6, *Psychological Types*, 1971.

Vol. 8, *The Structure and Dynamics of the Psyche*, 1960.

Vol. 11, *Psychology and Religion*, 1958.

Vol. 13, *Alchemical Studies*, 1967.

Vol. 14, *Mysterium Coniunctionis: An Inquiry into the Separation and Synthesis of Psychic Opposites in Alchemy*. 2nd Edition, 1970.

Vol. 16, *The Practice of Psychotherapy*, 1954.

Individual writings, with relevant volume of the *Collected Works* (see above):

'A Review of the Complex Theory,' *CW* 8, paras. 194-219.

'Synchronicity: An Acausal Connecting Principle,' *CW* 8, paras. 816-968.

'On Psychic Energy,' *CW* 8.

'The Transference,' *CW* 16, paras. 353-539.

Memories, Dreams and Reflections. New York, N.Y.: Vintage Books, Random House, 1965.

Klossowski, Stanislas de Rola, *The Secret Art of Alchemy*, London: Thames & Hudson, 1973.

Laszlo, Legeza, *Tao Magic*. London: Thames & Hudson, 1975.

——, *Tao: The Chinese Philosophy of Time and Change*, London: Thames & Hudson, 1973.

Lieban, Richard W., 'Medical Anthropology,' in: *Handbook of Social and Cultural Anthropology*, Chicago, Ill.: Rand McNally, 1973.

Lockhart, Russell A., 'Cancer in Myth and Dream,' *Spring*, 1977.

Lowen, Alexander, *Bioenergetics*, New York: Coward, McCann & Geoghegan, 1975.

——, *The Betrayal of the Body*, New York: Collier Books, 1973.

Manning, P.K., see Fabredaga, H.

Meier, C.A., 'A Jungian Approach to Psychosomatic Medicine,' in: *Journal of Analytical Psychology, vol. 8, no. 2* (1963).

Mindell, Arnold, *Dreambody*, Boston: Sigo Press, 1981; London: Routledge & Kegan Paul, 1984.

——, 'Der Korper in der Analytischen Psychologie,' in: *Behandlungsmethoden in der Jungscher Psychologies*, Fallbach-Oeffingen: Bonz Verlag, 1979.

——, 'Somatic Consciousness,' in: *Quadrant*, Jung Foundation, 1981.

——, 'Synchronicity: An Investigation of the Unitary Background Patterning Synchronous Phenomena. (A Psychoid Approach to the Unconscious),' *Dissertation Abstracts International*, vol. 37, no. 2 (1976).

——, 'Synchronizität,' in: *Behandlungsmethoden in der Analytischen Psychologie*, Fellbach-Oeffingen: Bonz Verlag, 1979.

——, *Working with the Dreaming Body*, London: Routledge & Kegan Paul, 1985.

Moreno, J.L., *Who Shall Survive?* New York: Beacon Press, 1952.

Morris, Desmond, *The Human Zoo*, New York: Dell, 1976.

Mumford, John, *Psychosomatic Yoga*, Wellingborough: Aquarian Press, 1976.

Muktananda, Swami Baba, *The Play of Consciousness*, California: Shree Gurudev Siddha Yoga Ashram, 1974.

Neuman, John von, *The Mathematical Foundations of Quantum Mechanics*, Princeton, N.J.: Princeton University Press, 1955.

Neidhart, John, *Black Elk Speaks: Being the Life Story of a Holy Man of the Ogalala Sioux*, Nebraska: University of Nebraska Press, 1961.

Ogawa, H., 'The Concept of Time in the Mithraic Mysteries,' in: *The Study of Time III*, New York: Springer Verlag, 1971.

Ogden, Thomas H., *Projective Identification*, New York: Jasan Aronson, 1982.

Over, Raymond van, ed. *Taoist Tales*, New York: The New American Library, 1973.

Oxford, *The Concise Oxford Dictionary*, 6th edn London: Oxford University Press, 1976.

Perls, Fritz, *Gestalt Therapy Verbatim*, Lafayette: Real People Press, 1969.

Philips, A.I. and Smith, G.W., *Couple Therapy*, New York: Collier Books, 1973.

The Psychotherapy Handbook, ed. Richie Herink, New York: Meridian, 1980.

Rawson, Philip, *Tantra: The Indian Cult of Ecstasy*, London: Thames & Hudson, 1973.

——. and Laszlo, L., *Tao Magic*, London: Thames & Hudson, 1975.

——. and Laszlo, L., *Tao: The Chinese Philosophy of Time and Change*, London: Thames & Hudson, 1973.

Reich, Wilhelm, *Character Analysis*, New York: Farrar, Straus & Giroux, 1968.

Rolf, Ida, 'Structural Integration,' in: *Confinaia Psychiatrica*, vol. 16 (1973).

Satir, Virginia, *Helping Families to Change*, Hays, Kansas: The High Plains Comprehensive Community Mental Center, 1972.

Shunryu, Suzuki, *Zen Mind, Beginner's Mind*, New York and Tokyo: Weatherhill, 1976.

Simonton, Carl I. and Simonton, Stephanie, 'Belief Systems and Management of the Emotional Aspects of Malignancy,' in: *Journal of Transpersonal Psychology*, vol. 7 (1975).

Simonton, Stephanie, see Simonton, Carl I.

Siu, R.G.H., *The Portable Dragon, The Western Man's Guide to the I Ching*, Cambridge, Mass.: M.I.T. Press, 1979.

Smith, G.W., see Phillips, A.I.

Spino, Michael, *Beyond Jogging, The Inner Spaces of Running*, New York: Berkeley, 1976.

Stapp, H., 'Theory of Reality,' in: *Foundations of Physics*, vol. 7 (1977).

Steiger, Brad, *Medicine Power, The American Indian's Revival of His Spiritual Heritage and Its Relevance for Modern Man*, New York: Doubleday, 1974.

Steiner, Claude M., *Scripts People Live By, Transactional Analysis of Life Scripts*, New York: Bantam, 1975.

Tansley, David, *Subtle Body, Essence and Shadow*, London: Thames & Hudson, 1977.

Thera, Nyanaponika, *The Heart of Buddhist Meditation*, New York: Weiser, 1962.

Thomas, Lewis, *The Lives of a Cell, Notes of a Biology Watcher*, New York: Bantam, 1979.

Toben, Bob, *Space-Time and Beyond*, New York: Dutton, 1975.

Tsu, Lao, *The Tao Te Ching*, New York: Vintage, 1972.

Watts, Alan, *The Book*, New York: Collier Books, 1968.

Webber, Andrew Lloyd and Rice, Tim, *Jesus Christ Superstar, A Rock Opera*, Decca Records: New York: 1970.

Weizacker, K.F., *Physical Reality and Mathematical Description*, Holland: E. Reidel, 1974.

Weith, Ilsa (translator), *The Yellow Emperor's Classic of Internal Medicine*, Berkeley, Cal.: University of California Press, 1966.

Wilhelm, Helmut, *Change: Eight Lectures on the I Ching*, New York: Harper Torchbooks, 1964.

Wilhelm, Richard, *The I Ching or Book of Changes*, London: Routledge & Kegan Paul, 1973.

Yablonsky, Lewis, *Psychodrama*, New York: Basic Books, 1976.

Yu, Lu K'uan, *Taoist Yoga: Alchemy and Immortality*, London: Rider, 1972.

Zukav, Gary, *The Dancing Wu Li Masters*, London: Rider, 1979.

INDEX

Accidents, 24, 88

Acoustical tones, 96

Active imagination, 8, 16, 21, 30, 32, 103, 124

Acupuncture, 8

Affects, 4, 41, 44, 125; and dreaming -up, 43

Aggression, 95

Aion, 81-4, 85, 87, 89, 95, 139

Albedo, 135-6

Alchemical symbolism, 40, 134

Alchemist, 132, 139; and death, 118; European, 123; as process worker, 118-40; as a puffer, 128-9

Alchemy, 3, 94, 97; goals of, 121, 141; history of, 119; limitations of, 142; and meditation, 119; methods of, 120, 121, 137; and process concepts, 71, 72, 118-42; Taoist, 8, 52, 71, 115, 118, 119, 139; and Unus Mundus, 62, 63

Alcoholism, 117

Algonquin 'manitou', 83

Ally, 134, 139, 140

Altered states, 52, 133, 136

American Indians, 74, 75; traditions of, 139

Americans, 21

Amplification, 8, 9, 16, 25, 27, 28, 31, 44, 50, 53, 59, 61, 94-6, 107, 118; and alchemy, 124, 128, 137, 142; and archetypes, 110; in auditory channel, 16-17; of body motions, 33; of body phenomena, 80, 81, 107; of double signals, 26; in kinesthetic channel, 17, 25, 117, 124; mythological, 31, 68, 83, 95; in proprioceptive channel, 17, 25, 27, 105, 107; in relationship channel, 25; of therapist's reactions, 44; in verbal channel, 105; in visual channel, 16, 25

Analysis, 5, 40, 96, 97

Analysts, 141

Analytical psychology, 57

Anger, 37m, 114

Anima, 88

Animals: dreams of, 76, 87

Animus, 88

Anthropos figure, 68

Anxiety, 124

Aqua permanens, 130

Aquarian age, 74

Arab nations: alchemy in, 119

Archetypal: image, 109; patterns, 60, 61, 107; processes, 132; tendencies, 61-5, 66, 68, 132, 139

Archetypes, 60, 61, 107; binary characteristics of, 102-4, 107; in channels, 99, 101, 102, 103, 109, 110, 111-13; and coupling, 111-13; definition of, 99, 101, 102; and dreaming-up, 113; group, 113; in the *I Ching*, 99-102, 104, 107, 108, 111; as potentials, 139; as process, 110; of sex, 72; as time, 110; and wave functions, 61-3

Asimov, Isaac, 83

Associations: in dreamwork, 31, 95

Astrology, 74

'Athanor', 127-8

Neptune, 72
Neurolinguistic: programmers, 40, 104; programming, 9
Neurosis, 31
Newtonian: concepts, 67; era, 38
Nightmares, 139
Nigredo, 130-4, 135; and unoccupied channel, 133
Nirvanic experience, 52
Noises, 97, 132, 136
Nuclear war, 89
Numbers, 63, 67; in *I Ching*, 96, 97

Observation, 3, 55; of channels, 14, 28; as detached, 63-4; and primary process, 67; and process logic, 63; as tool for process worker, 5, 11, 28
Observer, 3, 11, 38, 55, 68, 74, 86, 88, 112; chronological, 64, 65, 66, 67; as fluid ego, 65, 66, 74; and process logic, 63, 64; as process scientist, 66, 86; in process work, 85; and synchronicity, 59
Oceanos, 75, 77, 79, 80, 81, 84, 85, 86, 89, 139
Ogawa, 81, 83
Omtéotl, 87, 88, 89, 95, 161
'One continuum', 63
One world concepts, 56-8, 59, 62, 63, 64; in alchemy, 138; and dream world, 62, 65; and meditation, 62
Operations, 36, 116, 117
Opposites, 74, 93, 98, 107-8, 130, 131, 132, 135; as yin-yang, 92
'Opus', 97, 119-20, 121, 123, 125, 126, 128, 135, 137, 140
Out-of-the-body-experiences, 18, 67
Oxford Dictionary, 91

Pain, 4, 9, 35, 53, 96, 138, 139; amplification of, 17, 81; in head, 36, 81; lower back, 34-5; stomach, 96, 103, 105; working with, 103, 105
Panacea, 52, 140
Paralysis, 8, 23
Parapsychological: causality, 101; events, 14, 57, 68, 94; phenomena, 19, 42, 67, 86, 112

Parapsychology, 9
Pauli, Wolfgang, 57
Peacock's tail, 134, 135
Pectoral muscles, 33, 34
Perception, 11, 19, 20, 60, 67, 94, 103, 114, 116, 141-2; extrasensory, 97; sensory, 19, 20, 23
Perls, Fritz, 8, 16; on relationship, 40
'Permanent water', 130
'Personal power', 134
Personality, 7-8, 14, 31, 133; transformation of, 119
'Philosopher's egg', 126-8, 134, 139
'Philosopher's stone', 121
Physical contact (*see* Body contact)
Physicians (*see* Doctors)
Physicists, 56, 67, 84, 86, 141
Physics, 3, 9, 38, 61-3, 72, 73, 84, 139, 141; and alchemy, 119; as a channel, 94; and energy concepts, 83-5; mathematical, 83; and process concepts, 63, 71-2; and psychology, 7, 8, 48, 54-9, 61-3, 66-8, 72, 73; quantum, 60; and Taoism, 71
Physiology, 119
Planets, 81
Political events, 68
Poseidon, 72
Postures, 8, 16, 31, 52, 132, 134; in hatha yoga, 52
'Potentia', 62
Pressure, 36, 140; neck, 35
Priest, 91
Prima materia 52, 119, 121, 124, 125, 126, 127, 128, 129, 134, 136
Primary: channel, 24, 25; phenomena, 98; signals, 130
Primary process, 12-13, 25, 26, 28, 32, 34, 37, 45, 46, 72, 92, 111, 134, 135; acceptance of, 38; and alchemy, 124; and congruence, 139; and dreamwork, 30; and edges, 79; and fluid ego, 65; and *I Ching*, 110, 112, 142; identification with, 24, 66; mirrored in dreams, 27; and *nigredo*, 131; observation and, 66, 67; and time concepts, 74, 75, 142
Process, 8, 11-12, 38, 48, 63, 72, 83, 84, 85, 117; and alchemy, 118-42; amplification of, 115; as

Therapist, 121, 133; and body contact, 49, 50, 51; as a channel, 40, 42, 43, 44, 45; and dreamed-up reactions, 41-4, 48-51; and exhaustion, 32, 49, 96; functions of, 10; as incongruent, 48; and malpractice, 51; problems of, 9, 49, 128, 129; programs of, 36, 41, 45, 88; and projection, 43, 95; student, 93, 94, 96

Therapy, 9, 132; as dreamed-up process, 41, 53; group, 48; and role reversals, 44; transformation of, 130

Thinking type, 20, 24

Thomas, Lewis, 57

Tics, 124

Time, 6, 20, 61, 63, 65, 66, 67, 73-9, 83, 85, 86, 90, 94, 102, 123, 137, 142; and the *I Ching*, 109, 112; mythical, 73; and the *nigredo*, 133; symbols of, 71, 75, 76, 77, 83

Tone, 16, 19, 26, 96, 136, 141

Trances, 117, 132

Transactional analysis, 9; on relationship, 40

Transference, 40, 41, 44, 97; counter, 42

Transformation, 97; in alchemy, 9, 118, 119, 124, 129, 130; and conservation principles, 85; of ego, 135; of identity, 139; of *nigredo*, 133; of process, 85, 126, 137

Tumors, 124; breast, 3-4, 5; lung, 116, 117; neck, 106, 107, 129; non-malignant, 116; stomach, 105

Typology, 7, 20, 24

Unconscious, 9, 16, 54, 67, 88, 103, 105, 120; communication with, 104, 105, 106; and Freud, 102; and integration, 135; as *prima materia*, 119; psychoid, 63

Unconscious, 13, 137

'Unio mentalis', 138

Universal: dream fields, 45, 47, 48, 59, 83; law of flow and movement, 67; processes, 45, 48, 54, 56, 57, 61, 83

Universe, 61, 62, 64, 67, 68; and alchemical processes, 138; as a channel, 22; dream, 63, 64, 65, 112; post-Einsteinian, 59, 68; in Taoism, 92

'Unus mundus', 62, 63, 138, 139, 140, 142

Van Over, Raymond: on Tao, 91

Verbal channel, 51, 105

Verbs, 3, 4, 5, 74

Vibrating, 133

Visceral experiences, 136

Vision quests, 132

Visions, 95, 97, 117, 124, 134, 136, 141

Visual channel, 4, 5, 14, 15, 19, 24, 25, 27, 35, 98, 103; and binary communication, 103, 104; description of, 15, 16; edges in, 25; extraverted, 18, 19; introverted, 18; occupied, 133; and sexuality, 52; and synaesthesia, 112

Visual type, 24, 27, 133

Visualization, 8, 35, 37, 84

Voice: as double signal, 32, 33; signals in, 117

Voodoo, 113

'Wakanda', 83

Wave: equations, 61, 62, 139; functions, 61-4

Wholeness, 93, 139

Wholeness and the Implicate Order, 67

Wilhelm, Helmut, 91, 92

Wilhelm, Richard: on *I Ching*, 91, 109, 110

Withdrawing, 33, 34

Working with the Dreaming Body, 85

World, 22; and American Indian tradition, 139-40; in mythology, 75, 77, 79, 80, 81, 83, 87, 88, 95; and Oceanos, 75, 77, 80; as post-Einsteinian, 62, 66; problems, 89, 142; as a process, 56, 57, 58, 63-8, 140; as static, 63, 65, 66, 67; stopping of, 88, 89; and Talmudic literature, 139-40; and Taoism, 92-3, 139, 140, 142

World channel, 21, 24, 25, 30, 55-68; in alchemy, 138, 139, 140; consciousness, 83; edges in, 25; extraverted, 21; introverted, 21;

Out of
Darkness

Out of Darkness

Janelle Wade

Treasure House

a division of

Destiny Image

P.O. Box 310

Shippensburg, PA 17257-0310

"For where your treasure is
there will your heart be also." Matthew 6:21

ISBN 1-56043-756-1

For Worldwide Distribution
Printed in the U.S.A.

Destiny Image books are available through these fine distributors outside the United States:

Christian Growth, Inc.	Successful Christian Living
Jalan Kilang-Timor, Singapore 0315	Capetown, Rep. of South Africa
Lifestream	Vision Resources
Nottingham, England	Ponsonby, Auckland, New Zealand
Rhema Ministries Trading	WA Buchanan Company
Randburg, South Africa	Geebung, Queensland, Australia
Salvation Book Centre	Word Alive
Petaling, Jaya, Malaysia	Niverville, Manitoba, Canada

Contents

Chapter One

Painful Beginnings

The haunting past, the doors that have been closed for so long, now must be opened. Decades of patient persistence by God brought me to this place—despite the worst efforts of the hordes of hell...

"Janelle, I want you to go back in your past and tell me what has happened to you," the man beside me said, the one the others called Mr. Russell.

"NO! I can't! It hurts too bad, and I don't want to hurt anymore," I said. "I'm too afraid. You don't know what you're asking!"

Wait, there is another voice in me, and yet another, and another! I thought to myself. *How many are there? And who or what are they?* There are no answers, only growls and hissing coming from somewhere within my innermost parts. *Somehow, I'm united with these voices,* I thought. *We are agreed that we want only to kill the idiots in this place quickly and cruelly.*

Suddenly, I feel the voices within me surface enough to shout, "They have no idea how powerful we all are. How dare they try that authority junk on her...she belongs to us!"

Oh no! That man sitting beside me is speaking again, I thought silently. He commands me to speak in Jesus' name. I know I have to obey because he has an authority from a higher power than the masters within me. I understand that, but it is so hard to speak. The words pain me, yet I have no will but to obey, and no power of my own is strong enough to stand against him and these strangers.

I looked frantically around the room for the one source of possible help left to me—my friend Mona. *She will protect me unto death. After all, she brought me in here,* I thought. She was just sitting there, looking at me with tears in her eyes, praying and agreeing with them. *I'll try anyhow,* I decided

"Mona, please help me, I'm so afraid!" To my dismay, Mona simply answered, "Janelle, what are you afraid of? Tell them." All that is left is to remember.

It began yesterday as I sat in my own house, minding my own business, when my long-time friend, Marie, knocked at my back door. She had changed her life style a couple years before, and she began spending her time in church, and as she put it, "serving her Savior." Naturally, we started seeing less and less of one another. Now here she stood, glowing with a joy and peace that I had never seen in her before. She looked great, what a sickening sight for my sore eyes to see. She came in and began talking about some so-called miracle services at the local high school. She even claimed that God had asked her to come to me and compel me to go with her to those services that day.

Quite frankly, in my state of mind, I had a place in mind for her to go to that was a very HOT place of torment. Instead, I found myself saying half-heartedly, "Would you like a cup of coffee?" It was unbelievable. As we talked, I repeatedly tried to get her mind off the reason she paid me this visit, but it didn't work. She was persistent, so with much unseen anger, I agreed to meet her in town and attend the meeting with her.

I would have done anything at that point to be rid of her. In fact, I had already made plans to go fishing with my husband before Maria came on the scene. Nevertheless, I found myself compelled to meet her as I promised. As my husband drove me into town, I even started to cry and complain that I did not want to go with her, and my husband asked, "Then why go?"

He didn't understand, and neither did I, that the choice was no longer mine to make. So there I found myself, sitting at something called a miracle service, mockingly waiting to see a miracle. I sat there in amazement. The first thing I noticed was the smile on everyone's face. Evidently, no one had ever told these people that Christians can't have fun—at least, that's what I had been led to believe. If these people had heard it, they didn't listen.

I had never heard "church music" like this before, and they were even clapping their hands—some of them even moved their feet in a dancing motion to the music—yuk! Then the ultimate surprise at that point was to see those with their hands raised begin to say, "Praise the Lord!" Now that really gave me a chuckle, but not without some tremendous reservations in my mind.

The people in the "amen and hallelujah corner" were really weird, speaking in some language that I couldn't understand. It certainly was not the prayer language that I had been taught to use by my master, satan; but still I could not leave.

A small-framed preacher jumped and waltzed all over the stage, shouting out the love of his God, and the cruelty of the devil, and how he had been healed of a heart condition and knew that God would heal others. Of all the things to say, he said God would save and deliver people of their sins and demonic possession, and then there was an altar call. To my dismay, people all over the auditorium began running forward for healing, salvation and deliverance. That did it for me. Whatever power these people had sure seemed stronger than what was within me—even if I was a practicing witch and sorcerer!

I was grateful when it was over and I could go home, but I also had a peculiar empty lost feeling that I'd been living with for many years. Now that uncomfortable feeling was seemingly bigger than when I had walked through those doors.

As the rest of the day went by, I became more and more aware that I had to go back that next day and watch again. Little did I know that there were people praying for me—God had sovereignly placed a hook in my jaw that I couldn't remove on my own. The next day however, I convinced my husband that he should go with me, along with my friend, Mona, and her husband. I was very apprehensive about the weird people with their strange language.

After the music and praise, there came the usual altar call. I wasn't afraid of the altar call, mostly because my friend Mona was with me. I knew she was already a Christian, but I knew she loved and respected me enough not to push me. Evidently, God had other plans for the day, because Mona was the first person to head to the front at the altar call that day! I watched in horror as she started down the aisle—I'll never forget the image of the bottom of her green and white polka dot dress swirling about her knees as she almost ran to the front. An even greater horror hit me as I found myself following that green dress as if I had no mind of my own. We were like driven people, desperate to get up on that high school stage to be prayed for.

People met us there and prayed, first for Mona, and then for me. I struggled to maintain my composure, to gain some form of control over the situation. When a man asked me, "Daughter, what can we do for you?" I opened my mouth to answer and became painfully aware that I had lost all control of my tongue! To my total dismay, I began to speak in some form of inhuman gibberish. I tried to say something, but the sentence of gibberish ended with a sob and "...nobody likes me."

They prayed and absolutely nothing happened. I decided to leave and started to walk off the stage, when a small blonde woman approached me and etched a cross on my forehead with her thumb, saying at the same time, "I bind you, satan, in the name of Jesus!" Then she disappeared from view, leaving me shaken and confused.

Suddenly, I felt like there were many merry-go-rounds spinning in different directions inside of me, and they all had minds and wills of their own—attacking one another and me. Dazed and disillusioned, I started to leave the stage again, fully convinced that there was no hope for me. I decided I would not live another day on planet earth in my secret world of fear and hell—death seemed to be my only choice. Suddenly, someone grabbed my arm and told me to go backstage to the make-up room where someone wanted to speak to me. Unable to resist, I meekly followed them backstage.

When I reached the doorway to the room, I found I could not enter. I just stood there, staring at a man who was sitting in a chair. His arm was resting casually on another chair, and he looked very confident. For what seemed an eternity, his eyes held mine with such authority and love that I wanted to run and hide, but I was unable to move. Finally, he said, "Daughter, you've been in the occult." Unreasoning anger raged in me at his words, and I commanded the forces of the powers of hell itself to come to my rescue.

I did everything I knew to do, using the knowledge and dark powers I'd gained after practicing witchcraft and sorcery for many years. Then I looked straight back into the man's un-waivering eyes and said, "I have not. All I've ever practiced is white witchcraft, and that's not evil."

I was amazed that this man never moved or showed even a flicker of fear—I thought surely he would at least have been knocked from his chair by all the demonic power I had just called down on him. Instead, he just held my gaze and said with even greater authority, "I said, daughter, you've been in the occult!" Then he began to describe my condition and my fears. It was like he scanned me from the top of my head to the bottom of my feet. His penetrating words of revelation and love nailed me to the floor where I stood.

Finally, I felt something in me shake loose in my mind, and for the first time, I wondered if my involvement in the occult could be the problem in my life, the reason I had not had a full night's sleep for so long.

The anger was gone for the moment, and hope illuminated a thought in my mind. *Could I become normal? Does someone love me without my forcing them to?* I was lost in the love radiating from those eyes behind the man's glasses. Finally, I entered the room.

Others were now pressing into the room, and I went with the flow and found myself flopping down on a chair directly beside this man with the glasses—all the while wishing I could be anywhere else than where I was now. The people began to chat and laugh, and I felt assured they had forgotten me. Suddenly, the man's hand shot out and his fingers rested on my forehead. Then he said the words that started this whole memory thing. Now I had no choice but to do as I had been commanded.

Through clenched lips, I managed to cry out in terror, "I'm afraid to remember, to see, to feel anguish, to hope!" Then the man with the glasses said, "Child, you don't have to be afraid anymore because the man called Jesus is going to be with you all the way." In that instant, I looked to my right and saw a vision of Jesus, with His hand reaching for me. From somewhere deep within, I heard a cry and gasp as my spirit stretched out to take His hand. Suddenly, I knew that I could do all things—even remember.

Fighting pain and paralyzing fear, I reluctantly obeyed, starting again, this time, at the very beginning.

I was born in the forties in the Midwest, to a mother who was very passive and a father who was a truck driver. I found out later that Dad was also a philanderer, but all I knew was that he was gone a lot, and sometimes Mom and my two brothers and me had it pretty hard.

When I was three months old, Dad just left and didn't come back, leaving Mom without food, money or a job to care for all of us.

Mom told me years later that she had considered taking us kids to a nearby river and ending it all, but she could never quite bring herself to do it. A family member came for a visit one day and offered us her home as a refuge. Mother gratefully packed us up and away we went to a most appreciated home.

I was too small to relate to surroundings at first, but the time finally came when I started realizing that our new home wasn't such a fun place to be, with its strict religious rules and many different family members.

A memory floods my mind, the warmth of the sun and the tickling blades of grass about my ears are lulling me to sleep, when, somewhere in the vastness of blue space, I hear the monotonous drone of an airplane high in the sky.

The next memory pushes the first aside, commanding an entrance. I am standing in the back of a coupe with my two brothers, waiting for my aunt to get out of a church board meeting.

Every dull second seemed to stretch into an eternity as we waited alone in that car. Each of us was beginning to react to the boredom of the situation when one of my brothers decided to alleviate the problem by showing me his privates and directing my other brother to do the same.

For me, of course, there was one small problem—they thought it only fair that I join in with this fun idea. However, my aunt had always made me very aware that I was on my way to a fiery hell, and I knew that what my brothers had in mind for me at that moment would surely take me there quicker than I cared to go. I vehemently denied their invitation.

Our aunt came out of the church and the situation was supposedly forgotten. However, upon returning home, I told my mother my tale of woe. She questioned both brothers about the matter, and of course, they expertly stuck together and denied the dirty deed with an innocence I'm sure merited an Oscar.

Mother, convinced that I had drummed up the allegations, turned me over her knee and gave me "what for" as she lectured me on the biblical view of lying, and the liar's sure reward of eternal judgement. Later, as I sat on the top step of the stairs, my brothers tormented me about getting even.

Even though it was all child's play, it was a rude awakening to the fact that sometimes truth doesn't seem to pay. I could not understand how the teachings in church could be so wrong when they said sinners would be punished for lying. Here I was being punished for telling the truth and the twin liars were victorious! *Oh well, I'm only three years old and who cares?* I was to find that question to be most in my heart from that time forward, "Who really cares about me?" I remember few things in the haze of those early years, and it doesn't seem fair to only say there were bad times. Somehow bad memories overpower the good ones, don't they? Especially if you are a super-sensitive child who has been labeled a cry baby.

The deep pain of my silent screams bring tears even now, *Would some one please ask me why I am crying? Don't ask me if you aren't going to listen. It hurts too much to think that someone might actually care—only to have them tell me they don't believe me.*

One of the earliest memories suddenly came to the surface, as Mr. Russell's eyes seemed to grow larger...

Lular was the unseen household ghost who haunted our childhood nights and stalked our days. The adults in our household loved to stick one of my brothers or myself down a cold air duct, telling us, "Lular wants you!" We knew Lular hated us all, and that he was always trying to get to us to inflict the most horrible torments to our bodies—his only desire was to tear us from limb to limb.

Many times, my brothers were forced to watch in horror as someone would run around the house as if they were being chased by Lular. They'll never forget the sight of the knife sticking out of the victim, with red blood all over their shirt. Of course, the gleeful adults failed to tell my young brothers that the knife was really stuck under their arm, and the blood was really watered-down ketchup. My brothers were tormented more than I, but the only ones having fun in these memories were Lular and all his fans. Even though my brothers bore the brunt of Lular's rage, I still have memories of fear concerning his power.

The unending stories and sightings of Lular, as he chased adult family members around the house, ready at any moment to destroy them or beat the breath out of them, became the terror of our childhood nightmares in that house.

Poverty in the Commons

When I was three, we moved into a small two-room house in what was called "the commons," and settled into poverty. Food was hard to come by a lot of time, because Mom didn't receive enough pay from her job to make ends meet.

When Mom injured her back and was forced to take time off from her job, our already serious situation became worse. We soon grew to appreciate welfare, especially at Christmas time. (We appreciated the fruit more than the gifts.) Even the small amount of money we received through the welfare program often made the difference between starvation and survival.

There were happy times there though, with Mom and her endearing patience, and games and hours of laughter. Those hard, oh so very hard days are buried deep within me as moments of treasure.

Was It Love or Stupidity?

One Christmas, I vaguely remember getting three Betsy-Wetsy dolls—one from welfare, one from an aunt and uncle on my dad's side that I did not know, and another from someone else. I ended up giving two of them to missions, as I always felt that the children in Africa had it a lot worse than even me. Another memory that sticks out in my mind is the Easter that I was in the third grade. Without my knowing, my brothers took their wagon up and down ravines, collecting pop bottles so they could buy me a new dress for church. The excitement I felt was mingled with hurt for my brothers because I knew they had nothing but worn jeans to wear.

About the same time, just before Mom's factory was to have its annual picnic, I was gawking at the prizes they had on display in the entry way when a man came up to Mom. He wanted to take my picture holding the bride doll that was to be one of the first prizes for a game in my age group. I had never touched such a beautiful doll in my life. They put the picture in the monthly newsletter and wished me well in winning it.

I was unable to think about anything else but winning that beautiful creature in the flowing white dress for days. My age group had to race over and under ropes to win. That was one time I was glad that I had a bit of tomboy in me.

The gun sounded and off I ran, stooping and then jumping, and never stopping, with a determination to bring home the prize—my precious doll.

I don't think I really believed that I could win, but somehow I did. They took me up on a platform to choose my prize. As I started to pick up my dream, I heard the grumbling of the little girl who'd placed second, complaining because she would have to take second choice of dolls, the plain old baby doll.

My heart started racing as I considered the choice I felt I *had* to make: receive my heart's desire or let the cute little girl get what she wanted. (Actually there wasn't much of a choice, because I would rather be disappointed than cause someone else to be.) I picked the "plain Jane" doll.

The judge looked at me with a puzzled expression and asked, "Are you sure this is your choice?" I just hung my head and said, "I'm sure." Mom even questioned me on my decision, as she knew how badly I wanted that bride doll.

To add to my hidden sorrow, some people didn't know what I was doing, so they called me stupid. I wish someone would have really known me. I wish they would have realized that there really was a good person inside "the whiner." I always seemed to be doing things like that. In my mind, it made sense to give.

One time, an underprivileged boy in my third grade class brought in a scarf for the Christmas exchange. One of the more elite young girls in our class drew his gift, and she just threw a fit because it came from him.

Earlier in the year, this boy had fallen off a cliff and lost an eye and disfigured his face. This made him even more of an outcast to most of the other students.

When I saw her disapproval, I immediately went into action, "oohing and ahhing" over his present to her. I had received the most beautiful necklace and bracelet I had ever seen in that same gift exchange, but I knew Mom would never let me wear it because of our religious convictions.

I wanted to try to talk her into letting me keep it—at least long enough to look at it—but when I saw this young girl's apparent dislike for the boy's gift, I could not bear the look on his face.

I literally begged that girl for the scarf, going on and on about its beauty. She gratefully exchanged presents with me and you should have seen the pride on the boy's face. Of course, again I was misunderstood and the kids teased me unmercifully about having a crush on this young man.

I get so mad inside when I think about it all. *Why did I do it?* Yet I know I could not stop. Was it love or stupidity? Perhaps I had a gift of compassion, or maybe I just was never allowed to think enough of myself.

I wish I could have just been normal—with all my good and all my bad—without such guilt.

Life With Aunt Helena

After several hard months at that house, our Aunt Helena moved from the country into a house in the city, and again asked us to move in with her family. To Mom, this was an answer to prayer again, because she was desperate to take care of us.

I don't remember the move itself, but I do remember that I soon discovered that my aunt brought new meaning to the verse, "spare the rod and spoil the child."

I don't want to remember those days; it just hurts too bad. I loved them all so much. Why did they hate me when I did every thing they asked? *Yes, You are there Jesus, I can go on with your help, but please don't leave me on this journey of memories or I die.*

One afternoon, my brother came into the room with some coins in his hand. As he offered it to me, I asked him where he'd found it. "On top of the piano," he said.

Knowing it was my cousin's money, I quickly refused to touch it, and I warned my brother that I would tell on him if he spent it. That evening I had to keep my promise. There came the confrontation and denial from my brother, and then we were both whipped viciously, to "beat" the truth out of us. My brother still held his ground, claiming innocence, and I held mine, claiming his guilt. We got another beating, with my aunt stating that she could not believe my brother to be a liar. I felt like I couldn't take another beating, especially when my brother was getting all the "brownie points," so I said what they wanted to hear.

Once I said my brother didn't take the money, I received yet another beating. I was not accused of taking the money; however, I had "lied." I couldn't win. The beatings didn't hurt as much as the fact I felt my aunt made me lie.

After all, my aunt said they had heard from "God." He must surely hate me. One day, my aunt told several adults,

"You know what would be funny? Let's make Janny take a bottle and tell her uncle when he gets home later. He would sure get a laugh out of that." Without any thought, I immediately said "No."

That was all it took. Aunt Helena pulled herself out of the chair and came at me with a bottle in her hand. It was positively forbidden for anyone to ever say no to her.

I knew I was in big trouble. She forced me to lay down on the floor and commanded me to suck the bottle. She threatened to switch me if I didn't obey her. So tearfully begging, I gave her what she wanted and sucked on the baby bottle until she and everyone else had a good laugh.

Finally, I was allowed to crawl away to drown alone in the shame of the moment. It didn't stop there—Aunt Helena went to church and gleefully told people, "Ask Janny what she did last night." In total humiliation, I slipped by her and tried to hide behind my mom, hoping everyone would think that I was not there.

I thought no one saw the tears or heard my screams. The fact that no one knew my anguish seemed to make it even worse. (Now I know Jesus knew all along, and He cared for me when no one else did.)

I can't get the laughter out of my head. "What's wrong Janny, you afraid of bugs?" More laughter. "Stop it!" my heart cries, as my lips remain tightly closed, trying my best to pretend the situation away.

It happened more often than I dare remember...clad only in our under panties, myself and two female cousins cowered close together in paralyzing fear. We helplessly watched my aunt's hands close in on us, and grasped between her fingers are big black bugs with huge pinchers that were ever searching for something to secure themselves to.

The last time, she used those sticky hard-shelled June bugs that cling to everything including skin, but they did not look as menacing.

We weren't allowed to make one move or sound of protest, as we endured the indignity of their brutal cat calls as they slipped these monstrous insects into our panties.

"What's the matter Janny, the cat got your tongue? Don't you move!" After what seemed like an eternity, they seemingly tired of their sport with us and left us, deserted in the midst of our fear and momentary relief...until the next time.

The "Cat o' Nine Tails"

One time I dared to put some lipstick on my lips at the rebellious age of four. Two cousins committed the sin with me. After a teenage cousin told on us, we were suddenly forced to face the reality of judgement—all five-foot-ten-inches of it, weighing in at about two hundred and fifty pounds—Aunt Helena.

My cousins just stood there looking at her without the slightest hint of fear (they didn't live there), puzzled at my reaction more than anything. They soon understood my fear.

Aunt Helena cut two switches and gave me "what for," then I curled up in a chair, knowing I was not allowed to release the tears, unless I wanted to get more.

She then turned to my other aunt and tried to give her the other switch to use on Judy, but she refused to take it saying, "They're just little kids—they didn't do it to be mean." Aunt Helena grimaced as she began to preach about a hell and how I was going to go there if I didn't ask Jesus to forgive me for trying to look like a Jezebel.

Mind you, my aunt believed my younger cousin, Billy, was not doing anything wrong because he was just a little boy playing. My female cousin, Judy, and I were sinning against God, however, because we were girls.

Aunt Helena further told Aunt Bell that God would hold her responsible for Judy going to hell if she didn't whip her. Aunt Bell held her ground as I sat with mixed emotions, wondering if she was right or Aunt Helena.

Aunt Helena said *someone* had to pay for Judy's sin and threatened to make me the scapegoat. Aunt Bell left in disgust as Aunt Helena turned back toward me.

Surely, I was always on my way to hell, and that's a heavy load to carry when you are only four years old. What a bad girl I was! Why couldn't I be good enough?

Aunt Helena called her favorite instrument of punishment her "cat o' nine tails." It was actually a light cord, doubled over and over again. What that whip could do in the right hand of anger is unspeakable horror, yet the terror in our minds over the fear of its usage or threat of it was somehow as bad, if not worse, than the beating itself.

I remember how the fear, always the fear, coupled by the frustrations of every day teasing and harassments, kept me in a state of despair most of the time.

My aunt would often wash our mouths out with soap, especially my oldest brother, whom she almost seemed to have a vendetta against for some unknown reason. We always prayed, and then my aunt's God would reveal what punishment to inflict on us lowly creatures bound for hell. I started hating her God, and I always wondered what hate was like when I heard her and the others at her church say, "God is love."

I still remember huddling in fear outside the bathroom door, sharing the pain with my brothers who just minutes before were ordered to remove all their clothes and to bend over the toilet.

Before Aunt Helena raised her instrument of punishment, my younger brother would usually start crying, as if he knew what they wanted out of him.

Being satisfied with his submission to her authority, my aunt would let him off easy, but not my older brother. He was tougher, and she hated the fact that she could not intimidate him in any way—so she would beat and beat him, weapon against flesh, over and over again, until I thought she would kill him.

Finally he would give out small grunting sounds when he could no longer hold back, which seemed to satisfy her. If she saw me crying as she came out of the bathroom, she would ask me, "Do you want some of it too?" Fear would overtake the anguish I felt for my brother, and I would sink down to the floor and try to hold back the tears. After what seemed like an eternity, my brother would come out with his blue jeans on, walking ever so painfully, carefully buttoning his shirt because he could barely stand the pain when it touched his back. *I love you, bro.*

The mind games never seemed to end. We were always walking on eggs, wondering what would set my aunt off again. All we knew was that whatever it was, we wanted to be far away from it. Times were tough back then, and Aunt Helena's big house became home for many of her family members. Another bedroom was needed to house the ever increasing family members, so they made a makeshift bedroom in an unattached garage that was about twenty five feet from the house for Mom and the three of us children.

They pushed back stored furniture, car parts, and junk to clean out a corner where two small beds and a dresser could go. This became our sleeping quarters. Ah, home sweet horror.

Mom now worked nights and I was forced to go to bed early, without my two older brothers or any other protection. Oh yes, they protected me alright. They pad-locked me in, "so no one could hurt me."

Little did they know what kind of enemies lurked within as the sun went down—*Mommy please come home!* One night, the Lord told Mom to come home because I needed her. She tried to ignore the prompting, but soon she couldn't stand the fear within her spirit for her child, so she came home.

She found me with my legs spread apart, with blood where she assumed my clenched fist of fingers had dug in. She thought that I had been masturbating. Did someone sexually assault me that night, or was I just reacting to fear? I couldn't tell my mother anything then, and I suppose I will never know for sure myself—all I know is that the mere thought of that garage scene still makes me shudder. Whatever happened, it must have been bad, because God did hear my cry and Mommy came home.

Mom insisted on a daylight shift and got it for her children's sake after that, and I was so glad. Another horror feeds the darkness within me—do I have to talk about it? *Jesus? There You are, I can now go on.*

Now, Mom was at work at the same time my aunt was gone, leaving us to other family members who liked to hurt us in another way. We had to please them—if we didn't, they threatened to tell Aunt Helena that we had been bad. Somehow that scared us much worse than what they had planned for us. We were in a "no win" game, holding our breath, hoping that somehow we would survive.

One female cousin especially liked my brothers to "play" with her. She wanted me to sleep with her sometimes so I could make her "feel good." All I ever wanted was her love—it seemed like every time I reached for love, there was always a condition or string attached to that love. The cost was too much for a little girl to pay, but I always paid. At the age of six, I started what they thought was my monthly menstrual cycle—it was actually an infection triggered by the secret sexual abuse I'd suffered.

Mom asked me embarrassing questions, and the doctor's exam increased my embarrassment and distress. Although I had been sexually molested, there were no visual signs or outward evidence.

No one had penetrated me, so they assumed that I was okay. Despite all their questioning, I knew better than to tell. After all, no one had really caused my body pain that I knew of with all their games. Besides that, I could not have withstood the guilt of being responsible for the punishment they may have received for what they did to me. So I remained silent.

I also wondered if anyone would really believe me, since no one believed me when I told on my brothers earlier on in life. It seemed to me that truth was not always the victor, and I knew too well what would happen if no one believed me.

I was not in the mood to face those kind of consequences. I had this tremendous love for them that went far beyond any pain I could suffer, and somehow I felt I couldn't stand to see them hurt.

God was at work in my life even in those dark days. One Sunday morning, a missionary speaker came to speak, and he brought all kinds of relics from Africa, including a shrunken head encased in glass.

As he spoke, I felt an irresistible tug at my heart to go to the altar. I told Mom, "Mommy, I want to go to the altar and pray." She asked me if I could wait until the man was finished, and I tried.

The stirring in my heart kept growing stronger, and again I pleaded with her saying, "Mommy, please, I can't wait." She hesitated, and asked me to wait just a few more minutes.

Finally I could stand no more, and this time I frantically said, "Mommy, I have to go please." She told me to go on.

I can still remember the look of disgust on the poor man's face as this little girl headed for the altar, but he never missed a beat. He just kept on talking as someone came up and prayed with me, while I wept with a broken heart. I had no idea why I went to the altar in the middle of a service, but to this day, I know that it was in obedience to Jesus.

Religious hypocrisy continued to shape and mold a part of our family destiny. Mom met a man named Johnny through the church who seemed quite taken with her, and she saw him a few times.

I was so jealous of this rival that I was thrilled when my aunt told Mom that she should not see this man any more. She sternly reminded Mom that the church they attended did not believe in divorce and remarriage. Along with that, Mom had her own convictions concerning remarriage. Goodbye Johnny. In just a short time, Aunt Helena met a man and remarried...I could never understand why it was always okay for some people to do things but not right for others.

One time a lady from the church asked my aunt if it would be okay for her to wear a watch that her unsaved husband had bought her for Christmas. Aunt Helena told her it certainly would not be okay, and that she would be in deep sin if she did. The poor lady kept it pinned inside her pocketbook so she would not offend her husband.

Just a short while later, Aunt Helena received a gold watch from my uncle. Guess where "God" told her she could wear it?—on her wrist.

Watching all this as a child sure confused me. Shortly after that, Aunt Helena was divorced from my uncle and met another man. "God" again allowed her to do something that He never seemed to allow any one else to do. Yes, she married him.

Along with her new marriage, Aunt Helena moved out of town to a new home, causing all of us to find new living quarters—which thrilled me to pieces. It was a pure joy being together with just the members of our little family.

Suddenly, we moved across town, light years away from the past. I would later discover that in reality, the past was very much alive right inside of me. I just closed another chapter of my life and waited as the doors flew open to another adventure. I desperately hoped this one would be better than the last.

Did You Have Painful Beginnings Too?

Did you pick up this book because you feel like you walk around in darkness? Perhaps you feel like chains from the past have locked up your happiness and ability to live life freely.

Maybe you are like me—when I was little, I actually thought I deserved the pain of physical and emotional abuse because there was something wrong with me. I thought that maybe I was some kind of "bad seed" that didn't deserve to really enjoy happiness.

Has the devil robbed you? He robbed me of the simple truth that God loved me while I was still a sinner. I was starving for unconditional love. I didn't understand that God loved me as I was, partly because many of the people in my life seemed to barter their love for me according to how I acted or responded to their demands. The enemy of our souls loves to use religious hypocrisy to twist and mangle our concepts of love and a loving God.

God will do for you what He did for me. He sent mighty warriors on my behalf to tear down the walls of deception. These ordinary people knew how to pray, and how to love me in practical ways. God is reaching out to you right now, just as He reached out for me across years of pain, sin and confusion with a love that overwhelmed every lie and evil that had been perpetrated on the little girl named Janny.

That love was a free gift, and it was mine, even though all I had to offer God was a broken spirit. Believe me, God hears your struggling prayers and He sees your desperate longing for freedom!

With God, all things are possible!

Chapter Two

Life After Near-Death and Incest

The first time I remember seeing Dad was the day he stopped by with his "other" wife and two small daughters. He had decided to take my mother, brothers and I to our grandparent's home.

I vividly remember sitting in the back seat of his car with my beautiful new found sisters, each of which was beautifully dressed and pretty as pictures. I was painfully aware that they could hardly stand the sight of me—they openly resented even an accidental brushing of my arm against them. I wasn't the picture of beauty, certainly not in their caliber of fashion, due to our religious doctrines. I was forced to meet a strict religious dress code calling for long sleeves, long hair, and long "ugly" brown stockings, held up by a garter belt. (How I hated those stockings!)

The girls bluntly told me I smelled funny, and the over-protective older sister told me not to even touch her sister because I would get her dirty.

I wasn't about to show them my tears, because something was hurting me even more than their cruel words or looks—it was the scene I witnessed in the front seat of the car that day. My dad was at the wheel with his "second" wife in the middle, while my mother sat in the passenger seat, leaning as close to the door as she could get to avoid offending Dad's second wife.

The problem was that I knew Dad was still legally married to my mother—there had never been a divorce, and neither of my parents had consulted a lawyer.

Reality became very painful to me as I sat behind them. I wasn't sorry so much for myself as for my mother. Yes, my daddy had two wives and we were being given this great privilege of going on a trip to our grandparent's house—no matter who it hurt. But my heart went out for Mom as she bravely suffered the humiliation of the moment so that we children could meet our grandparents. *Thanks, Mom.*

Several years later, Daddy drove up in his big truck and parked it on an adjacent street. I'll always remember that truck. I thought it was a block long, and this man at the door seemed to be eight feet tall.

I didn't recognize the man when I opened the door, but he said, "Hi Janny, I'm your daddy." Terrified at his words, I ran into the kitchen to where my cousin was doing dishes and clung to her as she went to the door. In amazement, I heard her say hello, and I realized this was the savior I'd waited for, hoping he would come to rescue me and make my life right.

Dad only stayed long enough to give us some money and make a promise to return the next Wednesday. I thought that day would never come. When it finally came, I was so excited that all I could talk about was my wonderful daddy who would be there to see me soon.

As the morning turned into noon, my excitement mounted. But as the afternoon started to fade, I grew anxious and irritable at my mother's warnings that I should not expect too much out of my daddy. Despite the fact that Mom and my brothers were preparing to go to church, I was determined not to miss Daddy. I took off running for a hiding place to wait for my knight in shining armor. I knew he would come for me, just as he had faithfully promised to do.

My mother knew this man better than he must have known himself, however. She had my brothers catch me, and after a stiff scolding and switching, I was whisked off to church in tears, knowing I would not see my daddy.

Mother was right when she said that he would not return that evening. I guess she too had lived through a lot of broken promises, tears, and failed dreams because of this man. She was trying in her own way to spare me those same disappointments.

A lengthy span of time passed by before I saw this man called daddy again. I was waiting alone on a school bus, all dressed and exciting about going to my first puppet show downtown with the rest of my classmates. (I had never been allowed "such nonsense" before.)

I was lost in a dreamy whirlwind of dancing puppets and laughter, when all of a sudden out of nowhere, my oldest brother burst onto the bus to interrupt my fantasy with his exciting news. The news made a decision for me that would cost me a dream come true, a puppet show.

Breathlessly he said, "Janny, Mom wants you to come home! Grandma and Grandpa are here from out of state, and they want to see all us kids, NOW!"

I'll never forget the struggle that went through me. Should I go on to the show or to see my daddy's parents, who I hardly knew? In the end, it wasn't much of a decision after all, because I could not stand to hurt anyone's feelings but my own. So home I went, reluctantly.

When I reached the house, I soon learned that this visit wasn't so much to see us children as to take care of a problem my daddy had gotten himself into.

Horror stricken, I listened as they told us how my daddy had been thrown in jail for running three cars off the road in a drunken stupor while trying to get to Mother and us.

He was facing prison time, so they took us all to a place to pay our respects to this man who "everyone told us—really did love us." The absolute pain of seeing him in that cell was forever burned in my heart. I'll never forget those eyes peering through the wire with tears as he said, "Janny, remember always, Daddy loves you."

Somewhere inside me a scream of fear for my daddy went off, though no one could hear it but me. That scream erupted within me upon every memory of him.

A couple of years passed before I saw Daddy again. I was now in the fourth grade and loving school. I felt more accepted and on more equal terms with the kids at that school.

I had good memories in the house there, especially the joys of having our own place and having Mom relatively to myself. It was in this place that I met my very first real friend.

The good memories weren't to last. Some time after school had started, Mom noticed a growth just in front of my left ear that seemed to be growing. When she took me to the doctor, he said it was an abscess. He said that he would not be able to do anything with it until it came to a head, whatever that meant. All I know is that it brought a new kind of fear into my life.

As the large, ugly pimple-like thing grew on my face, I was forced by the doctor to stop all activities—including school. For the next six weeks, I stayed inside at home. I can remember only two good memories from that time: my best friend Betty, who lived in the other side of our duplex, and my older cousin Jackie, who came to care for me when Mother worked. Jackie became my joy, my love and my hero—the most beautiful creature, other than my Mom, that I had ever seen. Six weeks after this growth started, they tell me that I got out of bed one morning and started crying for Betty, my neighbor.

As Betty came into the room, I started walking toward the window, not even noticing Betty's presence. Someone ran next door to call Mom home from work—what the doctor had predicted was now happening.

Mom hurried home in a cab, and asked the driver to wait on her as she checked out the situation. As soon as she saw me, she knew. I was beginning to twitch and talk totally out of my head. She grabbed me, tossed me in the cab and rushed me to the doctor's office. He promptly sent me to the hospital.

A quick examination revealed that the abscess had come to a "head," and toxic poison was rushing throughout my body. The next few days would determine my life or my death. Only God would decide my fate.

The memories that I have of the days that followed are scant but vivid.

Mother told me that the convulsive twisting of my body suddenly changed, and I began to jerk violently and my eyes rolled completely back into my head. At that point, Mom ran for the nurse.

My doctor raced to my room along with two nurses, pushing Mom out the door as they began a frantic attempt to save my life. During the next forty-five minutes, I had three experiences that are real to me to this very day.

I remember being unable to move or speak as the doctor pulled the sheet up and over my face. Through my opened eyes, I watched his troubled, sad face disappear behind the white of the sheet as he said, "We've lost her." Suddenly, I had a bowel movement and coughed, and that's when this memory ends.

The memory suddenly shifts to another scene. During those fleeting moments, I found myself wondering why I was on the ceiling, looking down at the bed as the doctor and nurses worked on something I could not see.

It all seemed very strange. but not scary at all. Peace was in all these memories, not fear. At one point, I remember passing my mother in the hall and hearing her prayers, but not seeing her. The next thing I remember is looking down at a wide sidewalk and noticing it was golden glass, with endless depth. It was the most magnificent and beautiful sight I had ever seen. Just as suddenly, I was beside a sea of crystal clear water, and I jumped in. (That was a miracle in itself. I was more than terrified of water—but all I felt then was peace.)

I noticed people in the water with me. We weren't swimming—we were just walking through the water, looking at the flowers and plant life. I was content to remain there.

That was my last conscious memory of that place. Was it heaven? I do not know—all I know is that somewhere deep within, there is a calm surety that I will be there again.

The prayer I heard Mother praying was, "God, You know how much she means to me, but You also know the future. If she will someday die and go to hell, then take her now. I release her to You, and should she live, I dedicate her to Your will to do with her whatever You want—even if it is to take her to the darkest places in Africa to be a missionary." I lived! The last memory of my hospital stay is Daddy. Since I was so near to death, the prison officials allowed Daddy to come see me for what they thought to be the last time. The guard who accompanied him on the long drive to the hospital brought him into the room handcuffed.

As I woke up, I heard Daddy pleading with him not to let me see him in handcuffs, but the guard apologetically told him he couldn't do that. However, he did agree to stand outside the door so Daddy and I could be alone.

Daddy brought me a necklace and bracelet, and he brought Mother a pendant, even though she wasn't there. He also brought me a little vase with a plant in it. When the guard said it was time to go, I remember tearfully saying "goodbye, Daddy" and begging the guard, "Please don't hurt my daddy." I didn't see Daddy again until about two years later when he took us to see his parents in another state. After we arrived, we were hurried off to bed, as it was late. Upstairs there were two rooms, one with two beds and the other with three big beds. They became our sleeping quarters for the duration of the visit.

Mother selected beds and matched sleeping partners, placing my two brothers in one bed, my brother's girlfriend with me in another bed, with my daddy in the third bed alone.

I felt sorry for my daddy and I asked if I could sleep with him, since he didn't have a partner. He was teasingly complaining about "poor old Daddy" and no one caring. My heart of love jumped up into my throat as I pleaded to sleep with him and was granted my desire. What joy that was for a love-starved little nine-and-a-half-year-old girl. Here I am, snuggled up in my daddy's big strong arms.

I was suddenly jolted out of that memory as I suddenly become painfully aware that the man called Mr. Russell, and the other people in this prayer room, are listening to my innermost hidden secrets.

After refusing to say more, I begin to sob violently, begging them to take me no further—I'm too ashamed.

Daddy's Don't Hurt Their Little Girls, Do They?

Well, do they?! Through my tears, I see Mr. Russell look at me with tenderness, yet with determination, "Some daddy's do, very sick daddy's do. Janelle, was your daddy like that?" Shaking to my bones, I looked at this man—unable to speak a word from my mouth, yet in my mind I found myself screaming, *What do you mean? How dare you ask if my daddy is hurting me! I love my daddy. Please Jesus, I'm so afraid to go on, yet the choice is out of my hands, so on I must go...." Turning to kiss Daddy good night, I smelled alcohol on his breath as he gave me an extra little hug and said, "I love you, honey."*

Secure in his arms, I began to drift off to sleep, worn out from the trip, when suddenly I felt Daddy's hand slip between my legs. I was immediately awake and began to slowly slip out of the position I was in, sure that my daddy was totally unaware of where his hands were. I certainly did not want him embarrassed.

I moved away from his hands carefully, so I wouldn't awaken him, but he moved and pulled me back to him tightly, almost as if to assure me of my safety in those arms.

I was sure it had all been my suspicious mind, due to what others had done to me in my life, so I began to relax again. Almost immediately, he began to undo the buttons in the crotch of my pajamas, and I knew then for sure that he was fully aware of what he was doing. Suffering the indignation and disappointment of the moment, I pretended to wake up to go to the bathroom, and called for my mother.

Mother helped me, and then told me to return to bed with my Daddy. I quickly told her, "I'm afraid of the ghost," and threw a tizzy, hoping to convince her to let me sleep with her. All the while, Daddy was begging me to return to bed with him.

After a firm shaking and a few whacks on the rear, I was allowed to sleep with Mom. I managed to sleep there for the rest of the stay, and the incident was forgotten, or was it?

After that, I avoided Daddy at certain times while trying not to be mean to him. He often asked me if I was mad at him for some reason. Other members of the family ridiculed and taunted me severely, telling me I was hurting my daddy and asking me how could I hurt his feelings like that.

The taunts still echo in my mind, *I hate you, Janelle! You are mean! Love your daddy! Love him, you hear!!!*

To make peace, I started warming up to him again, but this time, with extreme caution and craftiness. Later on, Daddy started visiting us on a more "semi-regular" basis. In other words, we rarely knew for sure when he would come in, but we always hoped it was soon.

By now we were living in a fairly large house and Mom was trying to keep enough food on the table and heat in the stove for our survival. I lived in the fear we wouldn't have enough for every situation.

Christmas holidays were always bleak with very little to look forward to. We knew there probably wouldn't be presents for us, nor did we even expect a tree. One Christmas, there were only two small presents under the tree that a man sold my brother and me for fifty cents. They were both for me, a little doll with an extra outfit.

I was torn between excitement and sorrow, knowing that my brothers and Mother would not be getting anything. Somehow that took the glitter off the gifts for me.

Birthdays weren't much either, just another day. The only thing that made birthdays special was Mom. She let us get by with a little more than usual that day, and would sing silly songs, and reminisce with us about happy times past and a hope for the future.

When the electricity was shut off for lack of payment, Mom would light candles and tell us exciting stories. Somehow, we hardly noticed the inconvenience of darkness. She would take us into her dream world, where life was so much fun and so secure that I tried to stay in that realm more than reality. Dreams and love seemed to be all we had.

The first night that Daddy came to visit us in that house, I was close to ten years old. I don't remember whether it was necessary or desirous for me to sleep with Daddy, but I did.

I hadn't forgotten that terrible night at my grandparents' house, but I missed him so much, and I was so afraid that it was my fault that he had stayed away so long, that I just didn't want to live without him anymore. After all, he brought Mom presents and made her laugh. We ate better, and we could be somewhat of a family and that felt so good.

That night I just lay there pretending to be asleep as he did his thing. There wasn't much pain since he didn't penetrate me, but the shame of what he was doing between my legs made me sick to my stomach. Even as he cleaned himself and me up the best he could without waking me, I was silently screaming, *I'm not asleep, Daddy! My eyes are closed, and I'm in that safe place where Mom's stories take me.*

From that time on, the encounters occurred each time he came home—which was now more frequent. Sometimes I would let him do things to me to keep him from my mother. After all, she was an angel to me, and I could not tolerate him touching her when they were not legally married. He was divorced from two women at the same time when he was in prison, and one of them was my godly mother.

He soon let me know that he was not fooled by my sleeping act, and this seemed to excite him more. He began whispering in my ear as he would satisfy his increasing demands of me. He would whisper, "You are Daddy's favorite little girl, you're my Janny. You like Daddy to do this, don't you? I see it in your eyes."

No, Daddy, I hate it! I would scream silently, too afraid I would lose him if I told him the truth. *You hurt me, Daddy. What you are seeing is love, pain, fear, a little girl's need for a daddy's real love.*

Then my secret torment would start up again in my mind. *Oh well, Janelle's a jerk anyway, with no good thing in her, so it probably is her fault. I hate you, Janelle! Do you hear me? I HATE YOU!!!!! I am going to get even with you some day, girl!*

One night it was so painful that I couldn't stand it, and I cried out, "Daddy, it hurts!" Of course he stopped that part of it, but I still had to lay there while he finished and tried to assure me that he would never hurt his little girl. He told me he just wanted to make me feel good. *Then why don't I feel good, Daddy?* I answered silently.

Jealousy even managed to enter my mixed up emotional state at that age. I remember how my feelings would get so hurt when I saw him cry for some other girls who I imagined didn't love him near as much as I did.

I remember thinking, *Here I am giving him everything he seems to want, yet he plays his guitar and sings songs with the names of his other little girls by another marriage, crying like a baby because he misses them so bad.*

Reluctantly, a deeply buried memory forces its way into my thoughts despite my embarrassment. *I don't want to tell these strangers about my shame!* Yet the memory forces its way out, the vivid images of the afternoon Mom was at work and my brothers were gone.

Daddy started wrestling with me and tickling me. It was so much fun to just be his little girl at those times (and not his "little woman"). Slowly, his face started changing and I saw that "look" in his eyes.

I felt a growing dread in me as he told me he was going to give me a licking. I started crying at the mere mention of a spanking, because Daddy never hit me at all.

As I began to cry, he started laughing softly as he held me down on the sofa tenderly, and said, "Honey, Daddy doesn't mean that kind of licking, what I'm going to do to you will make you feel good."

I laid there stunned, trying to figure out what he was going to do to me, yet knowing it was something sexual. I had to find an escape from this one. As he started to bend his head down, somewhere inside of me, I cried, *Jesus!*

At about that same moment, our door-to-door salesman knocked and said his name. Daddy cursed and jumped up, and I seized the opportunity to run.

I grabbed my panties and ran out the back door and down over the hill to my aunt's house and stayed there until Mom came home. Of course he came after me and pulled me aside to ask me why I ran from him. With tears in his eyes, he acted puzzled as he said, "Janny, you know Daddy would never hurt you, don't you?"

Not wanting to hurt him, I said I was sorry that I had hurt him and asked him to forgive me. Of course he did, but not without letting me know that he would stay away before he would ever bring any more pain on Mom or us kids.

The fear of losing him was always greater then the shame of what he was doing to my body.

One night, Daddy and I went to the church to pick up Mom. As we waited in the car, Daddy took my hand in his and scratched my palm with his index finger and I laughed because it tickled.

He told me that he was not just tickling me. He said that was the way a man asked a woman if she wanted to have sex with him. If she blew in his ear the answer was yes. Then he blew in my ear, encouraging me to do it to him.

I was so torn and confused inside. Here we were outside of church waiting on Mom to come out, and my daddy is wanting to do "stuff" with me right in front of God. I was terrified. I had been raised to believe that the church was the house of the Lord and God dwelled in it.

Along with my horrendous fear of God was the fear of losing my daddy if I did not let him "make me feel good." I was spared from making that choice when Mom suddenly walked out of the church. I gratefully ran up to greet her.

Daddy never mentioned a word as we joyfully went home as usual. He acted like nothing had ever happened. Well, maybe nothing happened to anyone else, but I was in total confusion and fear at what God may do to my daddy because of his disrespect for Him. Not once did I think God would be mad for my sake.

There were fun times, though, when Daddy took us out to Aunt Gert's house for dinner and visiting. We all listened as

Dad, and my uncle and cousin played their guitars and banjos, and we all joined in to sing old songs.

Of course, Daddy was always drinking, but it was such fun. I can remember feeling like we were a normal family as I sat in adoration as Daddy would sing songs. He was a good-looking man, about six feet four, with light hair and beautiful blue eyes that sparkled and danced as he sang.

He used to tell wonderful stories about his family and the years past, when he was married to Mom. Those are very cherished moments, when Daddy was just Daddy. I loved him more than words can write, yet not without unbelievable sorrow and shame.

On one occasion, Mom allowed me to go home with him over night, several miles away where he worked. While there, he had me stay with the family of one of his friends from work.

That evening, I learned that their little girl was another "special" little girl to my daddy. All she could talk about was how my daddy was her boyfriend. Heartsick, I kept silent until Daddy picked me up about three in the morning.

He was totally drunk as he drove me to his place, weaving all over the roads, but somehow we made it. As we entered the house, I started receding into a deeper state of fear than I had ever known. I realized that I was at the mercy of a man who was capable of anything in his state of drunkenness.

We went directly to his bedroom and he removed his clothing and got into bed, motioning toward me to do the same. I sat frozen in fear on the vanity bench, shaking my head in refusal as he grew angrier.

Somehow, there was a knowing within me that if I gave in and got into bed with him, I would be hurt beyond my wildest fears. After what seemed an eternity, Daddy got up in absolute disgust and said, "You little bitch! You are nothing but a big baby—get in the car. I'm taking your ___ back to your mother!"

Grabbing his bottle, he took a big gulp and away we went. We had only gone a short distance when he had to pull off the road and immediately passed out. I was left sitting there with his head in my lap and his hand up my dress. After calling his name repeatedly and assuring myself that he was indeed asleep, I carefully removed his hand and sat there, unable to move under the weight of his body.

After a long while, a state policeman passed by looking at me from his car, and I knew he would be back. Although fearful, I was grateful to see him. When he finally returned, my dad awoke with a start. With his glib tongue and persuasive personality, he convinced the officer that he had worked all night, and that although he'd thought he could make it home, he'd discovered that he couldn't without pulling over for a short nap. He let us go.

I Felt Like One of the Kids for the First Time.

Some time after this, Mom cut my hair and for the first time, I felt like the other kids just a little bit. I really was hungry to be accepted as one of the kids and to live a normal life.

My last memory of Daddy was when Mother took the opportunity to get away with us children and visit her ex-sister-in-law in another town. We children had just been tucked in for the night on the front room floor, when a knock came at the door. It was Daddy, drunk as usual, wanting his family. As I lay there, he went into the kitchen with my mom and aunt to talk. Both of them started telling him he needed to get saved and change his life. I couldn't see Mom and my aunt, but I could see Daddy sitting in a chair with his hat on his knee, crying like a baby.

I had never seen him like this, except one other time when he was visiting us at our house and started seeing snakes and monsters and hell itself. That time, he just kept crying for my mom to help him. It was a horrible sight and a night of fear for us, but tonight, what was going on here tonight at my aunt's house felt different somehow. Something inside told me to pray.

I remember hearing my aunt tell Daddy that God could forgive all that he had done, but Daddy just sat there with his head hung down, crying even harder and saying, "I can't. I've gone too far, I've done too much."

No one except God and I knew that a little girl was laying in the other room crying, and wanting badly to hug her daddy and tell him, "No, you haven't, I forgive you." Unfortunately, she had been trained to "know better" than to interfere. After all, she had been taught well that children were to be seen and not heard.

Sometime later, I finally confessed to my mother what Daddy was doing to me. I did not tell all, because I could not stand the pain in her eyes. After all, they were making some kind of plans to perhaps get back together in the future. I felt so guilty about bringing that hope to an end.

After we returned home, I began having horrible dreams of Daddy being killed in one way or another. I woke the entire household up with my cries and screams of fear for my daddy's life.

Mother tried to hold me and convince me that I was just having another bad dream and console me back to sleep. About two months later, however, I awakened to see Mom sitting on the edge of our bed with tears in her eyes. I looked straight at her and asked, "He's dead, isn't he?" She said, "Yes."

Later I learned that Daddy had been killed in a car-train accident, along with a young female companion and her eighteen-month-old little girl.

How I ached inside over the fact that I had told on my daddy. What kind of monster was I? If I had not told on him, he might still be alive. After all, I could have stood what he was doing to me. As always, the voice within me said, *Janelle, you're nothing but a big baby. Don't you forget, I hate you— do you hear me? I hate you!!*

At the funeral in my grandparents' state, we said our last goodbyes to this man I called Daddy, but barely knew. As I walked away from the coffin with my mother, I remember looking over my shoulder for one last look when, all of a sudden, I heard a scream that still echoes in my mind—then everything went fuzzy.

Later, when I came to my senses, I was told that the scream was from me, and they thought they might have to take me to the hospital. I have no idea why I screamed, but the vibrations from that scream are still felt in my heart to this very day. Goodbye Daddy, or is it?

Mr. Russell and the other people keep prodding me on, as if they were sent to strip me naked and examine every inch of my soul. *Why won't they release me to leave this chamber of horrors?* I thought in my pain. *Where are you, Jesus??* He is still holding my hand. Onward we go.

I glared at those people, but I knew it was the only way to freedom. Obediently I began the journey through the turmoil and pain of my years between twelve and eighteen.

Were You a Victim of Abuse As a Child Too?

Did you ever wonder, like I did, *Do all daddy's touch their daughters and sons this way?* Has your heart been broken in two? Was your childlike innocence taken away, violated by the very one who claimed to love you?

Did you learn things a little child should never know, against your will and despite your most desperate cries? Were your inner thoughts haunted by fears and anxieties thoughtlessly planted by the words and actions of others? Have you been chased and tormented by your own *Lular* in your imagination?

If you answered yes to any of these questions (even privately in your innermost secret place), then I know you are bruised, broken and hurt by the abuse.

You probably believe, deep down where no one can see, that it's your fault. An abused child is a desperately confused child living in a world that has been turned upside down. The ones you are taught to trust are the same ones you learn to fear.

When I was a little girl, my tender heart was paralyzed by the confusion and fear that seemed to dance in my head like madmen. Like me, you may think that you were born bad, that you brought it all on yourself somehow. Or you may simply hate God like I did.

My image of God was that of an evil tyrant, who waited to punish me for any step I took which was out of line somehow. He stood over me day and night, with pounding fists and cruel whippings. I thought the abuse had to come from Him (whether the hands delivering the punishment were those of my dad, my aunt or my cousin) because I deserved it somehow.

Has the abuse you suffered caused secret wounds to form and swell within you? Did you put part of yourself where the rest of the world can never reach? Oh sure, like me, you give the world bits and pieces of yourself, but never the *real you*.

Maybe you have suffered for twenty years or more like I did. Did you lock the *real you* away forever, because you hurt too much? I did.

I wondered, *Who would want the **real me** anyway*? I learned later that Jesus did!

After I discovered that God wasn't an evil tyrant after all, I felt the pure, loving touch of a compassionate Father who longed to hold me and bury each scar in the blood of His son, Jesus.

When I dared to ask Him why, He helped me come to understand that His eyes of compassion followed me even in my darkest fears and deepest shame.

Years after my childhood, I came face-to-face with my God, the One I now call "Abba Father." He knows I need to be loved and cared for.

There came a time for me, and it will come for you, too, when Jesus asked me to expose those secret places and invite Him in. I was afraid. I feared that in time, He would come to believe "it was no use."

But in those times when I felt too bruised and battered for repair, Jesus became my healing Balm of Gilead Who restored my soul and set me free to live again.

Let Him take you, hand in hand, as you walk together to examine those dark places of hurt. His love will wipe away every tear, and finally—you will feel a real Father embrace your wounded heart.

Chapter Three

Mother
Remarries and
I Learn to Dance

With Daddy gone, life seemed to settle into an everyday humdrum with little to look forward to. The most exciting experience I'd had was when Mom cut my hair and let me enjoy a little more acceptance from other kids at school.

The year before, my fifth grade teacher called me to the front of the class, opened her desk drawer exposing a hairbrush, and said, "I bought this for you. I would be glad to comb your hair every morning if you would be willing to come in a little early."

To my horror, I listened as my classmates' giggles turned into a full roar. The teacher tried to calm down the situation, but it would take days before their jeers would stop.

I'm convinced now that my teacher meant well, but at the time, I hated her act of kindness and took it as a very personal slam. Some good came out of it however–my mother cut my hair.

We moved across town into a very small house, mainly to be closer to church, since Mom did not drive. The one thing I remember most during this time in my junior high school years was the day my brother was taken from us and put in a detention home after his first and only brush with the law.

His probation officer actually told us that although he did not believe my brother's crime merited incarceration, he wanted to take the opportunity to hurt our older brother whom he hated, and as well as "to spare his younger brother from his bad influence."

The pain and anger I felt on the loss of my brother was something I would live with for several years. I ached to have him home on family holidays. In many ways, he had become my very dearest friend. Forever he would be one of the deepest loves of my life.

The thing I remember most about school was how I would walk home from school for my usual lunch consisting of a slice of bread, coated with butter and sugar, and then soaked in coffee.

I hated those times when the school officials asked us to keep a record of our meals for the week. I guess they wanted to study the food groups or something. I would look in my health book and make up my diet—I'm sure my teacher knew I was spinning a tale. All she had to do was take a good look at my frail body.

Mother Marries a Southerner

Midway through my seventh grade year, something happened that changed the course of my life yet another time. Mom met a man and fell in love. I thought he was the strangest man I had ever met, and I mean strange. He made dumb jokes, and he talked with a stupid accent. He was something every true Northerner abhors in their family, a Southerner.

I couldn't help thinking, now what will everyone think of me? I was so embarrassed.

"Surely, Mom, you can't like him, can you?" I asked one day. She just looked at me intently, then said, "Janny, wouldn't it be nice to have a daddy?" No! I yelled.

After all, this woman was a mother, a bed partner, bath partner, and my only friend for twelve years. I wasn't about to give her up, especially to this nut.

One day, he brought two of his five children with him, a boy and a girl. I immediately took to the boy. He seemed to be scared and was afraid to talk. He looked so lost and hurt sitting there in those old patched blue jeans, that my hurt saw his hurt and I reached out to him from my heart.

The girl, however, was a well-dressed, round-faced spoiled brat that I instinctively recoiled from and was determined to hate.

Mother knew this man for only two weeks before she announced that they would marry soon. I felt that my life was shattered.

I was no longer the center of Mom's life, and I couldn't understand why she wanted to be with him and not me. The most hurtful thing was the broken promise. Mom, trying to make me a part of her wedding, promised to meet me so I could help her pick out her wedding dress.

After school, I waited and waited, and finally I started to walk home. I had gone several blocks when Mom and this man pulled over to pick me up. I was excited because they had remembered me!

My joy was short-lived. As I climbed into the back seat, my heart broke when I saw a large box sitting there. Apologetically, Mom said, "He wanted to be the one to go with me, so we went ahead and got the suit."

At that moment, I felt like I was back living at my aunt's house—I had just been beaten and forbidden to cry, with the threat of another beating for being such a big baby.

I was whipped and I knew it. Mom married this man after a month's courtship. Knowing well the stories about stepdaughters being raped and molested, or at least abused by their stepfathers, I assumed the worst.

My thoughts turned to my cousin, who just a short time earlier, had been found to have been sexually used and abused by her stepfather since the age of three over a period of ten years. I knew it was true because I was there. How well I remember going to their house when Mom worked nights.

My uncle would take his flashlight and check on each of us to make sure we were asleep. There were two rooms upstairs and no doors, just long open rooms.

I could see his shadow as he got out of bed and headed my way. My cousin slept with her little sister in the same room as my uncle, since my aunt worked nights also. I would lay in bed with my boy cousins in the connecting room, stiff in fear. When the boys fell asleep, I was left to wait.

Here he comes! He checks the one boy, then the other. Slowly, he crawls into bed behind me. I remember laying there quietly, pretending with everything in me to be asleep, hoping he will leave me alone.

He puts himself up against me and I struggle in fear to remain calm, despite the pain between my legs. Just when I think he is never going to give up, he stops. As quickly as he got into bed with me, he gets out ("without doing any long-lasting damage to my body," I always told myself).

I watch his shadowy figure turn from the bed and get into bed with my cousin. *Please, Jesus, help her...I love you, Cuz.*

He was found out a short time later and received a prison term for his dastardly deeds. Somehow that made me happy. Someone said, "Boy, it's a good thing Janny's daddy didn't live to see this, he would have killed someone." I remained silent, keeping a "secret" that they don't know.

The same day Mom married the stranger, we moved into his home way out in the country. He showed me the room upstairs where I would be sleeping with his daughter (who I secretly hated). As we entered the room, a little gray-headed woman stirred in another bed. She raised herself up on one arm and then lay back down. She was my new stepfather's mother, a woman I would learn to call Mam Maw.

He told me to get into bed and left me in the darkness of this place with strangers. Then he returned to his bedroom to take my mother as his wife. I cried all night in confusion and fear for my future.

Even though these people took some getting used to, I found it not so bad to live there. I was used to surviving through all kinds of situations, and I knew I would survive this one.

My biggest relief came day after day, and night after night, when I discovered that this man, my mother's husband, did not "like" little girls and most likely would have killed anyone who abused one of us.

He was a man's man. Later in life, I would to learn call him Dad with much love and respect, but for now I must defend my fears.

The past haunted me, and now my mother wasn't even mine anymore. I guess she was starved for love, too, and wanted a future so badly that she just hoped and prayed everything would work out for the best.

Memories From the Altar

During a church service one night, I found myself really listening to the sermon. I realized that I "really" needed to give Jesus my life. Conviction came all over me as my heart began to race wildly. A fear that I could not explain came into my heart, and I could hardly wait until the altar call.

As soon as the altar was opened for prayer, I went down and fell on my knees. I began to ask God to forgive my sins and to come into my heart. Of course, He did just that. I still remember the sweet peace that flooded my soul.

The most memorable thing about that experience was the sense of pure love I felt for everyone—even Mom's girlfriend that I hated out of jealousy. I remember just flinging myself into her arms and asking her to forgive me, and then telling her how much I loved her!

Mom was like most church people, she had a favorite spot in church where she liked to sit, but one Sunday evening we sat in the middle row of pews instead of on the left hand side where we usually sat.

Behind us were my cousin Louise and her children, and down at the other end of our pew was an evangelist's wife named Lilly.

When the altar call was given, several people started forward, and one of them was my cousin, Louise. She handed me her eleven-month-old son and headed to the front. I had been praying for Louise and I was elated to see her go forward.

Out of the corner of my eye, I saw Lilly get up from the far end of our pew and head for the altar. Several people started crying almost immediately, because they had been praying for her to surrender to Jesus for some time.

The next thing I knew, my arms started going up in the air as if to praise the Lord. My stepsister, Connie, grabbed the baby in my arms and down to the altar I went.

I was barely on my way when I had a memory lapse of some sort, because the only thing I remember is coming to myself and looking up into the face of our pastor. He was on the other side of the altar from where I was kneeling.

He was looking at me with a look of awe on his face as he said repeatedly, "Yes Lord, yes Lord." At that point I must have had another memory lapse.

When I finally regained awareness of my surroundings, I was totally unaware of what had happened. I got up and quietly returned to my seat, dying of embarrassment and wondering what had just happened.

Lilly finally came to where I was hunkered down in my seat, trying to just disappear. She looked at me ever so tenderly and said, "Honey I tried, I really tried." I looked at her, not knowing what to say, so the child in me said, "No you didn't," and I turned away from her.

Ever since then, I've hoped that she knew that my reply was merely the defensive statement of a little girl who was very young in the Lord. Mom told me on the way home that Lilly got up from the altar three times before she finally left for good. All of this happened while the Spirit of God was on me.

The first time she got as far as her pew and went back to the altar. The second time she went clear outside and then back to the altar. The last time she just got up.

The next weekend, I went home for dinner with one of the girls from church. Her dad started talking about what had happened the week before, and I will never forget his cutting words to an already guilt-ridden young girl, "I think Lilly would have made it through if it hadn't been for you and all those theatrics."

I fought back tears and said, "I'm so sorry." The only consolation I have concerning what happened that Sunday night is something my mother told me. She said that through the years, that same pastor would stand up during camp meetings and cry like a baby as he told how he was present when the Spirit of God moved mightily on a young girl called Janny.

The harsh words of church people, coupled with the bitter past and an uncertain future would soon harden my heart toward the Lord. It's too bad that some of our most painful rejections happen within the family of God....

During my first short-lived experience with Jesus, I can remember having a vision in bed one night. I saw my spirit get up out of the bed, go down the stairs and out the front door to a honeysuckle bush in full bloom.

Jesus met me there and took me by the hand. As we walked around the bush, He talked to me. A brightness came from somewhere, even though it was night. At our feet, I saw the earth and the moon rotating around the same bush. I do not remember the conversation, but I know I will remember it someday, when it's the right time.

We Move to the Wrong Side of the Tracks

After spending a weekend out of town at my brother's house, I came home to learn that over the weekend, Mom and the new family had packed up and moved into town.

To my horror and embarrassment, we had moved from a beautiful home along a country lane, with rooms to spare and a lovely brick fireplace, to a dumpy house next to the river in what I saw as a "low-life part of town."

I was mad. For once in my life, I had it good with a life style that yielded me a little pride. Now here we were, moving into a poverty pit.

Shame overwhelmed me. Right or wrong, I was hurt and extremely angry toward Mom and her husband, because they had not asked of my opinion or even let me know about their decision. They just moved and I had no choice but to call this place home.

Things were crowded and, horror of horrors, I was forced to share a room with my stepsister. That really made me mad, but not for long. She ran away soon after that and got married at the tender age of fourteen. I was thrilled to get rid of her. Now I shed tears for her. *I love you, Sis.*

Now I attended the city school, and I quickly learned the cruel lesson that kids who lived on the wrong side of the tracks are not accepted, and they hardly ever cross to the other side.

I had to accept the harsh reality of "once poor, always poor." I soon stopped trying to reach through the invisible bars of society to embrace a better life style, I would live out the miserable life I had been dealt by a God I believed was unspeakably cruel.

Mother had no idea that her little girl Janny was a very sick young girl, emotionally as well as spiritually. Like millions of teenagers today, I was desperately crying out, "Somebody talk to me, I mean, please really talk to me!" *Nobody's there. HELP!* I would cry in my silent torment. *I've had it! The changes in my family life are too much for me, so out to the streets I go.... I need some love and attention, I can't bear one more disappointment. Nobody cares, so here I go. Watch out, world!!!*

In school, I was in the concert choir and played lead roles in two of the plays, but I had very little if any encouragement to achieve from the home front. Mom just couldn't do it, due largely to her religious beliefs, compounded by the fact that she was busy with two new babies at the age of forty, and a husband institutionalized with tuberculosis.

I'm sure Mom was totally drowning in all the confusion and fear so I don't blame her. She was trying to love us all and hold onto the hope that it would somehow all work out if she kept on loving us.

Looking back, I recall that some girls tried to reach out to me, but I was bound by low self-worth. The dean of girls at school tried to reach me too. She even brought me a bunch of her daughter's clothes to wear to school.

Her daughter was gorgeous, and I pretended that I was her daughter and tried to act just like her to be accepted. It didn't work. The kids knew what I was doing and did I get ridiculed! The boys called me names like "pig, street-walker and whore." At this point in life, I had not willingly allowed anyone to touch my body, nor had anyone tried since my uncle.

I had been a "good girl" so far. My tormented heart cried out, *Why do the kids call me such things?* Was it because I was poor? Was it because I had to walk five miles round-trip, back and forth through town every day? Were they mistaking smiles of friendship for a "come on?"

I didn't understand, I was a fifteen-year-old who just loved everyone and I wanted to express it, and have someone receive it as "love."

After a near escape, we had been dumped into poverty again and I knew it would take an act of God to take us through...only I wasn't so sure about a God Who seemed to have put us in this mess in the first place.... Inside, I had reached my limit. I desperately longed for some love and attention, and it wasn't coming from home, church or school. I felt I couldn't bear one more disappointment!

My First "True Love" in the Bourbon Beauty

One evening, I was walking up town to the skating rink when a burgundy Mercury with "Bourbon Beauty" painted on the side pulled alongside me. A young man, who I later learned was twenty years old, stuck his head out the window and said, "What's happening, Baby?"

I felt my heart melt as I drowned in the blue of those eyes. From that moment, I would never be the same. I was in love, and it was my very first "real" love.

We never actually dated, but if he didn't have anything better to do, he would pick me up and I would be his for an hour or two.

I remember walking the streets in the evening after our first meeting, hoping he would want me. We lived just below the main street through town, and I sat out back on the steps straining to see every car that passed by on the road.

With each passing car, I desperately hoped it was him, that he would turn down our street or honk—just to let me know he was still around. I was nearly always disappointed, and I would cry myself to sleep. I hated rejection. I hated its unbearable pain. I spent those lonely nights in inner torment, asking punishing questions with equally punishing answers. *Why can't anyone love me like I love them? Am I ugly? Probably! Am I stupid? Most assuredly, or I would not be alone and hurting all the time. People can't help if they can't stand me—it's my fault. I'm always the guilty one. I hate you, Janelle. Do you hear me? I hate you!*

The pain was made worse by the knowledge that I had given myself to the man in the "Bourbon Beauty." I didn't do it because I wanted to. I just didn't want to lose him. I thought, *Surely, if he sees how much I love him, he would want that love.*

In the end, I thought to myself, *"The guys are right—you must be a pig and a whore. Daddy was right when he said I 'wanted it.' He said he could see it in my eyes."*

I decided it was all my fault and that I deserved the pain. I would love him for several years, but I finally realized I had to survive and escape the pain of his rejection.

I began running around with some kids I thought were on a higher level of society. Somehow, we found a place in another city called "The Inn." It was a restaurant with a dance floor, catering mostly to black people.

My new-found friends and I started frequenting this place and dancing. How I could dance! I had finally found something I could do better than most people. It felt good to be number one at something!

We were all white kids, but we begged people to take us there anyway. We loved it. I guess I took it too far—I didn't realize it wasn't "right" to like people of other races. The Jesus I was raised with said everyone was special and made in His image. I thought everyone knew this.

We lived just up the hill from a black family. My brothers played with them and so did all the other kids, and they called them friends.

The only personal memories of black people I had to relate to were two little girls I went to school with who befriended me on occasion.

The other memory is of the time one of the girls from the black family down the street stopped by to show us the tiny bundle she was carrying.

I stood on the side, stretching to see, when suddenly, she turned to me and walked over to expose the most glorious roundfaced new baby girl I had ever seen. Not only did she let me see her, but she put the baby in my arms for a moment. Wow, I was in love. That memory still brings tears of joy and thanksgiving for that precious young mother, wherever she is.

I was ignorant about prejudice, but I knew anywhere I found injustice in society, I would retaliate.

I was now called "Nigger Lover" because of my new friends. I came out of a dark pit, determined to love everyone—especially the underdogs of this world. I would defend the underdogs I met in my life at all costs, even when it cost me my reputation, and that I did.

What I couldn't understand was why all the other kids got off the hook while I became the scapegoat? Why were my other white friends so ashamed of these new friends?

Naive is what I was, but then I was just a kid. In the end, the police got involved because we were under age (and probably because we were white). They closed the place down after the authorities dragged me into court to tell my age and verify that "juveniles were staying after hours."

No one bothered to ask why no black high school students were called in to testify. They didn't have to. I know the truth. I was a white female, and they were trying to spare me from "those black monsters."

After this, I had no strength left to try to climb out of the pit that I had helped dig for myself. So I didn't even try very hard.

The only good thing in my life after that were the trips to see my real dad's family, two states away from the scoffing and taunts of my tormentors.

What peace I felt in the solitude of those country mountains where no one knew me. I could be anything I wanted to be. I developed a new personality there, and I even had a different name, "Nell." This new "me" was loved, and I felt it.

The precious days I spent there with my grandparents and my aunt and uncle helped me to realize there was more to life then I had ever seen nor hoped for. Granddaddy was a mountain man who was well respected by all his neighbors, and held in high regard by all who knew him. He wasn't liked for his money, because he didn't have all that much. He was respected for his honesty.

He was a giant of a man to me. He always told me I was his favorite granddaughter, and I believed him. He could never get away from me, even when I was a little girl. He was my greatest pleasure and I adored everything about him—and still do to this day.

If he slopped the hogs I was with him. If he cleaned out a fence row, there I was. Even if he went hunting with his dog Tigger, you would see me in knee boots—desperately afraid of snakes, but determined to be anywhere Granddaddy was.

We would take long walks, he and I, and talk of places he had been and things he had seen. He had even met Frank James, Jessie's brother, once.

After walking a good distance, we would rest under a big tree in the woods and I would sit in amazement as he sat there and called the black birds to the tree.

"Caw, caw, caw!" Granddaddy would say until the tree was filled with black birds echoing his call to them. Never in my life could I get enough of this man with gnarled calloused hands and sharp blue eyes growing dim with age.

Barely able to see, he would take his magnifying glass and read the Bible every evening, no matter what. He was devoted to God and was probably one of the finest men that ever would grace planet earth.

On many occasions, he had me shave him. As I shook in the fear of cutting his endearing face, he would moan and groan as if I was indeed tearing his face apart. He loved to tease me and I loved every bit of it.

He adored me with real love and I never had to be afraid to sit on his lap or be half-undressed in front of him, or worry that he would come up to my room at night. He never was in any way improper to me. Wow, did I finally have a role model of a man! I somehow knew that he was one in a millon, and I thought I would never be able to find another like him. Grandma was a different story. She was not the soft-spoken, good natured person that Granddaddy was, but she was a jewel of a woman who knew what hard work was, and she knew how to laugh.

Several of her brothers were known as child molesters, and so was her dad. I often wondered if Grandma had been the victim of sexual molestation as a little girl. I loved her in a different way than I did Granddaddy, but I truly loved her just the same.

She caused me to be defensive where he was concerned, because she nagged at him all the time. Not that he didn't do things to get on her nerves, especially the older he got, but he was such a sweet heart.

They became my heroes, along with my aunt and uncle through my teen years. I've often wondered what would have happened if I had just stayed down there with all of them.

My dad's sister and her husband were wonderful to me. It almost seemed that they were the parents that I had always dreamed of having. I admit that I almost idolized my aunt and pretended that she was my real mother. She had dark hair and big almond-shaped emerald green eyes, and olive smooth skin—what a beauty.

Many times I watched the reactions of men in town when we went shopping on the weekends. When they spied her, some of them would straighten up their backs and put on the biggest smiles they could put on their faces in admiration of her beauty. She wouldn't even notice them doing it, and would just think they were being friendly.

I would crack-up, laughing inside at her genuine naivete. My uncle was the cutest thing that I'd ever seen in my life. He was feisty, ornery, and the biggest tease that I had ever met.

He would take brutal harassment from my aunt and I, most of the time in good humor. Remember, I said "most of the time." We were pretty mean to him, but he managed to always pay us back.

I loved this couple with all my heart and sensed that I was more like my aunt than anyone else that I had met so far on either side of the family. The people even mistook me for her, even though I had brown eyes and was not near as beautiful as she.

We fished and camped out all summer long each year for about four years. They had a hobby of collecting Indian relics, so we would go out all day with a sack lunch to hunt for arrowheads until dark. I loved it. What peace and fulfillment I felt.

We would drink all our drinking water up in just a few hours time in that blistering heat, and I can remember several times going to a spring-fed river or stream nearby and drinking right from it. I wouldn't have dared to drink from any river or stream back home, but there in the country it just seemed right.

Each time I had to go home, I would cry. I hated to get on that bus, but I always went back to what I determined was hell and resumed the old personalities of Janelle, Janny, Babe, Jan, Preea or whatever person someone wanted me to be.

I hung on to being Nell as long as I could, but the only problem was that no one knew or recognized her, so they thought I was trying to be someone that I was not. I would just slide back into whatever personality the people around me wanted me to be.

I believe "Nell" was more "me" than any other personality I was, and I liked her because she was decent, kind, fun-loving and adventurous, and she liked who she was.

Later in life, all my partying friends called me "Nellie." Somehow that comforted me and lulled me into thinking I was being loved, and that I was all of a sudden right with my life style. People seemed to like the "new me." That feeling of acceptance was a familiar feeling to the Nell inside me, so what could possibly be wrong with what I was doing?

Whenever I came home from my long summer visits, I heard gossip from cruel mouths that said I had gone away to have a black baby, and then gave it away. *Won't they ever give up?*

Finally, I quit school and started working as a car hop at a nearby restaurant. I tried to make my own way, even though I was still at home. There wasn't much discipline over me, so I pretty much went where I wanted.

When I was about seventeen, we learned Aunt Helena had what they thought was a stroke. The left side of her face was paralyzed and she desperately needed someone to care for her. Since I had quit school, I seemed like the best candidate to care for her for a few weeks.

It was a good time for me, even though it was a lot of hard work, since she couldn't do anything but cook a little. I went home on the weekends and came back on Monday.

She was always so glad to see me and I believe the time shared helped me understand why she hurt us so badly. Matter of fact, she never knew or accepted that she had abused us, so I just kept my thoughts to myself. I loved her enough to not want her to feel guilty.

In those days, she shared how she had been beaten with a bull-whip as a child, and how she had suffered from a severe lack of everything in those days.

I would sit and listen with tears running down my face as I realized that she, too, had been a victim. I was sure now that she never hurt us as badly as she had been hurt. She always vowed her love toward us children and I honestly could see that she was oblivious to what she had put us through.

During this time in my life, I was in denial because no one ever told me I could cry for me. All I was told was what a big baby I was, and how I was selfish, always thinking of myself. I didn't have many adult memories of my aunt, so as my own life started to be my focal point, it seemed like I was able to put all the anger and hurt of those painful childhood years behind me.

The past always seemed to reach up and touch every good thing that tried to come my way and either taint it or destroy it, often through my own actions.

After I came home, I awoke with a very uncomfortable feeling in my lower stomach that worsened as the day went on. I went to a doctor who, without examination, said it sounded like I had an infection or abscess, and prescribed some high-powered sulfa tablets.

After a couple of rough days, I was in the kitchen helping with dishes when I felt a release inside, and I ran for the bathroom. It must have been an abscess because it was now draining.

Several months later it started again, but this time I could not take the pain. For two days I kept my legs hiked up on pillows. The inside of my groin was swollen so badly that I could not go to the bathroom or put my legs together.

Finally, Mother took me to our doctor who attempted to examine me, but couldn't because of all the swelling. He gave me shots and medicine, and told Mom to bring me back for three more days of shots before he'd try the examination again.

Three days later, my condition had so deteriorated that Mom insisted I see another doctor. I was crying and pacing in horrible pain, so the nurses knew something was seriously wrong.

The new doctor, to my fear and dismay, told the nurse to prepare me for an examination. He gently but firmly told the nurse to hold my hand and not let me move, no matter what. I knew that "what" was going to hurt.

I remember screaming as perspiration popped out all over my body, and I prayed for death. After he finished, he and Mom took me immediately to the hospital, where they gave me shots to kill the pain. The shots worked so well that I was convinced they had remedied the problem; after all, the pain was gone.

It took me back when they told me that they were going to take me into surgery the next morning to "check me out." I began to cry and beg, as the doctor tried to convince me it was just a precaution. He said he just wanted to check me over good while I was knocked out from the pain. That sounded better, so I settled into the embarrassment of being prepped for the ordeal.

The next morning as they prepared me for the surgery, I made the doctor promise that he would not let them cut on me. With much fear, I let him convince me that surgery would be the last thing that they would do. The next thing I knew, I was awakening to the most unbelievable pain; it was worse than before the shots. I would have been grateful for sleep or death, whichever came first—it wouldn't have mattered to me, as long as I could escape this pain!

Awakening back in my room for the first time, I heard the pastor's voice say to Mom, "Will she ever be able to have babies?" Mom's words screamed through my mind as she said, "They don't think so." I opened my eyes and looked at them at the foot of my bed; then I grabbed my stomach and yelled at Mom, "You let them cut my belly!"

Later, Mom told me how they took me to surgery, and after a long time they brought me out with drainage tubes attached to bottles that were filling up with poisonous substances draining from my body.

They brought me out to take more X-rays, and then wheeled me back to surgery. Many hours later the doctor came out to my very shook mother with the news that her daughter was deformed inside. Complications from the deformation had created a football-sized abscess.

The doctor excitedly drew her a diagram of my internal organs and explained that I had two sets of female organs—one on each side, and my right kidney was deformed and throwing off poison into my system.

They removed my deformed right kidney, and one of two ovarian tubes. They also performed a hysterectomy and an

appendectomy! They thought I would never have babies because the remaining ovary and uterus were not in the right
place.

I couldn't help but think, *Why didn't they just let me die?
Haven't I suffered enough of God's rejection? Am I being
punished again by not being able to have babies?*

My life hung in the balance for four days, and then I
started to come back. There was one solace to the horror I
had just been through: I was finally able to see my family eat
their cruel words, words like, "You big baby, you're not sick,"
and, "Janny, you're a hypochondriac!"

I guess I showed them I had not been faking it...well, at
least not all of it. I had learned that it felt good to be babied,
and when you're sick, people feel sorry for you. I embraced
"self-pity" as a way of life to get attention (which I thought
was love).

Suicide had been in my heart and mind since Daddy had
died, and now I desired it more. Every time I tried to do
myself in, I would chicken out, and that made me mad. I did
enough damage to hurt me, but not enough to finish the job.

After the surgery, I don't remember much of what I did. I
drank and partied and the usual rebellious kid's stuff, but I
found I liked drinking more than most. Many times I would
not remember where I had been, and I had memory lapses of
hours, days, and experiences which I did not understand.

There just wasn't anyone to talk to then, and besides, I
don't know if I would have known what to say if someone
would have been there to listen.

I thought all my inner turmoil was normal, even the horrible sinking knowledge that I would never be a mother, and would probably not live very long. I began to think I should "live and let live." After I turned eighteen, I got a factory job in a small town about twenty-five minutes from home. For the first time, I really felt the freedom of being "my own person," and it felt good.

One night, one of the young men at work asked if he could take me home and I hesitantly said yes. I already had a eye for him, but he was such a flirt that I kept my distance.

We drove around after work, and he stopped to get his favorite liquor, Southern Comfort, which he mixed with fruit juice. I drank a little of it, but not much.

He kept driving, and I had no idea where we were going, so I began to get nervous. Finally, I asked him, "Please, just take me home like you promised." He just said, "Come on, I won't hurt you."

Shortly after that, he turned into a driveway where there was no house and pulled the car into a barn or big garage. I knew I was in trouble. He turned to me and said, "I heard you don't like to park, is that true?" I said, "Yes, that's true, so why don't you just take me home please." Then he put down his drink and began to pull at my clothes, all the while touching me in places he had no right to touch. I started panicking. I knew that I was in terrible trouble in this deserted place, and I didn't even know where I was. I did the only thing I could do, and that was to fight like a cornered animal for my rights.

Every time I tried to get up, he would throw me back down and pin my arms back behind me. He was so strong that I could not get loose. He had managed to pull my slacks and underwear down almost to my knees and he had already exposed himself. Finally I managed to free my arms and turn over on my side. In the process, I managed to open the door. It was in the dead of winter and ice was thickly crusted on the ground. I could feel it tearing at my fingers as I scratched and dug into the ground trying to pry myself free of this maniac's clutches. My hands were hurting so badly from the cold ice that I figured they were frostbitten by now.

After fighting in this position for for so long, my body was beginning to ache from all the slamming around I was getting.

Finally, I just relaxed and said, "You go ahead and do what you want, but I'm warning you that I have two of the biggest and meanest brothers in the world. They will hunt you down and get even for me."

He suddenly stopped, and with a cruel laugh said, "I believe you mean that." Mustering my coldest stare, I looked him in the eyes and said, "You'd better believe it." At that point, he hesitated and then let me go. I got myself together and he took me home. The next night at work, he was real sheepish around me, but I could tell he wanted to talk to me. After work, he asked if he could take me home and I said no. Then he said, "Look, if I promise that I will be good, and your girlfriend and her boyfriend can follow us, will you let me take you home?" I said yes, and at least we remained friends, even though I would not date him after that.

Another time, my girlfriend and I went with a couple of guys to get something to eat after work. The guys sat up in front and she and I were in the back seat. It had rained that evening before we left work, and to no fault of the boy driving, we went into a skid down the highway.

I will never forget it. As we skidded out of control toward a culvert, I screamed, "Jesus!" Suddenly, it seemed as if a giant hand came out of nowhere and scooped that little car up and slammed it into a mud embankment, and then set it right back up on its wheels.

The windshield was cracked, but other than being shaken, we were each intact. My girlfriend, Val, asked me, "What did you say?" I just stared at her, embarrassed that I had screamed out the name of Jesus.

Val persisted and so did the guys, because they just couldn't believe what had just happened. When I finally told them what I had said, that was all they wanted to talk about— not the wreck, but how "this Jesus" had intervened.

I was always put on the spot somehow about Jesus, and to the people around me, it seemed like I knew Him personally— even though I did not live for Him. I could never get away from Him, even though I tried. Oh how I would try....

During those crucial years, I felt lost in a vacuum of fantasies. I was just acting out various parts of a play, trying to escape the harsh reality of my broken dreams. I was chasing the vain hope that I could reach the "right side" of those ever-widening tracks of society.

When Rejection Is a Constant Companion...

Rejection came early in my life. Sometimes, I think rejection was the only constant companion I had. It certainly influenced my decisions about how I would live my life.

Rejection comes in many forms. Unfortunately, you and I probably know most of them firsthand. I felt it through my mother's divorce or remarriage—the children in one out of two marriages in this country suffer through those same feelings too right now.

Mom's remarriage was a giant intrusion into the security of my life. I resented this stranger who suddenly "took my mother and best friend away." I felt rejected.

It turned out that my stepfather was a very godly man who became, in time, the earthly father I had always needed and wanted. Through him, God gave me room to be a little girl again.

Poverty causes rejection too. Maybe you know the rejection and heartbreak of being a "second-class" citizen because your family couldn't afford the best clothes, cars, or house. God healed the hurt and rejection poverty brought by showing me that He was always there. He had actually felt my pain and rejection. Best of all, He cared, and He did something about it.

Chapter Four

I Enter the Occult, Marriage and Motherhood

When I was nineteen, I received a letter that I had waited for seemingly forever. My two half-sisters had somehow managed to find me, and to my great excitement, they lived only an hour and a half from us.

They wanted to get together with my brothers and me as soon as possible. I began systematically aggravating Mom to get me there. I will never forget my increasing excitement on that trip!

As we got closer to their apartment house, I thought I would explode! I could hardly contain my joy! When we finally arrived at their place, I stepped into their house with that familiar fear of being rejected again—especially after all these years.

To my surprise, I met only open arms. It was heaven! Love starved as I was, I finally felt acceptance!! We talked and talked, and yes, talked some more! Yet even in the middle of my dream come true, the enemy of my soul was hard at work.

On one of my visits there, we went over to a friend's house where we talked about things like tarot cards, candles, and Ouija boards. Some of them could sit in a circle and mentally bend up a card table.

The three of us were naturally interested in hearing from our dead father. We felt sure that wherever he was, he would be pleased that we had finally made the contact.

My sisters, along with their friend, pulled out a Ouija board and started asking it questions. To my amazement, it started moving and it even gave the correct responses.

Sure, I thought they were moving it, but another part of me believed in what they were doing, so I gave it a test. One sister urged me, "Ask it something in your mind, don't even speak it, and see if it's real or not."

Silently, in my mind, I asked if I was pregnant by my fiancee, and it said, "Yes!" Remembering what the doctors told me after my surgery, I doubted the authenticity of this prediction.

Then I asked it how far along I was, and it said, "Two and one-half months." Then I asked if he would marry me, and when. The board said, "Yes" to marriage, and gave the date of October third. My sisters were screaming with excitement over the specific answers I'd received, but they were just as disappointed that I would not share the questions with them. A week after I returned home, a doctor gave me a pregnancy test. The following week, I fearfully called his office to get the results. The rabbit had died. I was indeed with child.

The doctors of yesteryear had been wrong. Getting off the phone, I told Mother what was going on and that I was pregnant. She had no idea of my suspicions, but being the loving mother she was, her first concern was for me.

She stood there, clasped her hands together and said, "Oh, Janny, I'm so glad the doctors were wrong." I noticed that she said it with moisture in her eyes and a break in her voice.

Jimmy and I made our wedding plans quickly and set a September wedding date (I never mentioned what the Ouija board said). A couple of weeks before the date, my fiancee called to see if we could postpone the wedding for a week, due to his pay period.

Of course I agreed, not realizing that would put the wedding day on the third of October. Later, as that sunk in, I thought thanks to the Ouija. In my ignorance, I was almost sure that Daddy was indeed the one guiding me from the spirit realm, and I sure needed a father's guidance.

The day I told Jimmy about my fears about being pregnant, we were in his car. He just sat there saying, "Man, how did this happen,? I don't want a kid, I'm not ready. What can we do? I don't want to get married, I'm not ready to settle down. What about college, what about my life?"

At the time, I felt so guilty and sad for him that my hurt didn't come out. Then the longer I thought about it, the hotter I got. I let him have it and went back to my home town and to my parents. I refused to see him, and I even avoided talking on the phone to him. I didn't need any more rejection and hurt.

A few days later, I went to my doctor and found out that I was pregnant by about two months. Now what?

As soon as Jimmy found out that I really was pregnant, he came after me and tried to talk me into marrying him. I refused repeatedly because I knew he was decent and wanted to marry me out of responsibility. Somehow he convinced me (and himself) that we wanted to marry each other for love.

Then Jimmy took me to his mother's and left me with the task of telling her I was pregnant. He was too afraid to stay, and left while I shakily told this woman I hardly knew that her son and I "had" to get married.

She was a gracious lady and to my much appreciated amazement, she took the news kindly and offered any help she could give to the situation.

I'm not sure what I thought marriage should be, but moving into a small apartment with a stranger wasn't even close to any storybook romance that I had ever read.

I was lonely, insecure and horrified at the change that took place in the person I had just married. Where's all the glamorous glory of love now?

I quickly found out that his ideas and mine were very different—concerning everything from eating, to watching television, to what love was all about. He was a great guy, but we couldn't overcome the fact that he was from one side of the tracks, and I was from the other.

The next few months of marriage brought many new changes. We gave up the apartment after a couple months and moved in with his mother. This was a real issue for me, not that I didn't love her, but I was a young pregnant girl from a dysfunctional life and home who had suffered severe rejection, along with low self-worth. I felt so inadequate in every way.

Those years proved to be what I call my learning years. I was always trying to bring myself up to what I thought I should be. Now I was going to be responsible for a little baby too.

For the next few months, I enthusiastically prepared myself for motherhood. I was thrilled that the doctors were wrong. Indeed I would have babies.

My firstborn was a boy, and that little rascal came feet first into this world, almost costing his mother her life. He was five months old when I found out that I was pregnant again, and this time I was not real thrilled. In fact, I was terrified because of my near-death experience during the first delivery.

I can still remember my husband's response the day I left the doctors' office, "Why did you do such a stupid thing?" (as if I was alone in the endeavor).

Guilty again, Janelle! I hate guilt! What I lacked in the first birth, I made up through the second. He was an easier birth, and I found out that I didn't have to learn to love him or care for him, it just overflowed out of my heart to him.

At times I almost felt a different sense of guilt for my eldest, knowing what he suffered as I learned to have a mother's heart. I adored my babies. After all, they never rejected my love—in fact, they were always demanding my attention. I was loved...what a great feeling!

My husband and I were so young with totally different aspirations of life, that our marriage was always rocky and painful.

I always felt rejection on all sides from him. He may not have meant to, but he brought back all the feelings I had tried to overcome as a kid from the wrong side of the tracks who never quite measured up.

He had no way of knowing or realizing that I was trying to rebuild a future from the pieces of my devastated past. He was not guilty for creating it. All he knew was he was married to a very unstable young woman who whined and cried all the time.

On many occasions, Jimmy wouldn't even hug me or kiss me for weeks, let alone show any other signs of affection. I'm not saying he was bad, but the hurt of his rejection took me to a deeper state of despair. The thought of divorce was ever growing in my mind.

By now I had started working in a factory and the men were abundant with their attention. I had always been embarrassed by my nose, so I went to a plastic surgeon and he gave me a new one.

Did I feel prettier afterward? No—I felt worse. When the men on the job began following me with their eyes and making wolf calls, I couldn't imagine why—but I did start looking back. That was the beginning of the end for my marriage.

One day I was introduced to a young man straight out of the Viet Nam war zone whose father was dying of throat cancer. My heart went out to him and so did my desires.

I went home and told my husband I wanted a divorce, and all of a sudden he noticed me. He even stopped watching television and reading the paper. I finally had his attention.

Jimmy could not imagine why I would want anyone else when I had the best—him. Well, "him" was always in front of the television watching sports, while at the same time reading sports books or the paper, then falling asleep. In the evening, I was blessed if I got two or three entire sentences out of "him." I filed for divorce, but discovered I was two-and-a-half months pregnant, so that stopped the divorce for several months—but I still saw this "new" man of my life.

Here I was, pregnant with Jimmy's third child, and this "new" man paid me more respect and consideration than my husband.

After the birth of my last son, I remember laying in the hospital room alone, waiting for my baby's daddy to come, ever aware that I was having second thoughts on the divorce, which would be final in a few weeks.

As I waited for Jimmy to come see his third son, I lay there thinking about calling off the divorce. Jimmy didn't show up for a long time, and when he did, he didn't even want to go see his son. He said, "Why go look at him, you see one of our babies, you've seen them all. They all look alike."

He couldn't see it, but an anger rose up in me that I had never known before, and a pain for the baby just born. I vented that anger on myself out of habit. I always took the blame for every one.

Finally, he ran down the hall for a glimpse and returned a minute later with, "I told you, he looks just like the other two," and he was gone.

Well, there went any desire I had to drop the divorce.

I found out a few weeks later that I was with child again. Here I was, twenty-five years old with three babies under the age of three-and-a-half, pregnant again, divorced, with a boyfriend. Let me die, please! Of course, it would not be that easy for me.

My ex-husband and I began to struggle in conversations over who would get what. Of course he got the furniture and I got the babies and the privilege of finding a new place to live if I could not afford this place. Was I a mess?! I didn't know how to drive, I had never had a checking account, I didn't even buy groceries on my own—Jimmy had controlled all the money.

More times that I can remember, we would be in the grocery store and I would walk out on him mad. If I wanted some sort of food that he didn't like, I was never allowed to buy it.

He took food out of our basket and put it back on the shelves, or openly made fun of me for not knowing the cuts of meat. Pork chops were pork chops. I had no idea what "center cut" meant. When I asked for a roast, I was terrified when they would ask me what kind. I could only tell them, "Just a roast, you know, the kind you bake in the oven with carrots and potatoes." Horrified, Jimmy would intervene with a look of total embarrassment for the "thing" he had married.

How blessed could one young man be with a wife like he had, but I will say this for the man, he challenged me to grow beyond the side of the tracks that I had grown up on.

Somewhere inside, I determined to learn how to set a table instead of throwing all the silverware in the middle of it. Why, I even learned what a napkin was. You should have seen me the first time I saw a cloth napkin. I didn't know what to do with it—I didn't even know what it was. As usual, I watched everyone else and did what they did. Thank God that there were people who knew the right things.

I struggled to manage two toddlers and a baby when I went to a local doctor to see if I were really pregnant. To my dismay, he shook his head saying, "You look to be about four months pregnant."

He cursed as he told me that I should never have been allowed to have more than one child, since I had only one kidney. Then he strongly urged me to have an abortion.

What?! I didn't even know where to go—abortion was very illegal at that time. I later found out that several women had been "helped" by this doctor to terminate pregnancies. Oh, believe me, I thought about it, but I was in so much confusion that I just didn't have it in me to make the decision.

My ex-husband moved back into the house after the birth of our third son while we waited for the divorce to be final. After it became legal, the boys and I were to find another place to live. I was scared. A couple of months after the divorce, we talked and decided to try to patch things up for the boys' sake.

My problem was that I still had a boyfriend that I cared very deeply for, and the boys' father was still interested in doing his own thing for a while longer. What a pathetic mess we had gotten ourselves into! I was in total confusion.

The night we made the decision to reunite, I saw my boyfriend for the last time. When I told him goodbye, we both cried. He had been very good to me and was planning on marrying me, but I had made up my mind.

I just couldn't deal with the hurt I felt I was causing everyone including myself. As my friend walked away, he kept turning around and asking me if I was sure I was doing the right thing. With tears in my eyes, I assured him I was, but in my heart I did not have that assurance, only hope.

My "ex" returned home, and I told him the good news. He seemed elated as he reassured me that I had done the right thing. The next statement he made, however, hurt me so badly that I could only cry. He said, "Now, you can't expect me to stop running around with my friends out of town right away. It will take time for me to get used to married life again."

My heart sank in hurt and disappointment, but I had nowhere to go and I had committed myself. I would live with the hurt of the moment and play a waiting game with him.

One evening, Jimmy was walking through the kitchen as my sister and I sat at the table talking. As he passed through, I wrote on the Formica-topped table in pencil. The table belonged to him, and I knew it would irritate him, but I never dreamed of his reaction.

He grabbed me and started shoving me around as he screamed at me that I had better not ruin his table. As he threw me into the bathroom, I heard my sister yelling and begging him not to hurt the baby in me.

I was defenseless, and trying only to protect the baby in me. He stopped before he hit me, but the next day I started spotting blood at work. The bleeding grew worse over the next few days, but I still went to work.

Two of the girls at work told me that taking quinine could help abort a baby, so I said, "If you get me some, I will take it." The next day, one of them brought me a bottle of the pills. I took them for the next twenty-four hours, but stopped the next day. I didn't think it was helping, and I was also afraid for my own well-being as well as the baby's.

Several days later, I started hemorrhaging on the job so I called the doctor and he said, "Go home tonight, mop the floors and wash down your walls. You need to do what you can to help abort it."

Later that same day, I got so bad that I called my regular doctor in my home town. He was shocked to learn that I was pregnant and said, "Get in here, now!" My sister went with me, as I now had my driver's license, but she would return home alone. I was placed in the hospital on the spot. Bless her heart, she had no driving experience and no driver's license! She had to drive my car home on the back roads.

By then, I realized I wanted more than anything to keep my baby. I had already broken off with my boyfriend and was trying to make things work again with the children's father. I spent that night in hard labor and in the early morning hours, I aborted my four-and-a-half month old baby boy. I didn't cry at first, but I suffered from the shame and guilt for the part I played in killing my son. To make matters worse, I wasn't sure who his father was. Poor baby, I'm glad he is with his Creator, at least where he is, Someone wants him. I'm so sorry!

I went to the doctor one day because I wasn't feeling very well, and he suggested that I have a check up. The Pap smear came back with some suspicious-looking cells, so we decided it best that I have a hysterectomy.

I was heartbroken because I really loved babies. I would have loved to have had more later, or at least to have had the option.

I was only twenty-seven years old when I had my "second" hysterectomy. Because of the deformity inside me, I had two sets of female organs, and that created some interesting situations.

I laughed after the birth of my first son, David, when a nurse came in to gather information for the hospital records. When she asked me how many and what kind of surgeries I had previously had, I told her that I had had a hysterectomy at the age of seventeen.

The nurse smiled and said, "Honey, you could not have had a hysterectomy and just had a baby." I tried to explain it to her, but she would not listen. About that time, my doctor dropped in and informed her that indeed I was telling it right. I had the surgery, and after that, it seemed like many surgeries would follow, and many more hospital stays.

Jimmy and I finally seemed to get along extremely well for several months living together in the house, so we decided that we would try marriage one more time.

Right after the wedding vows, things started slipping away again, until we divorced again. This time it would be final within a year.

We Don't Have to Be Trapped by the Past!

Perhaps the most exciting scripture in the Bible for people like me is found in Second Corinthians:

Therefore, if any man be in Christ, he is a new creature; old things are passed away; behold, all things are become new.

II Corinthians 5:17

Choices made in the past trapped and tormented me every day of my life until I let Jesus take control of my life—and my past.

Early on, the devil saw the depravity and wantonness in my life and soul (he had done a good job). I had wandered away from the Lord, and he saw his opportunity to set up his kingdom in my life.

If you've wandered away from the love and protection of God, you are an accident waiting to happen. Don't fall for the enemy's innocent-looking tricks....

The enemy whet my appetite for the supernatural, preying on my inner compulsion and need for a daddy's love. He supplied me with bits and pieces of information through the Ouija board. I found it exciting to ask personal questions of an "innocent board game" that seemed to have all the answers.

When a child has been sexually abused or abused in other ways, the child's normal instincts about danger and safety are warped. Their basic need for love leads them into dangerous situations they otherwise would have avoided, had they never been abused.

Has your past driven or enticed you to seek out "love" in any form you could find it, even if it was the kind of love or thrill most people would label as "taboo?" I tried to buy love by giving myself to a man, desperately hoping I wouldn't be rejected. Later, as a married woman, I yielded to my fears of rejection and aborted an "inconvenient" baby to grant the wish of someone else. Each time I left more scared than before.

The day came when the Son of the Most High dispelled the giant darkness over me and He broke the chains of the past in my life. He wants to do the same thing for you, now.

Chapter Five

A Single White Witch With Three Sons and a Drug Addiction

After Jimmy left, I discovered that the life style of a divorcee wasn't so glamorous, especially with all the pressures of being a single parent.

The first year after the divorce, Jimmy and I maintained an on-and-off relationship that was determined by how serious we were with whoever we were dating at the time.

Jimmy and I had begun frequenting the night clubs in Fort Wayne, especially the clubs that had well-known groups and singers. We prided ourselves on knowing the right people who would regularly introduce us to these groups.

Jimmy moved to Fort Wayne and the gap widened between us as I started sinking more into the terror of knowing I was alone with the responsibility of raising three small boys. I had never been very good at handling my own life, let alone the lives of others.

Those weeks and months are a blur of despair, dominated by thoughts that perhaps history had indeed repeated itself as I found myself reliving my own childhood. But this time, I was in my mother's shoes, and believe me, I didn't have what it took to fill them.

Insanity was hovering over me day and night, compelling me to commit suicide. It was totally beyond my comprehension to grab life and do something with it.

My life was an emotional roller coaster. I was high one moment, with the next thought, word or deed taking me to the depths of despair. My emotions always overrode all logic—my own as well as that of others.

My friend, Jane, thought she could help me by taking me to a lady she knew who was a card reader. At first I was skeptical, but then she convinced me it would be okay since this lady was a "Christian". Indeed, she was a dear person and she truly tried to get out of the reading, but I was relentless with my begging, so she agreed to do it.

She said it took too much out of her and she was too old to spend that kind of energy. She also said she wasn't certain about what God thought of her doing it, and she was "too old" to want to make God mad.

She began the reading, and I sat in amazement at how thorough she was. She started first with my past, then she moved to the present (that was what I was so desperate for), and finally she read the future.

She would hesitate, and then move on with a worried look that caused fear to rise up in me. She tried to reassure me by saying she couldn't tell me what she saw because the times were not for me to know. I might try to change certain events, and they had to happen just the way she saw them.

She told me that I had a strong Indian spirit guide who would take me where I needed to go, because I was a "chosen one." She said I had great natural gifts to communicate between the spirit plane and the natural. I went back to her again, because I found this woman totally fascinating.

From that time on, I started buying books on spells, magic, candles and curses. I was convinced I had finally found the source of power I needed to get my desires in life.

I began to spend more and more time with my half-sister Celia, and a girlfriend named Marie. The three of us started calling ourselves the Three Musketeers, because where one was, you would usually find the others close by.

The other two were both married at about the same time. They had their own lives, but their husbands fished and hunted "all" the time, giving them a lot of hours to fill up, and we started doing just that.

We were always together, laying in the sun, playing canasta or throwing booze parties. Finally, they started hitting the bar scene. (I had already gotten into it with Jimmy and some friends from work). It was the only way to bury the loneliness the three of us were feeling.

My sister Celia was still very much in love with her husband, so she rarely did anything without his approval. However, she had her moments and her husband deserved every one of them.

Marie was a different story. She had long since tired of her husband's abusiveness, so she would go anywhere that she could find a way to go with me, while always remaining faithful to her husband.

She was just out for a good time and unlike myself, she had gone to school with everyone in those places. It was just like the "good old school days," always laughing and reminiscing over memories of old crushes and most embarrassing moments. At this point, I would just listen and pretend to be a part of their past.

At about this time, my sister gave me her Ouija board and the three of us began to play with it. For some, it may have been "just a game," but to us it became a way of life.

Even With the Thrill of the Moment, I Can Remember Fear...

I bought a book on card reading and decided I was indeed a natural. I could see things in cards concerning peoples lives that would even shock them. It was just all too easy.

It seemed there was always something more to learn about reading palms, holding seances, mind reading, etc. Before I knew it, I had the title of "witch" to go with my activities, and somehow that made me feel important.

Marie, Celia and I would spend evenings around my kitchen, working the Ouija board. We were amazed that we could do it so fast and well.

For fun and experience, we would often take a album cover and place our fingers lightly on top of it and watch as it slowly started moving. It would pick up speed and—without any help from us—fling itself clear across the room. Even with the thrill of the moment, I can remember fear.

One evening, after laying in the sun all day, I put on my most seductive "hot pants outfit" and the three of us headed for our new hot spot, a bar downtown. I had been stood up by a date, and their husbands were away on yet another fishing trip, so we decided that we deserved to party our blues away.

As we entered the bar, the men ogled each of us, but then one of them recognized Marie and pulled her aside to ask about me. The young man seemed to be quite taken with me, so Marie introduced him as a former friend and classmate of hers whose name was Rob.

My girlfriends and I went into the back room, ordered our drinks, and began to watch the people playing pool. Then the young man I now knew as Rob came back and asked to join us. He was very personable, handsome, and a "fun kind of guy."

I liked him, but I tried to play hard to get. (I felt he might be a playboy.) Earlier that evening, I had been stood up by another guy named Allen who I had dated a couple of times. I was more interested in that rejection and humiliation than in Rob.

As we sat there sharing drinks, it became easier to talk about the frustration of the evening. Rob suggested that we get some beer and try to track down Allen and tell him off.

We unanimously agreed, so off we went. Part of me was very hurt, but I was already enjoying the attention of Rob. We went to Allen's house and he was having a party.

I was so angry that I let him have it royally. He tried to explain that things got carried away when some old girlfriend had showed up. He said he just couldn't leave her, or give up the chance that they might work things out.

Turning on my heels and with a flip of my long, black hair, I returned to the car. I was holding onto my pride, but I was still embarrassed. Here I was, a woman with three children chasing a single man about five years her junior, who had just made a fool of herself. My friends in the car reassured me that I had done the right thing. (Then, why didn't I feel better?)

We spent that night at Marie's house getting howling drunk and acting like teenagers. When a friend of Marie and her husband, stopped by, I doused him with a container of water as he entered the kitchen. I had been hiding, standing on a chair with the water.

He thought that was hilarious, so he got even by dousing me good with a can of beer. Rob pulled me into the bathroom and promised to be a good guy and wash my hair if I would just slip out of my top. Not knowing why, I did as he asked and was pleasantly shocked as he gently bent me over the tub and washed my hair. After towel-drying my hair, he helped me get back into my jacket. I was stunned. For the first time, a guy saw me in a very vulnerable position and didn't make one suggestive remark. Maybe that was when I fell in love, I'm not sure.

As things quieted down and people went home, Marie went to bed, and Rob layed down on the floor and stared into the face of my youngest son. My littlest was about two-and-a-half years old, and he had fallen asleep on the floor after coming back from the sitters.

Rob just stroked his sleeping face and said, "Man, Janelle, you and Jimmy have the best-looking kids in town. This little guy is a doll." If I weren't in love, it was certainly not for lack of trying.

No man had ever taken time to see beauty in my sons. I always knew my sons were beautiful in their own way, yet here was a stranger softly touching my heart through my son.

Rob never touched me that night except to kiss me. Then as light broke the sky, he was gone and so was my heart!

To my surprise, he came by my house the next night. My sister, who lived upstairs in an apartment, and my girlfriend Marie were there, so we all went out back to talk to him.

We barely got out the back door when a friend of his pulled up. He was stoned out of his mind, but he sure seemed fun. He was cracking us up with his joking around, and I liked him.

In his back seat on the floor was a big baggie, stuffed with what looked like dried grass. At first, Rob made excuses for him, and especially that his friend brought the bag to him.

Finally, one of us asked Rob if the grass was marijuana, and he admitted it was. He told us we should not be afraid of it. He said it was more harmless than drinking and that we should try it. Of course we each said no, but we didn't object to them doing their thing.

For women who had earlier talked about marching in a protest against the legalization of marijuana, we were awfully quick to shut our mouths and accept that it just might be okay.

Rob never pushed us—he just kept inviting us to try it. After all, it was only making him happier—not a "druggie" like we had expected. A druggie to us was someone who stood around in oblivion, saying, "Wow, man" to things that were only seen in his head.

We never expected to see someone really enjoying themselves and not getting hurt. After a few minutes, Marie and I agreed to try it. Rob rolled another one and lit it.

Now I was a strong smoker and if desperate enough, I would smoke any brand; but nothing had ever tasted as bad as this stuff did. I choked and gagged, but kept right up with the rest of them. Absolutely nothing happened, so I thought it surely wasn't for me. I didn't even get a giggle out of it. The backyard party broke up and once again I was back to the normal side of my abnormal existence—but now I had a longing to see Rob that I could not get over.

Finally, he called to ask me out the following Friday, and I said, "Yes, yes, yes!!" He came by sometime after eight and off we went. He picked up something that looked like a deformed white cigar, put it in his mouth and lit it. Then he asked me to join him, assuring me that it was only marijuana. He reminded me that it had no ill effects on me last week, and he said he wanted to teach me how to smoke it to "get off," only to relax me of course.

I was a little nervous as we drove out to his dad's farm about four or five miles in the country, but somehow he had won my trust so I began doing as he told me.

I can't remember which "hit" did it. By the time we arrived at the farm, I was high and I never wanted the evening to end.

The farm had sand dunes on it, so he drove up to them and built a fire. We spent the evening "touching the moon" and listening to "how keen the night sounds had become." At one point, for no apparent reason, I started laughing and could not stop. It felt so good (to my tortured soul) that I insisted that we go see Marie and Terry and share this new found high.

Marie and Terry came out in the back yard with us and began smoking a freshly rolled joint. Terry was sure that there was nothing to it but what people made up. At times, I began to choke and laugh at the same time, and the three of them joined in.

Terry suddenly said, "Did you see that?" Rob said, "What, man?" and Terry said, "That pig that just ran across the yard." Well, that's all it took. We were lost in frenzied laughter—not knowing that the hook had been sunk deep in our jaws and we were being reeled into the world of darkness in a way we had never known. We waited like night creatures for night to fall so the kids could be put to bed and we could party.

At the time, I thought it was good to date Rob, because he was never out of "good stuff," and what he didn't have he could get through the guys he knew. Some of those guys were into heavy addiction and dealing, but I never said a word, because I couldn't imagine life without Rob (and especially without a high).

All of a sudden, I belonged to the tight-knit group of druggies and partiers. I felt it was better than the aloneness I felt. I would work part of a day and party as many nights as I could with Marie and my sister (who was now smoking dope with us as often as she could).

My sister, Celia, lived on a country road about nine miles out of town on a farm. This made it possible for Terry, Marie's husband, to plant some marijuana in with her garden. One afternoon after spending the day at the beach, the four of us—Terry, Marie, Celia and me—went back to Celia's house to try some of our home-grown harvest. That stuff was so bad, that I ended up on the front porch, watching a bird soar and climb up over a rainbow that seemed to arch across a cloudless sky. I thought I would stay there. It was so peaceful—but the drugs were inside. If there was one "hit" left on the joint, I wanted it to be mine.

I lived for only one thing, and that was to "party!" As long as I had my children fed and in bed safe, I felt that I was entitled to my own fun. Terry took an old television set and gutted it. Then he took a piece of frosted Plexiglas and put it where the picture tube had been. He took a flat board and drilled holes in it to hold a string of blinking Christmas lights and mounted it on the back of the empty television set.

He put his stereo on top and as the music played, we would sit for hours in a stupor and get lost in the rhythmic sounds and hues of colors dancing around the room and our minds. Druggies came from all over town to sit in front of that thing and get lost in music and laughter.

One night, we were doing some hash with a few very tight friends when I realized that my mind was suddenly "going faster then light itself" and I was being "rushed" to a different dimension and time.

Transported Through the Hash to the Cross

Somehow, I managed to get alone just in time to totally be lost in a vacuum of energy that seemed to explode before my eyes. Then I came face to face with a man or what was left of a man hanging on a cross. He looked like a skinned rabbit or squirrel—all that was left for skin was wet tissue mingled with his blood.

I was at his feet in a crouched position, with my arms curled over my head trying to protect myself from his blood that was dripping down on me.

Each time a drop hit my arms, it made a sizzling sound, like drops of water hitting hot grease in a skillet. I kept looking up at his badly beaten face, and I knew who He was and what He was saying to me, even though He didn't speak a word.

He was saying things like, "I'm doing this for you, baby. You have been made in My image, I created you for My pleasure."

While this man was calling me His child and telling me how wonderfully made I was, the world was calling me other things that can only be left to your imagination.

Suddenly, someone called me back from this scene and I spent the rest of the evening trying to put the whole incident behind me, but with little success.

One evening while I was getting high with Terry and Marie, I found myself going on a trip. The drugs took over, and I could not stop.

I saw myself running through a huge field of daffodils, and far off in the background there was a glorious snow-capped mountain. At first, I was having the time of my life running, singing, and dancing around the trees scattered about the field. Then a feeling of terror suddenly penetrated my being as I realized I had no body.

Something instinctively warned me to find my body, because this paradise was not what it seemed to be. I began trying to find a way back, but to my misfortune there seemed to be none. I began to wail and scream for help as loudly and fearfully as I could, but no one could hear me.

Finally I just started to cry when I heard Marie say "Janelle, Janelle, are you all right?" As I came to my earthly senses, I began to cry with gratitude and explain to Marie what had just happened. She had no idea where I had just tripped to, she just felt like I was in trouble. Did I stop doing drugs, of course not. It just got worse as my drug dependency worsened.

The Noose of Darkness Draws Tighter...

It was always difficult to get up and go to work, with the fact that I had to get three boys up, dress them and then rush them off to a baby sitter.

Thanks to my new love affair with drugs, I lost any real desire to work and my life lacked terribly in the area of commitment to anything except my sons—and even then I didn't like to be bothered.

The partying went on for about a year and a half. Rob lived with this girl, then that girl, but somehow, he always came back to date me for a week or two here or there. I always made myself available for him. I felt I needed him. I had some stuff (dope) stashed, but it was running low and I was missing Rob badly.

One evening when my sister and Marie were visiting, a strange thing happened. Marie brought in a small book she had bought at the grocery store. There was a beautiful cat with a golden candelabra on the cover, and it said, "Get what you want, cast a spell, try white witchcraft."

It said to get someone to come to you that you wanted to see, you should make a doll of the person's clothing or carve one out of wax.

I went into my kitchen and found a box of wax bars used for canning purposes. Of course, I had never canned so I didn't have any idea of how the wax got there. I was just grateful to have a second choice in doll-making.

The three of us proceeded to make dolls, they of their husbands, and me of Rob. They laughingly made theirs, but I made mine with much more seriousness.

As I carved, I became more and more amazed at how much this doll began to resemble Rob. So were my companions.

There were certain words I had to say while I was carving the doll. Then I had to light a candle and say some more words as I took the doll and passed it over the flame (being careful not to burn the feet for fear of burning Rob).

Then I noticed the footnote at the bottom of the page—it said "to have all power, you must use blood." No problem. I simply pricked my finger and had all the blood I needed to smear on the area of the doll that would indicate the area of Rob's heart!

No sooner had I done all this than we heard a knock at my back door. I jumped, and glanced at the clock, wondering who could be at my back door at eleven o'clock.

I went to the door cautiously, as Marie and Celia looked on. I opened the door and there Rob stood, big as life.

I was so taken back in fear that I slammed the door in his face and said, "Oh, my God!" Rob carefully opened the door as he spoke words that sent a chill clean to my bones, while at the same time they caused a delicious sense of power to overflow my being. He said, "I don't know why I'm here, I just felt compelled to come." Rob sat down at the kitchen table, and the three of us joined him in awe of the moment. We excitedly explained what had just happened, and he joined in the electricity of the moment.

As we talked, he gave me parts of his clothing and body that I really needed to complete the spell of the doll, including his blood. What a night to forget!!

That night, I left the natural to embrace the supernatural, not realizing that the door I had so easily opened would

take a long time to shut, and the journey I was about to em-
bark on would take me further than I cared to go. With my life
opening up to a new dimension, I found my thinking changing. My perception of life and death took a new and exciting
direction. I found myself thinking, perhaps ideas like reincarnation, were worth looking into. Maybe my life was the payment due for "bad karma." That would explain the "why me's"
away. Somehow, I thought I might make sense of all this sorrow after all.

The "three musketeers" seemed to become more and more
interested in the supernatural. Of course, since I was alone, I
took a much deeper interest in it all. I just had more alone
time than they did, and the spirit realm was filled with beings
to "play" with. Then why was I not having fun?

Wooed and Frightened by
Manifestations of the Dark Realm

On many occasions, an eerie coldness would settle in the
room with no explanation, while manifestations of whispers
and cold breezes would kiss our cheeks or ruffle our hair as
we would "play" the Ouija.

Most often an evil spirit would end up taking control of
the board, spelling out obscenities. During these times, it
seemed like a war would go on between spirits, and one
that made us think it was good would always come to our
rescue.

Without any help from any of us, our "spirit guide" would
begin to frantically start spelling out, "evil-boys." We would

ask it if my sons who were sleeping in their bedroom were in danger, and the planchet would repeatedly move to "yes."

We would immediately get up from the table and check on my sons in their room. Other than finding the same eerie coldness in their room, they would be intact, so we usually passed it off as a fake warning—but not without much reservation.

On several occasions, we would go into my bedroom to watch the mirror saying certain words. We used the mirror to see how many past lives we had experienced and what or who we were in them.

We sat spellbound as the mirror seemed to mist over, and either a face or demonic creature appeared where our faces had been.

Many times other people would stop by and we would let them watch the mirror with us. They usually got so shook up that they would break out in a cold sweat and say things like, "Man, this is too heavy for me. I gotta get out of here."

During this time, I began to meditate heavily while trying to learn to levitate objects and exert mind control. I read that I had to exercise my powers or I could lose them, so I would sit alone for hours, after the children were in bed, and listen to music by candlelight, commanding the power of the flame and fire to obey me.

I would go into a trance-like state as I watched the flame of an ordinary candle leap higher and higher until it would flicker at least eight to ten inches in the air. I watched, spellbound, as the flame would separate and then dance in circles back to the wick.

It seemed like I was being compelled to spend more time in my room, sitting in a yoga position on the floor with a cloth spread out before me.

On the cloth I would have my candle and book of spells, along with more wax, a knife, and any personal belongings of the person I could get my hands on. Sometimes, there were even precious drops of blood.

If people did not supply me with their blood, that was no problem. I seemed to have plenty of my own to use, after all, I must have "all power." Some of the spells required that I drink blood to strengthen my power. Not having the stomach for it, I did the next best thing. I would cut or prick myself and suck the blood into my mouth on those occasions. This seemed to appease the spirit that started making an appearance.

On many nights, my cat would look on while I danced nude by candlelight before a host of beings that I would tantalize and mock, knowing how desperately they wanted my flesh and to be flesh.

Those were times that still bring horror to me, especially the remembrance of the dance that would suddenly take on a voodoo frenzy and end with the master of the spirits overpowering me for his pleasure.

I shall not linger here any longer, since my mortal mind dare not remember the details of the sickness between man and spirit.

God can you forgive me? In the distance of my lost state, I heard a voice, perhaps of the man named Russell, who is calling all of these evil memories up and out, saying, "Yes, Janelle, God can forgive even this." With hope, I gather new strength and carry on.

The Craving of the Love-Starved Often Leads to Addictions of the Flesh and Spirit

Whenever I attempted anything, I went at it full force. With my background of hurt, confusion and brokenness, I was a natural candidate for drugs and the occult. Combined with my "all or nothing" approach, I was on a headlong road to destruction.

Are you hooked on drugs or the illegal "power" of occult practices? The drug world supplied me with friends and the acceptance I had so craved as a child.

The occult offered me what I thought was some control over my destiny—I felt I had been at the mercy of others long enough. I wanted to be cherished and to be special so badly that I was willing to sell my soul for it.

You may be nodding your head right now as you read these words, because you can feel and share the hurt behind my words.

I'm writing this book so that you can find out what I discovered: even in my growing love affair with drugs and the dark world of the occult, Jesus was beckoning to me.

When my conscience would scream out, "I'm no good!!" He was there, softly whispering above my self-loathing, "Janelle, you're special to me, just as you are. I love you, Janelle, and you don't have to sell your soul for it. I want your heart just as it is—broken and bruised."

No matter how deep you've gone into the dark and magical arts, no matter how dependent you are on drugs, alcohol or other people, Jesus is telling you the same thing He told me: "You've been lied to, but I'm here to give you truth."

Chapter Six

If the Devil Ever Comes A'Callin'...

The man they call Mr. Russell and the other people are still listening, and I've never had anyone listen this long before, I think silently to myself. *They must think me mad and that's okay, I've wondered about that for years too...but now I'm beginning to understand. Thank you Jesus, yes, I'll go on....*

Mother was a fine woman of God, and she continued to pray for me. During our visits, I told her how I had worked the Ouija board and talked to my dad's spirit, and how I had made a doll of someone and saw how the spells worked.

Mother told me she was concerned about what I was doing, but I was too excited about my new-found power to pay attention to her, so I dismissed her fretting as an over-religious caution.

Then she said something that managed to stick, even though I was convinced I was right and she was superstitious. She told me, "Honey, if the devil ever comes a'callin in person, then grab a Bible and say—I plead the blood of Jesus, or, in the name of Jesus." Then she assured me that "at the name of Jesus he must flee."

On spiritual matters, I listened to Mother, even if I didn't obey. I knew she was right-on in her belief. The days ahead proved Mother's fears to be well-founded, but I was too lost in my new pursuit of power to change my course.

More and more, I locked myself away in my room with candles, books, and dolls—meditating and talking to my "spirit guide" or other spirits that I would visibly see.

It seemed pretty good, except the "evil spirits" dogged me at night. I could not understand why, since I had put hexagrams in all my windows to ward them off. That was the most "powerful" protection I knew about then, but I also tried other methods of protection people had told me about. (One used salt, and another used papers with certain words on them placed in strategic spots throughout my house.)

The nights became longer and harder to sleep through as each night would bring some new spirit-being and more fear. In the beginning, I would clutch a Bible to my chest as I sat up in the bed with the light on.

As I held the Bible, I would do as Mother had suggested. But then, as night after night of torment went by, it became evident to me that Mother's "God" was not greater than the devil, and now I had nowhere to turn. (I didn't realize I was in the same situation as the "seven sons of Sceva" in Acts 19:14. The demons recognized God, and my mother, but they didn't recognize any of God in me!)

The spirits often came in droves to run up over my bed as I sat unable to move. They growled and hissed words that were not human. Their appearance varied, with some having snouts and others having dog-like noses, but they all had the sharp, jagged teeth and fangs. They all seemed to have tails, and some had distorted paw-like feet and hands, while others walked on cloven hooves. All of them ran swiftly on two legs, they had hairy bodies much like monkeys and as much agility.

I still remember the feeling of dropping off into exhausted sleep only to have the presence of a demon pin me to the bed and try to suck the life out of me.

Unable to move, I would hear a scream rise up on the inside of me as I fought desperately to breathe and shake this "thing" off of me. All the while, inside me I was saying "Jesus!"

I woke up night after night, shaking and soaked in a cold sweat—only to drop off to sleep and have it start all over again. I found myself living in continuous terror with no way to get out.

Finally, a doctor prescribed some powerful sleeping pills for me that made me literally pass out. They made me slur my words within five minutes, and within fifteen minutes, I was out like a light. Night after night, in the midst of a demonic attack or just before I went under in a pill-induced sleep, my heart would silently groan, *My precious children, where are you in all this mess? Oh, there you are, asleep. Please, Jesus, protect my babies.*

Death Seemed Like My Final and Only Solution

The hopeless cycle continued to the point where there seemed to be nothing left for me but suicide. I reasoned that the children's father would take them and life would be much better for them then.

No one would really miss me, and somehow I found solace in thinking that some people would hurt, and I could get even with them by killing myself. They would then have to live with the guilt for the rest of their lives.

Time and again, I tried to do myself in. I tried it with razors, but I couldn't stand pain, so no real damage was done. I also tried drug overdoses. One time I took half a bottle of sleeping pills, thinking it would do the job, but then I became fearful and called Marie. She came and took the pills away from me.

Before she left, she made me drink coffee and told me off, then she left me alone to cry myself to sleep. The next morning, I stopped by her house and sheepishly picked up the bottle containing the rest of my pills and headed to my mom's with my children.

I tried to finish the job at Mom's by taking the rest of the pills. I got scared of dying again and told Mother. She called the doctor terrified, but he just got mad at me and told

Mother the pills weren't strong enough to kill me, but I would probably get mighty sick. Mother asked what she should do if I got sick and he said, "Let her, it will be a good lesson." I lived.

Several times I remember locking up the house, only to return home to find every door opened wide and with that familiar cold, eerie breeze creeping through the house. Of course, no one was there, at least no one you could see with mortal eyes.

What am I saying? You may think I'm crazy—I even have a hard time believing in the sanity of my mind. How can I trust you to believe me?

The powers I had tapped into made it possible to turn on lights without touching a switch and to open closed doors without moving.

I could command my phone to ring and know who was calling. I would often say hello using the caller's name—before they told me who they were. This usually scared them, but they always laughed. Marie and I could call each other and the phone wouldn't even have to ring before the other picked up the phone.

We had a special bond between us that seemed to allow us to communicate without words. Some people called us psychics because we would often begin a conversation and end it without really finishing one sentence, in front of other people. We called it "mind talk," and we wouldn't even notice we were doing it. We could easily bother people, and that in itself thrilled us.

There was a book on witchcraft that told me how to be initiated by various rituals, none of which seemed to fit my stomach. To become what I desired—a blood covenant witch" there had to be a ritual of blood, preferably of a white rooster. I also needed someone "higher" than me to make me an initiate, only I didn't know anybody who qualified.

Still convinced that I was only into white witchcraft, I decided it wasn't so important to have animal sacrifice. Besides that, I was fairly ignorant of what I had gotten myself into and was never willing to kill anything.

Black witchcraft, satanism, and voodoo...these words frightened me, so I "played like" I was innocently stepping over barriers that "white witches" call off limits.

With candles, words and my own blood, I did a ritual out of a book, while a hoard of grotesque beings looked on. I added my own words and chants and proclaimed myself a blood covenant witch. I was proud of what I had accomplished, but I didn't fully comprehend the gravity of my folly.

I was getting what I wanted—or was I? In the safety of daylight, I laughed at what I thought were my powers, but at night I was fully aware that the power was beginning to overpower me. My will was getting lost somewhere in between heaven and hell.

I knew deep within that I must find a Savior, so I kept seeking by candle, Ouija, and cards for that person.

Starting Over With Ed "the Rat"

One evening, I went to a bar hoping Rob would be there. He wasn't, so I went over to Marie's and got blown away. By now I had tired of waiting for Rob, yet I knew I loved him so much that it was destroying me. The pain of loving him and not having him was more than I could bear alone.

While I was at Marie's, the phone rang and it was my oldest brother. He was downtown at a local bar with a bunch of people and asked me to come down. As I drove to the bar, I knew that I was in no condition to be driving my new car, a Nova three-speed, and I was terrified that I could not keep my thoughts together long enough to park it.

Somehow I managed to park the car and collect myself enough to enter the sleazy little bar to meet my brother. As usual, he was drunk, along with his wife and many friends. He made introductions. Then I sat down with a friend beside my brother's booth trying to figure out just why I had come down here.

Music was playing loudly as people danced. A young man suddenly approached my table and asked me to dance. I took one look at him and sized him up, and quickly said, "Get lost."

He had shoulder-length bushy hair, a scraggly beard and a cast on his ankle. All this was bad enough, but he even had an earring dangling from his one ear.

As he turned to walk away, he told my brother how much he liked me and asked him to put in a good word for him. To my shock, the people sitting with my brother were this guy's brothers, sisters and their spouses. So when my brother pleaded with me to dance with this guy named Ed, I agreed.

As he took my hand and pulled me to the dance floor, I noticed that he had beautiful green eyes and a gorgeous smile. I saw him as just a kid gone "wild" that had no desire to be anything but obnoxious—which he was.

To my horror, he sang loudly to me as he danced and I couldn't wait to finish and sneak back to my table. He left me alone for awhile and I decided to go, but I was in worse shape than when I got there, and my brother knew it. So like a good brother, he asked Ed if he would see me home. Of course, Ed jumped at the chance. I will never forget the embarrassment I felt as we left. I was hoping that no one saw him get into my car.

After taking me home, he just walked on to his house, which was only about two blocks away. The next day, Ed came to see me and to meet my kids. He also brought me some flowers in a glass. He never stayed, but I was quite taken by someone giving me a gift for no reason. The boys instantly liked him and he liked them. Still, I wasn't going to get tangled up with a younger man who acted like a hoodlum and was nicknamed "Rat." He started calling me and coming over to visit until finally he just stayed. The boys had a friend and he was great about babysitting them, since he couldn't work until the ankle healed.

It felt good to not have to be afraid to go to sleep at night. Ed had been raised Catholic and was totally against my involvement with witchcraft. He did not appreciate me calling myself a witch. He made me put all my dolls away, so I carefully wrapped each one in special cloth so as not to damage them, and put them away. I still worked my Ouija, read cards, levitated, and held seances though. One night, not long after Ed and I met, Rob called out of the blue. "Hello," he said. "I'm in town and I would like to see you, can I come over? I'm only about a block away at a phone booth."

I panicked at first because I was still in love with him, but Ed was with me and I was now very much involved with him. Disgustedly, Ed said, "Is that Rob?" as I motioned for him to be still.

All of a sudden it was quiet on the other end of the phone. Then Rob said, "Is Ed with you?" I couldn't speak. Then Rob said, "Goodbye" and loudly hung up the phone.

In just a few seconds, I heard the squeal of tires and looked out my window in time to see Rob's Corvette fish-tailing as he went around the corner and out of my life forever. (Why was I so sad about that when he could have had me?) I turned to Ed and pretended to have no emotions about the incident.

My family and friends began to realize that Ed and I were a twosome. He was almost seven years younger than me, and so wild that my friends couldn't stand him. They were relentless with their questions about why and how I could be interested in the likes of him.

They just didn't know how alone I was, nor how tormented I had become. After all, they had husbands to curl up to at night, and they never had to punch a time card or pay a bill.

Ed wasn't afraid of anything and would fight at the drop of a hat. Even though that embarrassed me, at the same time it comforted me because I didn't think anything could get past him to hurt me—whether it was spirit or flesh. Somehow I managed to lull myself into a false sense of security.

Ed kept drinking heavily after he moved in with us, but he seemed fun-loving enough, and at my insistence, he cut his hair, trimmed his beard and got a job. Those were my requirements for marriage, so we agreed to a wedding date a few months away.

I should have known that something was wrong during those months—there were enough signs. One time, Ed went out drinking with his friends, and Marie came and took me out to look for him. Finally, we came back to my house and found Ed drunk, eating at the table.

I stood across the room trying to fight back the tears, and I asked him if he loved me. He just cussed at me, so I asked him again. He turned around and started laughing at me. Then he threw a full glass of milk on me.

As I fought the humiliation of his personal insult to me in Marie's presence, I reassured Ed that I loved him no matter what he did. He turned to me again and said, "You mean you would love me if I threw another glass of milk on you?"

When I said, "Yes, you know I would." He said, "Good!" and threw the second glass of milk on me. Marie didn't want to leave me, but I assured her I'd be okay, so she went on.

A few days later, he got drunk with an old girlfriend and came home angry because she would not come back to him. He ended up throwing a can of beer against my cabinets and walls, scratching the wood. One time he really scared me when he threw a big iron skillet containing hot grease at me. Fortunately for me, I moved and it hit the wall. Such were the joys of love. Why I didn't leave him? I don't know, except I was so insecure that I thought anything was better than nothing. When Ed was good, he was very, very good, and when he was bad, he was BAD!

We began preparing for our wedding and bought new furnishings for our house and really got to know one another. Things began to calm down a bit between us as we started the process of committing our lives to each other, and as we got to know one another's family.

Just before Ed and I married, a couple of guys moved to town named James and Bill. They claimed to be in witchcraft and that they had been sent to groom me for greater things.

Bill, I could stand, but James was horrible. He reeked with evil. We ran into them occasionally and James always ended up talking to me about my natural gifts in witchcraft and how I should seek further guidance.

I told him at that point that I was trying to get out of practicing. When he heard me say this, his eyes lost any human quality and his voice changed as he warned me of the danger to my children if I didn't go on with the craft. Somehow, I always took his words as a threat.

The Night Death "Knocked at Our Door"

Finally, the wedding day came and we were married in a beautiful lawn setting in his parents' yard. (We could not yet be married in the Catholic Church because I had been divorced and the papers had not yet come in from the Vatican to annul my first marriage.)

Only a week after we returned home from our honeymoon, our family survived a horrifying experience. We took the three boys to the drive-in and got home late, so I hurriedly put the boys to bed.

Ed got ready to take a shower, as my youngest son (who was four years old) started screaming to sleep with me. I didn't know what to do, since the little guy had never done anything like that before, and he had never slept with me.

Ed told me to get him back to his own bed as he took his shower, but instead, I let him lay at the foot of the bed, thinking I would put him in his bed as soon as he went to sleep.

Ed finished and came into the bedroom, and he was angry because my son was laying at the foot of our bed. At first, Ed protested, but as he saw the fear in the little guy, he conceded and let him stay.

I headed in to check one last time on my two other sons and they were asleep, so I gently kissed my middle son on the forehead, and then turned to my eldest who was snuggled up asleep in an old heavy army sleeping bag, laying on top of his bedspread. He looked so cute that I softly chuckled as I smoothed his tousled hair.

Before I left the room, I looked around thinking how nice it was that the boys had such a nice, single big bedroom. It was big enough to comfortably hold three twin beds, two antique dressers and a six-foot long toy box. It also had four wide and long windows in it that made it a cheerful room during the day.

The house had four stories counting the big basement and full attic, but we only lived in the first floor, and rented the apartment upstairs. After admiring my sleeping sons and their bedroom, I returned to bed.

Ed and I had just turned in when I remembered I needed to check the alarm. I got up to turn the light on when I saw light shining into our bedroom window. My first thought was that someone was peeking into our window. We lived on a hill where the street curved, and there was no way that a car could be that close.

That was the last sane thought I had that night. In the next moment, I heard a roaring noise in my sons' bedroom followed by the sound of rafters being ripped apart and glass breaking everywhere.

The dresser came off the wall in my bedroom, and then it slammed back, smashing everything to the floor. Mirrors and pictures were falling off the walls, and windows as far away as the back porch were breaking and cracking.

Everything seemed to happen in slow motion, then I heard the most horrifying sound of all—silence—total silence.

Where were the cries of my sons?! I thought, *Oh, God, no, I can't live without them!!!* In agony, my mind raced back to James' threats.

He had all but warned me that he and his masters would kill my kids if I tried to get out of witchcraft. Demon spirits had been tormenting me night after night, and I had been checking on my sons as many as two or three times a night. And I hadn't forgotten the warnings of the Ouija.

My oldest son often came out to the kitchen where we were holding a seance or working the Ouija—crying his heart out incoherently, as if sleep-walking with his eyes open. He would beg me, "Please, Mommy, don't...don't do that!"

I was afraid he had had a nightmare about the many beatings I had given him, so I always tried to calm him down before he revealed to my friends what an abusive mother I was behind closed doors.

Now I wondered, *Did he have other reasons to fear, were demons trying to kill them?* As I jumped out of bed that night, all these thoughts and more screamed through my head and drove me to my knees. Horrid screams came out of my mouth that I had no control over. Suddenly, my little boy was at my side screaming as loudly as me, and I reached out somehow and embraced him.

Ed threw on some jeans and rushed out of the room to find my sons, yelling over his shoulder for me to "stay put." He didn't know that I couldn't have left the room if I wanted to. I didn't dare see my sons' dead bodies because I was so near insanity that I would surely never come back.

The next scene I saw was Ed and my second son at our bedroom door. My son was unhurt, only in shock. Running down Ed's bare chest was blood—a lot of it—and there was no sign of my oldest son.

There was yet another scream as Ed picked me up and threw me in the bed and told me to stay there. Suddenly, a young man with blond hair came into the bedroom crying, begging me to forgive him. I found myself out of bed again and back on my knees, begging the God that I hated for mercy for my son, pleading for his life.

Ed told me later that when he first entered the boys' bedroom, my middle son was standing in a pile of debris in the middle of the room, in total shock.

Ed went to my eldest son's bed and threw off an antique record cabinet that was on top of him. He had been flipped completely over in the sleeping bag. His feet were now sticking out where his head had been.

When Ed started pulling his little lifeless body out of the bag, he suddenly realized his hands were filled with something hot and sticky, so he pulled them out. They were covered with blood. Without thinking, he wiped them on his chest and brought me my other son. He then went back to carry off my son's body so I couldn't see him if I managed to wander in.

He had just pulled him free from the sleeping bag and was trying to carry him out of sight from the growing crowd of concerned neighbors when the police arrived.

As the police tried to check my son, one of his toes moved and they thought there was life, but couldn't find any vital signs. Finally his little leg moved and Ed stood him up without thinking, and asked him if he was all right. My son just stood there looking at him, wiping blood out of his eyes asking, "What's going on?"

The next thing I saw, after what seemed like two eternities of pain and fear, was my precious son standing at the bedroom door, bloody but whole. My other two sons who were huddled together ran to him and led him into the bathroom to wash off the blood.

Somewhere in all the hysteria, I picked up the phone and called the children's grandmother and my brother.

The police took my son and me to the hospital in a squad car and the children's grandmother took the other two boys home with her. At the emergency room, we learned that my son only had a small cut on his head that didn't even require stitches.

After returning to the house, we were told that a car had become airborne on the street near us. It "flew" through the air about a half a block to our house, and crashed right through the boys' bedroom—only three inches above where they lay! Then it continued its flight through the side of the front room.

The car belonged to two young men who were out partying and missed the curve. I knew better. Those young men were at the wrong place at the right time, and a power greater than they knew used them as pawns for their purpose.

The car's impact knocked the house off the foundation a full six inches. The boys' bedroom looked like a war zone, with nothing left standing but one bed normally occupied by my youngest son. He would have been crushed if he hadn't been in my room. A piece of wall measuring nearly two foot thick and almost as big as the mattress was laying on top of his bed. My heart sinks at the thought of what could have happened had my youngest son not cried to sleep with us, or had we refused to let him stay in our bed.

The bed used by my second son, Vinnie, was broken down with debris all over it. Glass and pieces of wood were sticking out everywhere in his bed and mattress. How he came through without a scratch is a miracle. The explosion knocked him out of bed and onto his feet as the car passed three inches over his head. As I remember it, unbelievable gratitude floods my soul.

My eldest son's bed was a shambles, totally buried in debris and large pieces of glass and lengths of rafter. The beat-up and bloody sleeping bag had saved his life. Trembling, I followed the police as they showed me the ugly black tire skids directly above his bed where the car had passed through.

There had to be divine intervention. A big antique dresser with a round mirror above it originally stood between the bed and the wall. All we ever found of that dresser was a front panel from a drawer. The rest of it was splintered and scattered all over the room. The boys' clothing was ruined and strewn everywhere along with all their toys. With the light of day, the reality of what had happened hit me as we turned the corner and I saw a car-sized gaping hole where the front wall of my sons' bedroom had stood the day before.

The car took the entire front wall and three huge windows out as it passed through the side portion of the front room wall. It even ripped out the front door and frame. The curtains were shredded with glass and debris, and so was my "new" front room furniture. I could only wander through the devastation of the rooms, gasping and weeping and full of gratitude for my Mother who never stopped praying.

As I rummaged through the broken picture frames, toys, and clothing, I was constantly reminded of how three precious boys could be dead, and thousands of shudders shook me to the foundation of my soul. After that, the continued memory nearly always caused my heart to faint.

We stayed with Ed's mother for the next few days. Then Ed and I moved back into the house temporarily to protect our furnishings from theft. My sons stayed with their dad and grandmother.

I certainly didn't need the separation and I'm sure they didn't either, but I was unable to make decisions on my own. I just obeyed others desires.

Are You Trapped or Tormented?

My descent into the occult and the destruction of drug addiction unleashed a terrible havoc in my life. Had I known that my first "high" would lead me to become an addict, or that my simple "fun and games" with the Ouija board would lead to such evil torment or life as a witch, I would have never done them.

When the world offers us its "pleasures," it never gives us the whole picture. Satan will never show you the end of the road—he knows if he did, most of us would run for our lives. He hooks us through deception, and he keeps us through fear.

There was hope for me—even in my darkest hour, and there is hope for you today, no matter how deep or hopeless your personal pit of despair may appear!

The occult seemed to have all the "answers," so I walked through its door. In the end I was a puppet on a string. Sure, the devil was careful to make me think I was "a natural," but I was just another pawn for his devilish use. I allowed myself to dance with the devil and he was not too eager to let go.

In the middle of the devil's onslaught to possess my soul, I desperately needed my mother's prayers. She was faithful to pray for me and plead for my life before God. Better still, I later learned that my savior Himself, Jesus Christ, continually plead my case before His heavenly Father. Even in the middle of my cries and torment, the answer was on its way.

I believe God has people who even pray for those of us who don't have "praying mothers." They may not know our name, but the Holy Spirit helps them pray for us with deep groanings and petitions that are powerful and unstoppable.

Turn to Jesus now, don't wait another moment! There is no escape from the enemy's web except through the all-powerful love of Jesus Christ and the heavenly Father. I promise you, as a terrible sinner, a "loser" and former witch and drug addict, nothing is impossible for God! He forgave and saved me. He is waiting to instantly set you free too!

Chapter Seven

Living Under the Fear of Demonic Torment and Attack

After we moved back into the rear two rooms of our house, our friends started coming by to view the damage. By then, we had pretty much cleaned out the bedroom and put all the salvageable stuff into the front room, which now served as our storage room. We didn't have any electrical power in the front of the house anyway.

Our friends practically ran out of the house saying they felt "something evil" in it. A couple of friends brought two dressers to us and left faster than they came. They said,

"Janelle, we can't stand the horrible smell and evil presence here."

My cat even shied away from the two front rooms, especially my son's bedroom. She growled and hissed as if something unseen was about to get her. With hair bristled, she would slink back out of the room.

The following weekend, Ed went to the store and didn't return. I was terrified of losing him too, so I called Marie and she took me out to find him. We never did.

Late that night, Ed came home drunk, talking about the old girlfriend that he could never stop loving, and how she was in town and they had been together.

Stunned, I stood there so hurt that I could scream. Instead, I looked at him and calmly said, "That's okay, this weekend I will go find Rob." I turned to walk away, but Ed grabbed my arm and shook me as he screamed, "You —, I will make you sorry you ever said that!"

He started beating me and throwing me all over the front room in the darkness. I was thrown against one piece of furniture after another. Time and again, I picked myself up, only to be slammed down to the floor.

At one point, he picked up an endtable and hit me with it, knocking me to the floor. Then he straddled my body and began to choke me and slap my face and head. Over and over, he yelled, "Say you're sorry!" In total fear and brokenheartedness, I said what he wanted to hear. Then the tears started to flow and he let go of me and helped me up.

Ed kept asking me why I made him hurt me all the time, while helping me up. Painfully and very slowly, I made my way to bed, barely able to stand the touch of my nightgown against my bruised skin. I crawled into bed beside him and curled up in a ball of pain. To my total despair, I felt his body wrapping around me and I knew what he wanted. Kissing the nape of my neck, he reassured me he still loved me and said he thought we should make love before going to sleep.

A scream of silent terror went through my mind, but I forced my voice to remain calm and finally talked him into going to sleep. He passed out quickly, but I lay weeping as I wondered what I had gotten myself into this time. *What evil have I done to deserve a life that mocks me so cruelly?*

The next day, I could barely move for the stiffness in my body. I finally managed to get up and look in the mirror. I could see that my body was covered with large black and blue bruises from head to foot. There were yellow stripes mixed with bruises up and down my sides, and my face was swollen almost twice its size. And I actually felt worse than I looked!

When I went to work the following Monday, I was forced to put makeup on most of my body so the people at work would not ask questions. Some of the marks I could not hide and they knew something was wrong by the way I could hardly move. I just said I'd forgotten about having our television at the end of our bed and had fallen over it on the way to the bathroom in the dark. After that night, Ed seemed to settle down some, not that he ever stopped drinking, but he pretty much took me along wherever he would go from then on.

When all the investigations by the police and insurance adjusters were in, the only question still unanswered was how the car got to our house. To reach us, it first had to hit a huge maple tree, or at least pass through its branches; or go through a telephone pole or its guidewires enroute to our house, but it had done neither.

After determining the damage, the insurance company and contractors agreed that the house would have to be destroyed, since it had been knocked off its foundation six inches. We would be leaving this house of horror for the final time.

We Move "Out of the Frying Pan Into the Fire"

A few weeks after the decision was made to level the house, we found a nice looking two-story home to move into. We were desperate to get the children back to some normalcy, as well as ourselves.

While we felt this would be the start of something new and positive, I couldn't figure out why I hated the new house. Something just wasn't right to me. I liked what I saw—it was what I felt that bothered me. I sensed a familiar eeriness, a peculiar coldness there. I felt like a trespasser in this place, as if the house belonged to someone else—and that someone or something wanted me "out!"

While we were there, the noises began and mysterious voices talked in the night. Then we started having nightmares that always were accompanied by night sweats. There always seemed to be someone watching or following me.

The boys didn't like the house either and I had trouble getting them to sleep. My half-sister, fifteen years my junior, often came over with my niece to baby-sit. They were always terrified by the time Ed and I returned.

My sister used to wake me up, scared half out of her wits, to tell me she saw a man walking down the hallway. Once, she even felt him kiss her. The only witchcraft I practiced in this house was card reading and a few seances; I had gotten rid of everything else.

The drugs and demonic manifestations began to merge together in my life. On one occasion, Ed brought me a dime bag of marijuana from work and I quickly rolled a joint for myself. (I was still an addict.) Ed didn't like pot much, he preferred to drink and take pills. On this particular night, I talked him into taking a couple of hits. The stuff turned out to be some heavy-duty pot.

I was "blown away" after taking three hits of it. Ed hit it a second time and got scared. The only thing I knew to do was to get him into bed, so we made our way upstairs and down the long corridor to the back bedroom. Ed was almost crying and I was laughing hysterically at him.

When we finally crawled into bed, Ed became even weirder. As he laid there, his heart would literally raise up, like a fist on top of his chest with only skin covering it, and it beat wildly. Then his eyes turned from green to yellow and he began to talk in a garbled language.

Ed's heart would settle down for a moment, and his eyes would turn back to green long enough for him to look at me and begin to desperately cry and beg me to help him.

It was impossible for me to keep a normal thought together for myself, let alone make a decision for him. He just kept switching back and forth as I kept laughing—yet I knew I had to get Ed help.

Finally, I picked up the phone and called Marie. I knew she and Terry were now into some "bad" stuff and she could tell me what to do.

When she answered the phone, I tried to be coherent but nothing made sense, so I just told her I was going to take Ed to the emergency room. Marie began to plead in a demanding kind of way for me not to do it.

"Nellie, the police will get involved. Don't, please promise me you won't! Promise me, now!" she begged me. Bewildered, I promised her I wouldn't go to the hospital. She then told me to get into bed and just hold him until he calmed down, so I did.

Ed's body felt like a water balloon to me, but somehow I survived his changing between personalities, or whatever he was doing. After that night, Ed refused to do pot again.

I tried one more time to smoke some of the bag, but it was too much for even me. I had no idea what it had been laced with, but I had never smoked anything like it. Ed sold the bag to his friend, Frank, who was a total addict. A few days after the sale, Frank complained to Ed that the dope wasn't any good and he didn't even get a buzz.

Ed and I looked at each other and laughed, and said, "No way." After a couple of days, Frank walked right by Ed at a party, and when Ed spoke to him, Frank just kept walking on as if in a trance. Concerned, Ed caught up with him and asked him what was happening.

Frank almost cried when he finally recognized Ed. He said he had gotten back in the bag and had somehow lost his vehicle several hours earlier, or so he thought. Sure enough, he had been downtown and had forgotten where he had parked his car. He didn't even know where he even was. Frank and Ed finally found the car abandoned in front of the courthouse.

More and more, Ed and I ended up in the bars on weekends. We were on two separate party levels. He was drinking and I was hooked on both alcohol and drugs. We started running into James and Bill more often too.

Bill began teaching me new tricks and knowledge in witchcraft, but I still couldn't stomach James. He was arrogant, and cruel with a capital "C." He always talked about how he had no soul or heart. To him, love was an emotion for human "weakies." He claimed to have conquered his human frailties.

James told us he lived solely on instinct, just like the animal he was. He could talk about his bestiality with his German shepherd dog as easily as he talked about being a satanic high priest and warlock, or his taking of life and drinking blood. He was disgusted with my own humanity as well as that of everyone around him, yet everyone went to his parties and drank with him.

Bill was nicer and more subdued than James, yet you could tell he was as turned on to witchcraft and as proud to be a warlock as James was. Where James could never reach me, Bill could. Even though Bill was James' homosexual lover, I still found myself drawn to him. Not by looks, because Bill certainly was not good looking, nor was he manly.

In fact, he was totally controlled by James—even when he didn't want to be.

I'll never forget the evening James joined Ed and I at our table in a bar. James sat down across from us and Bill took a seat at the bar. As we sat there, James did everything in his power to get me on his side (or at least get me under his control), but I would not budge.

He mocked God and Jesus to argue with me concerning my "holding back" on satan. After all, he said, "Did God keep your home from getting destroyed by that car?" I remember watching him as he sat there with demonic glee dancing in those blackened eyes.

Finally, when he realized his words could not hurt me, he sneered and leaned across the table and said, "You would make a greater witch than you can imagine with that feistiness. I find you sexy and hot. I would give anything for you to have sex with me. You have such an animal spirit."

Angry and horrified, I said, "You mean you want to have sex with me, knowing I'm married to your friend, Ed?" I looked at Ed and said, "Ed, do something!"

James leaned even further over the table and looked at me with those piercing eyes, and said, "I would love to have sex with you." Then he turned to Ed and got about three inches from his face and said, "But I'd rather have sex with your husband."

I was horrified. I sat there for what seemed like an eternity thinking he was actually going to kiss Ed, and Ed wasn't even trying to stop him! You could have cut the silence with a knife. Finally James quickly sat back in the seat and said with glee, "Of course, we could make it a threesome."

James knew, and I knew, that he had just slapped me in the face with the fact that he had Ed totally under his control—I had just lost an invisible battle.

From then on, I felt a tremendous jealousy toward James, almost as if he were the "other woman." After that, Ed always made a way to be near James, and Bill would occupy my time consoling me and instructing me in things I wanted to know about witchcraft.

James didn't totally give up on me being something of a protege. He was always telling me how he had been sent to groom me, and how proud he would be to take me back to New York and present me to the large coven of witches there.

He watched me at a distance as Bill taught me mind control, astral projection, and the fine art of speaking in ancient languages so that my rituals would be more powerful.

There was never any fear with Bill, because he was always with me in my learning. He would astral project with me, he allowed me to read his mind, and he spoke back with me ever so gently with the new words.

Bill was a good teacher, but I always knew who the real master was, James. He could make Bill a whimpering "basket case" with one glance or word. They convinced me that I had been truly called to be a priestess, so naturally they could prey on my longing for power and special status. I was a prime target for all their flattery.

One night, when Ed's cousin threw a big party at his house, Bill said it would be fun to march around the house and make it into a shrine for satan, and we said, "Okay." We were game for almost anything wild, so we prepared ourselves.

We held a candle waist-high in front of us, and formed a line behind Bill. As we marched, Bill had each of us saying the chant he had just taught us. We said it over and over again until we finished our march.

Six of us marched seven times around the house. Some of the people, including James, did not march. They just looked on. When we finished, we all stood out front at the stroke of midnight and sang. It was halloween, and we thought we had done something really wild and crazy.

A few days later, Ed's cousin and his wife woke up choking on the smell of sulphur. They jumped up and tried to locate the source of the smell and open windows. They looked out the upstairs window of their bedroom and saw hot coals burning down on the ground.

They went outside to see what it was, and put some of the hot coals into a bowl. The next day, they took them to a local college to find out what the substance was. The chemist said as near as he could find, it was not of this earth. He said it was more like some form of brimstone.

We were all amazed over what had happened, but when we saw the upside down cross that appeared over night at the uppermost point of this two-story house, we were each just a little terrified. We stood in quiet awe, not knowing what to expect from our folly. Of course James and Bill thought it proof that satan was god.

"Wait a minute!" I said. "This certainly is no longer *white witchcraft*, is it?" James gave me a sly laugh as Bill tried to console me by saying, "Witchcraft is witchcraft, so don't worry about what kind, okay?"

"But I won't serve satan, understand?" I said. James made some snorting sound and walked away in disgust as Bill tried to sooth my fears. Bill was a great recruiter. On one occasion, James cornered me into a conversation on my religious beliefs. "Who do you consider your god to be?" he asked. I answered, "The Creator of all things and the Father of Jesus." James snarled at the name of Jesus. Then with a smirk, he said, "I suppose you believe in the virgin birth?"

When I told him I believed that Jesus' mother was Mary, and that Jesus died at Calvary on a cross, James answered with mocking anger, "Crucifixion was a form of capital punishment back then—read your history books—many people died on a cross."

He was right there. Many had died on crosses. I then said in defense of Jesus, "But Jesus rose from the dead on the third day after His crucifixion," and James grinned slyly and said in a soft, sure voice, "That proves reincarnation."

I had no answer for his last remark because that seemed to make a lot of sense to me at the time, especially since I had been studying reincarnation.

I looked at him and said in a small voice, "But Jesus shed His blood for the remission of our sins." At that statement, James flew into a rage and held his hand up as if to stop me, and screamed, "Don't talk about *that* blood!" After spewing out a mouthful of obscenities, he walked out.

From that time on, we started losing contact with Bill and James, and it wasn't long before they moved back to New York. They were two very strange guys who were terrible creatures of the night. I somehow knew that they truly were sent to me, but in all my "natural abilities," I just wasn't bad enough—thanks to Mom's prayers and God's grace. We moved again just a few months later, and this time we bought a big two-story home with an apartment on the second story. It was right on the banks of a river and that pleased both Ed and I, plus, my young sons loved to fish.

Naturally, as soon as we settled in, we rented the apartment to a couple of young guys. It wasn't long before they moved out and a couple more young guys moved in.

We kept one room upstairs that we could shut off as a bedroom for my son. We could lock the doors to the apartment from our side, so we really didn't have to be concerned for the boys. Suddenly I began to notice strange noises, and this time, lights would zip around the room out of nowhere. The stereo would turn on by itself and do things like change its own channels and volume levels. Now that tended to spook people—especially baby-sitters.

Because of this and the recurring nightmares I had of the boys being trapped by fire in their bedroom, I moved them downstairs into our small den.

Ed and I then put all our junk furniture and boxes upstairs in the boys' former room. The only thing we left up there was a twin bed, just for company. Of course, everyone was afraid to sleep up there, so it never got used.

Our front room was directly below this room. I used our sofa as a divider and set it directly under the register connecting to the room upstairs.

One night, after I'd had yet another surgery, I was unable to sleep so I got up and started watching television. As I sat on the sofa, directly under the register, I heard something run across the floor above me and then jump up and down on the bed that was still up there. I even heard the springs squeaking under its weight. Then, it came to the register and started spewing out horrible grunts, unearthly words and growls.

The hair pricked right up on the back of my neck as I froze in fear. While my mind tried to explain away what I'd heard, I remembered that the young men had just moved out of the apartment. Even though they still had some of their belongings there, no one was staying up there.

I finally got my brain to function again, and I pretended to not hear its goings on. I got up and walked to the television and pretended to turn it down. I then walked way around so that whatever it was couldn't see me, and then crawled over the back of the sofa. (Now that in itself was no easy job. I still had the clamps in my incision.)

I slipped into our bedroom and quietly, yet forcefully, awakened Ed and begged him to investigate. We sat down again on the sofa and settled in to listen. After a while, the noises finally began again.

This time Ed heard it and went to get his gun. He opened the door leading to the stairs and waited to hear it again. He was determined to shoot whatever it was. Meanwhile, I begged him not to go. I just had a knowing that whatever it was, it was not of flesh and blood; therefore, a gun would not protect Ed.

He would not listen, so up the stairs he went while I waited, the breathless coward, at the foot of the stairs. After what seemed forever, he came down the stairs reassuring me that he had found nothing.

In the days that followed, Ed set traps for everything from mice to squirrels; he even set a bear trap. There were no holes in the wall where anything could enter, the register was the "straight through the floor" kind, and the door had been shut and locked.

We never did find out what it was; however, the next day, I went into the apartment and found an ashtray with a big fat demonic looking creature sculptured on the side, plus other books and paraphernalia of the craft. It seemed like no matter what I did or where I moved, I was unable to kick this thing.

We Escape Death Once More...

About this time, my health began to fail and my doctor sent me to a clinic to a horde of specialists. They determined that I would need extensive surgery, so two doctors operated on me at the same time.

My bladder had ruptured into the wall of my vagina and my bowels had ruptured on the other side. To make matters worse, my bladder had fallen and had to be tied up. During surgery, the doctors found a hernia and a floating piece of bone that was not connected to anything. The doctor told me it was a floating rib.

I wanted to die. I couldn't sit or lay comfortably. If I got the one part of me comfortable, it was stressful on the other area, so I couldn't win for losing. *Oh well*, I thought, *it's just another day in Janelle's episode of her own General Hospital*.

Then my youngest son started getting nodules behind his ears and on his neck for no explainable reason, so the doctor sent us to the hospital to have a blood test run. My husband was at work, so I packed the three boys up in my Nova and headed for the hospital. We had only gone a few blocks when a car pulled out in front of us, causing me to run off the road and into a tree. My five-year-old and my eldest boy were in the front seat with me, and my middle son was in the back seat.

During the collision, I watched, in what seemed to be slow motion, as I held my arm out to protect my sons in the front seat. When the latch on the passenger seat did not hold, I watched with horror as my son in the back seat flew up over the seat and hit the windshield face-first, and then was thrown back into the back seat, only to be thrown into the windshield again.

As soon as the car stopped, I jumped out and helped my two sons out of the front seat. I knew that the oldest had hit the dash pretty hard, but my main concern was for my son in the backseat.

Blood had spewed all over the car and I knew he was in trouble. I helped him out of the back seat as a man ran out of his house and ordered my son to lay down on the ground. The man said something about my son losing too much blood, and he said we had to get it stopped. He applied pressure to his nose in just the right places until the ambulance got there. We arrived at the hospital and the boys were checked by the doctor, when he finally got there. The oldest boy was banged up and in shock, but he would be okay. My youngest boy was not hurt at all because somehow, my arm had held him secure.

My second son had chipped teeth, a broken nose and severe blood loss, causing him to be admitted for the night. Had that man not been there to stop the bleeding, the doctor said my son may not have made it.

Once again, my mind was tormented with the answers to the questions that refused to go away: *Why me? Why all the chaos? Was there a connection between the dark world and the recurring sickness hitting me and my family? Are these constant "accidents" really accidents, or are they attacks from the spirit world?*

Even the Most Evil of Men and Spirits Tremble at "the Name"

Anyone who has dabbled in the dark arts or toyed with the devil's power knows it well: the enemy's manifestations of lurid evil are his greatest stronghold over them.

God supernaturally caused me to doubt that satan was "all powerful" as he claimed. Despite the enemy's violent attacks against my mind, my senses and my family's safety, God made me genuinely doubt my "gifts" as a witch.

Don't let the enemy fool you. If you're convinced you are "in too deep" to get out now, you have underestimated the sheer power and intense love God has for you. Yes, of course there is a genuine spiritual war. But understand your oppressor.

Satan's manifestations and attacks against me and my family were demonic ploys of intimidation to frighten me away from Jesus. Yes, I was afraid, but God, in His infinite mercy, protected me and allowed no real harm to come to me or my chilren.

You may be in the terrible state I was: my fear seemed to keep on growing, but at the same time, I came to realize more and more that I had to find a way out of the madness—that way was Jesus! God's Word says that He is the Way, the Truth, and the Life.

The more doors you open as you get involved in the occult, the more fierce is the struggle to preserve what little sanity may still remain. I began to wonder if I would ever sleep without demonic dreams.

The devil knew my eyes were being opened—I became aware that his "gifts" to me as a witch were really poisoned talons that had embedded themselves within me. *The simple fact that I was being attacked was a sure sign the devil was losing his servant!*

God Himself crushed satan's evil kingdom in me. He crushed it bit by bit, with His own hands. Even when I despaired that I had thrown my soul into satan's miry pit forever, as I looked to God, I found that He was already reaching down to pull me out!

The words Jesus said from the cross 2,000 years ago are for me and for you today, "Father forgive them, for they know not what they do." Jesus, clothed in all our sin and shame, was speaking on our behalf.

Listen to me: the devil may merrily dance around someone like me or you, chanting, "You are mine! I will never let you go!" But there is nothing he can do or say to defeat the command of Jesus Who stands on holy ground and commands that our souls be made free!

You can know what it is like to live without torment or fear. You can be free! No matter what, there is always hope in Jesus!

Chapter Eight

She's Had a Hypo From Heaven and Won't Be Right for Days!

Soon after we moved into the house, Ed was working one night and I went over to Marie and Terry's house to do some drugs. There were six of us, two friends of Terry's and then of course, the three musketeers—Marie, Celia, and I.

The stereo blared in another room as we sat at the kitchen table getting high. We were each drinking our favorite kind of booze and passing joints around.

Of all of us, I suspected that Terry most likely was already high before we joined him.

He was so hooked on drugs that he should have gone to a rehabilitation place long before now, although we doubted that he could ever get free. He would just pace and pace like a wild man, and it looked like he would never find happiness on this earth.

This particular evening turned out to be different than any other. It began when we started discussing seriously the things that bothered us about our lives. The further we went into the conversation, it became more evident that we all agreed that none of us felt as if we had ever known love.

Terry remembered my story about going to Golgotha that time I spaced out, so he asked me to share it and I did. Mind you, as far as I knew, Terry didn't have much, if any, church or Christianity in his life. He must have really been taken with what I had seen.

They all sat quietly, listening with only an occasional "Wow, man" as I told them how Jesus looked and how much I felt love coming from Him. After I told the story, Terry jumped up and left the table to go to his bedroom. We all assumed he was going for more pot or something, but after what seemed like an hour, we found out he was looking for something entirely different.

Terry returned with a Bible he had received at his graduation, saying, "She's right, she's right! I watched Billy Graham twice this week on television, and he said the same thing, 'God is Love.'"

He threw the Bible down on the table and opened it to the Gospel of Saint John. He started counting how many times the word "Love" appeared on the first page.

He finally said, "See, you can't even count all the love's in this Bible." We all sat down and said a prayer inviting Jesus into our hearts. (No one had ever told me that the Holy Spirit would go to a drug party.) The next day, we all gathered again at Terry's to see who really meant the prayer the night before. Each of us sheepishly dropped by, sort of embarrassed to open up for discussion the events of the night before. Everyone except Terry, that is.

In utter amazement, we watched as he excitedly talked of his commitment and how he had the best rest that night that he had ever had.

As he talked, he left us totally in shock to go into his bedroom. He returned several minutes later, and in his arms he had a grocery sack filled with drugs and all kinds of paraphernalia. Why, he even had my favorite pipe in there! (I couldn't help but think, *How dare he give away that cute little homemade pipe we smoked our hash with?*)

"What's the matter with you Terry," we asked, "have you lost your mind?" Inside me, I think I heard a groan. I was not ready to quit using, and I knew one of my main sources had just abandoned me when I heard Terry say, "I don't need this stuff anymore!"

One of the other guys stepped forward and asked if he could have it. Now this was the guy who, just the night before, ran outside and fell on his knees and cried, "Forgive me, Jesus."

Now here he was taking the sack of goodies, saying, "I told God that I would give up drinking, but I'm not ready to give up my dope yet."

Terry said, "Take it and get it out of my sight." I'm sure that was the moment I heard an even bigger groan—I secretly wished he would have given me a choice in the matter, but he didn't.

Terry headed for the door to go to work, when all of a sudden he turned around and came back to the kitchen. He had his cigarettes in his hand, and threw them across the table saying, "I don't need these things anymore." Then he took off for work. I couldn't tell Marie's reaction, but I was clearly stunned over the events of the past twenty-four hours. *It won't last*, I thought. Terry was too dependant on the stuff. Somewhere deep within, I hoped against all odds the he was for real, because we all knew that he was on the brink of insanity, and what he really needed was to go into rehabilitation and dry out.

We watched him closely over the next few days to see if Terry would go into withdrawal. To our utter amazement, he didn't have one bad reaction. Not only did he get saved, but Jesus had healed and delivered him!

That Sunday, I took him to the only church I knew to take him to, my mother's. After the sermon, I watched in awe as Terry made his way to the altar to make his public commitment to Jesus Christ. He had settled it for all time and I knew it, because Terry was the kind of guy who took commitment very seriously.

I took him back to Marie at her mother's house and dropped him off. Marie and her entire family were devoted Catholics and bless their hearts, they were about to get blown away.

Marie told me later that Terry came in like a ray of sunshine and she got so mad that she left there alone in her car to yell at God. Soon a beautiful light came down and filled her vehicle, and Jesus said, "Marie, I want you too."

Guess what...Marie gave Jesus all of her heart. Now what was I going to do? I was raised to believe that Catholics could not be born again, and that they had caused the death of millions of Christians. They were therefore "the arch enemies of God." I even half-heartedly tried to hate the Catholic religion.

I had been taught to feel sorry for the people, because they were being deceived into hell with no hope. Now here stood Marie—a "born-again Catholic" who was determined to serve Jesus with her whole heart.

Well there went all hope for my drug habit. I was not a happy camper, to say the least.

Marie and Terry began going to a United Brethren Church of about a hundred-and-fifty to two-hundred people, and I followed them figuring I should at least try. I also went to the altar and made a public commitment to Jesus, but I spent most of my time going backward instead of forward.

Ed wasn't about to become a "born-again Christian" and he wasn't real thrilled about what I was trying to do.

One evening I was sitting in church and he came in after me. To my horror, he had a lit cigarette in his hand and was as drunk as a coot, asking loudly for me. I was so embarrassed. I knew it just couldn't work out with Ed going his way and me going mine, so I slowly stopped going.

This also put a damper on my relationship with Terry and Marie, because we were headed in different directions. I just couldn't live it, and the horror at home was worsening as the spirits began to reveal their true selves as demons—complete with name tags and torment. One night as I knelt on my knees by my bed, a demon who was about four feet tall bent over my back and started spewing threats in my ear. He said they (the demons) would all show themselves to me if I didn't "shut up this stupid !@!#! bawling out to God."

The being assured me God wasn't listening, since I belonged to them. "After all, He has never talked to you like we always have," he said.

I was convinced they were right. I told Jesus that I wanted to pray, but "they" wouldn't let me. So sorrowfully, in much fear, I stopped praying.

Many nights later, I saw a figure in our darkened bedroom. Again, it was about four feet tall with hair all over its body, and it was standing in one of the corners near the foot of our bed. It just crouched and stared at me through its fiery red eyes. I knew he was a guardian of some sort. After all, I had sent enough of his kind to do my bidding—now one had been sent to guard me. The torment got worse. One night I was asleep in bed, when I felt Ed start snuggling up behind me, bothering me. I woke up angrily, thinking that Ed was attempting to take his liberties with me, and he knew better than to try this when I was asleep.

Suddenly I felt an all too familiar breathing on my neck as strong arms tightened painfully around me, making it impossible to move. I tried to move several times, to no avail.

After I fought with all my strength, I suddenly broke free, slinging my arm clear around behind me. Nothing was there. Ed was curled up next to the wall, snoring softly. Fear raged through me, as I shakily woke Ed and had him hold me the rest of the night. On another occasion, we were asleep in the middle of a hot summer night when my phone rang. I picked up the phone by the side of the bed and heard my girlfriend, Kandy, excitedly saying, ""Janelle, get up! The fan's on fire!"

I looked at the fan on our dresser at the foot of the bed, and sure enough, flames were shooting out over our bed as the fan blades continued to spin.

I nudged Ed and said, "The fan's on fire, get up!" Then I fell back to sleep. The phone rang again, and this time Kandy was screaming at me as she again warned, "Get out of bed— the fan is on fire!"

This time I really woke up, and I yelled at Ed to get up now! The phone was still in my hand, but there wasn't anyone on the other end. I don't know who warned us, but it wasn't Kandy.

Ed and I jumped out of bed only to find our heads in a cloud of smoke, forcing us both to hunker down, choking. Hurriedly, Ed went for the fan as I groped for the door. As I opened the door, Ed unplugged the fan and went out the door with it, still in his underwear.

He returned to the room to open windows to vent the smoke out so he could find out why the "very expensive" smoke detector installed recently did not go off (it was directly above our bed).

We even had the sales person stop by to check it out, and we watched as he lit a cigarette and softly blew the smoke toward the sensor on the detector. It went off immediately and loudly, leaving us again with an unexplainable incident that almost cost us our lives.

By now, demons went everywhere with me, even trying to discredit my sanity or blatantly trying to kill me. I was always arguing with them for my soul and life.

It seemed like I was always just "a hair's breadth away" from a wreck or accident. Weird and strange things were always happening to me and to those around me.

The phone would ring and horrible beings would be on the other end, growling in an inhuman garble. Ed was now finding notes with messages scribbled to him, signed by demons—either in me, or using me—or else they were just notes from beyond the reach of mortal man. Either way, I never remembered doing the writing.

My nights were spent in fear and horror. My days were filled with wanderings and fears of the night yet to come. My life was a vicious merry-go-round of terror, fear and hopelessness. I knew all too well that it's easier to get on that ride than to get off—especially when it was heading straight to hell.

Up to this point in my marriage to Ed, I mostly ran around with him, but he now worked nights and I worked days. I was getting lonely. I always had what some call a sixth sense. I always seemed to know when someone was talking about me or doing me wrong. I usually chose to believe them when there was a confrontation, but somewhere inside me I knew the truth. Of course, I was unable to face the truth I sensed, so I believed their lies, or did I?

Ed started getting home later and later, especially on Friday. I sensed that he was beginning to run around on me, but without solid truth I couldn't be sure. I tried to give him the benefit of the doubt.

It was difficult though when I saw cars with women in them come by my house and turn around in the driveway. Especially when I watched them pointing at our house numbers, clearly mouthing the words, "This is it, this is where he lives."

Then there was the time he supposedly went to a union meeting with a promise to come right home after it was over. The promise was especially important because I had family visiting from out-of-state who wanted to visit with us.

Ed left around eleven o'clock that morning and he didn't return until after midnight. I couldn't believe it—he wasn't drunk and he had even taken a shower.

I let him tell me a lie about how he had gotten drunk and had to sleep it off on a back road. Then he told me that he stopped at some truck stop and showered because he had gotten sick all over himself.

When I asked him why his clothes weren't soiled, and whose perfume I smelled (it wasn't mine), he said he ran into his sister and she hugged him. I knew the truth would be unbearable, so I let him convince me.

Another time I followed him undetected from his place of work in another city to a bar, only to have the female owner of the place glare at me and refuse to wait on me. She looked just like one of the women who always showed up pointing at my house.

Ed was shocked to see me, but he covered it over quickly and excused us from the bar. I felt a sickness growing inside me that never left me from that point on, but I did nothing about it because I did not have concrete proof. The sickness was still doing something inside of me, though.

Finally I had enough of his flimsy excuses and I decided to do more than just threaten—I would do what he hated and feared the most. I went back into the bar scene with my friends from work—but this time, without Ed.

On a Friday night, Kandy called me up to ask if I wanted to go out like she had so many times before, but this time to her surprise, I said that I would go.

We went to a local night spot that had dancing, and met another girlfriend and a guy from work that she was crazy about, even though he was married.

After the place closed, we took some beer and went riding in the country, getting crazy drunk. The four of us laughed 'til we hurt. Then they dropped me off.

It was about ten 'til four in the morning and Ed wasn't home yet. I waited on the sofa in a drunken daze, thrilled at what I had to tell him when he got home. I had fun without him, and he deserved it.

About four o'clock he came in, just as drunk as I was. I got up from the sofa laughing like crazy at him, almost with too much joy. Ed sensed the change in my attitude and began asking where I'd been. I taunted him about pushing me too far, and I told him that now it was my turn.

When I saw the fear cross his face, that made the game even more delicious. From that point on, I knew I would have a more attentive Ed. Part of me just wanted to get even and totally dismiss his feelings, but I could only do so much because of guilt. I really did love him—at the least I was very married to him.

One night I was with Kandy and one of her friends when we picked up the brother of Kandy's fiancee, who was from another country. Kandy's friend was so drunk that Kandy had to drive, so I was forced to sit in the back seat with Kandy's future brother-in-law.

We were friends and I knew he had a terrible crush on me, but then he had an eye for a lot of Kandy's friends—after all, he needed a wife to stay in America. He and I were left in the back seat alone while Kandy and her girlfriend went into a liquor store to buy some more beer.

The car was parked in a busy place that was well lit, so I thought it would be okay. I was semi-attracted to this guy, but I was totally committed to staying Ed's wife. All of a sudden, this guy's all over me trying to kiss me, and I'm hand-wrestling him to stay away.

I wasn't mad at him, because I sort of enjoyed someone wanting me for a change. He finally grabbed me and kissed me on the mouth. As I jerked away, I heard a knock on the back window of the car—there on a bicycle, incognito, was Ed's brother who was a policeman.

He started calling me names and proclaiming how great his brother's love for me was in front of everyone there. I could have crawled under the seat but it was too late for that.

Ed had seventeen brothers and sisters, and most of them had large families of their own. If you hurt one of them, you've hurt them all. Ed would leave, but come back.

I couldn't believe him and all the tears—after all, his family didn't bother to ask me about all the lonely nights I spent while Ed stayed out all night with his lady friends. They certainly couldn't know, because his activities were in another city.

His brother was wrong, but it was the real beginning of the end for our marriage. Our finances were in poor shape because of mismanagement and booze, so we decided to sell our home. It sold right away and we moved to the country. I was hesitant about moving so far out in the country, but Ed thought it would be best as it would be closer to his work.

The house was a beautiful two-story house with nine rooms, all natural wood and with an open staircase, but it too was spooky. Ed had to take his .22 rifle and shoot the rats that were sitting on my back porch staring into the kitchen.

I could have been happy there forever and so could the boys, but our marriage was on the outs. I no longer had a desire to party and Ed did. I really wanted a life with Ed, but he was wanting his freedom.

The pressures of the crumbling marriage, compounded by my being laid off, began to take a toll on me. During this time, the boys would find me cowering in a closet or hiding in a room talking to things that weren't there, whimpering.

Ed wouldn't be there, and even when he was, he was usually passed out drunk on the sofa. My oldest son would call one of my friends and they would take me out and get me high or drunk, and then bring me home—just in time for it to start all over again.

I began to get confused trying to decide between reality and madness. I was so far gone that my darling sons and the love I held for them couldn't even keep me straight. They were just kids, yet they had to take care of a mother who was unable to keep it together.

The boys were also concerned about their stepfather whom they had learned to love so very much. They knew that he wanted to leave and that terrified them. After all, they sure couldn't find stability in their mother. It was during this time, just when everything was falling apart, that I went to answer a knock on my back door and there stood Marie. Somehow, that girl got me to go to the miracle services, and I ended up sitting helpless and exhausted in a prayer room with a bunch of people I don't know—*Do whatever you want with me people*, I thought to myself. Mr. Russell was sitting in front of me now, looking closely at me. I was still unable to move. He reassured me that I was doing fine and that Jesus was setting me free of demonic forces.

When I raised my head, my eyes caught sight of something in the mirror that I didn't understand. I felt a shudder in my soul as I looked again—sitting in the mirror was a green monster-like being with armadillo-like skin! Its long black hair stuck straight out the back of its head, and its eyes were red with penetrating fire.

I heard a roar come up out of me as I looked again and realized it was sitting where I was sitting. Mr. Russell said, "Daughter, is there anything else you need to confess?" I told him I didn't think so, because I had even asked God to forgive me for hating Him so much.

Mr. Russell led me through the sinner's prayer, but I was still unable to move. *What's wrong?* I wondered, *won't God forgive me?*

About this time, Mr Russell touched my forehead again and prayed, "Father, in Your Word You said that You would bring all things to our remembrance; would You do that for Janelle?" At that very moment, I remembered that to have "all power" as a witch, I had to have a blood sacrifice. Since I would not kill, I was forced to use *my own blood* if people didn't give me their blood to use to gain greater power over curses and spells.

Suddenly, I realized the gravity of what I had done: I had become a living sacrifice for the devil. I begged God to forgive me, and I quickly renounced what I had done, but still I remained tied to the chair.

The small-framed man who preached that day, Rev. Estie, entered the room and stooped down beside me. He said,

"Child, have you confessed all?" When I said yes, he said, "Then you should be free."

Then he asked, "Child, what is your religious background?" I thought that was a peculiar question—this man had no idea that a few weeks earlier I had stood in my dining room challenging God, saying, "If You really love me, then send me someone from the denomination I was raised in, someone who believes that You care more about who I am inside than what I look like on the outside—then I will believe You love me."

Now this man was asking me a question that brought back the conversation with God. I looked down at him and told him the name of the denomination and he dropped his head and said, "Dear Jesus."

With my heart racing I hoped against hope, surprised that this man even knew about my little-known denomination. When I asked him if he had heard of it, Rev. Estie raised his precious head and with tears in his eyes, he said, "Child, I was a pastor in that denomination for twenty-seven years when God filled me with His Holy Spirit and they asked me to leave."

"God, oh my God, Abba Father, You do love me, I am forgiven!" Suddenly, I could move, I could even laugh from a place within me where I'd never laughed before.

I had to hug everyone, first of all, Mona, my sister in Christ. Wow, I was a sister! I was so excited that I couldn't calm down. I felt like I'd instantly lost a hundred pounds and I was suddenly a ballerina, dancing proudly before my Heavenly Father. Rev. Estie took me out of the room and presented me to my husband, telling him, "Get her home, put her to bed—she's had a hypo from Heaven and she won't be right for days."

Ed went home with Mona's husband, as she and I were too hyped up to go home and stay. First, we asked if Rev. Estie was having church anywhere that night, because we wanted to go. He wasn't, so we hit the road to find someone to share our joy with.

Mona and I were acting like a couple of drunks; I felt higher than any high I had ever been on.

First, we went to Marie and Terry's house to tell them. They sat there, stunned, as I just gushed all over them about how Jesus set me free from demons, and how my problem all along had been that I was possessed.

I could tell they didn't really know what all I was talking about, and I'm sure they were wondering if it would last, considering all my backsliding in the past.

Mona and I didn't stop there. We headed out of town to see my Mom and stepdad who lived about twelve miles away. We realized just before we got there that we had driven the entire distance in second gear on a major highway.

Mom and Dad knew something had happened to me, but they didn't know quite what, and I could clearly tell they were skeptical about it lasting. They probably were hoping for any kind of positive change, because I was a basket case.

Finally, Mona and I headed back home, sure that our husbands would now be ready to hear about what had happened in that room. To my dismay, Ed wasn't the least bit interested.

His only concern was that I wouldn't turn into some kind of "Jesus freak" like Terry and Marie.

It was too late to be concerned about that. I was already soldout. For the next few weeks, Ed could barely stand me. He drank every night and stayed away as much as he could.

The man that used to adore me could not stand even the sight of me. Even as he slept, if I touched him he would sling his arm at me and say, "Don't touch me." He began to call me "Godzilla," and I couldn't understand why he didn't love me anymore—I was now a much better wife to him.

Perhaps I was too much for him. I'm sure I acted more like a zealot than a woman of God, and for that I would later be ashamed.

Ed walked out on us a little over a month after my experience, and there was no way I could convince him to stay or return after he left.

Grief like I had never known set in, along with a new depth of fear. We were two months behind on our light bill and I was laid off with nine dollars to my name and hardly any food to last us until an unemployment check came in.

Ed had taken our car to his sisters to get something done to it, and left it for her to use. When he left, he took our other car with him, leaving the boys and I with the "old" Chevy truck to drive.

I had to call someone to send a mechanic out just to get it running so the boys and I would not be destitute nine miles from everything. The mechanic got it running but warned that the linkage could lock-up on it when shifting from first gear to second gear. He showed me how to take a screwdriver and fix it, should it happen.

I soon found out that it would happen over and over again, on the way to church or any other place. I got so embarrassed at stop signs when I had to hold up traffic to fix it. The floorboard was partially rusted out and the doors squeaked loudly when opened, but I was grateful to have something to drive. Soon after that, I was called back to work at the factory, thanks be to God, so I felt a little more secure.

Night after night, I sat in my kitchen reading my Bible and praying, as I watched every car that came down the road— praying it would be Ed. Finally, one night I took Ed's picture and put scriptures all around it and laid it out on the kitchen table and I cried out to God to see "His" power in action.

I had seen satan's power when I made dolls or cast spells. Now I desperately needed to see a sign that God's Word was as powerful as satan's. I laid my hands on Ed's picture and said, "Okay, God, I need to see if You are Who you say you are. Bring Ed home this very night—even if he is not ready to stay. I need to know You hear my prayers."

I laid down on the sofa in the TV room where I slept most of the time, and waited. Just after I'd finally fallen asleep, I was awakened all of a sudden by a presence standing over me. It was Ed. His shirt was halfway pulled out, and he was drunk as usual, but I didn't care—at least he was there.

He looked at me and said, "Don't ask me why I'm here, and I'm not coming back." He stayed the night with me and left in the morning. But nothing could rob me of the peace I had, knowing God did hear me. I knew not to ever tempt God again.

A couple of nights later while I was in deep prayer, I had a vision that my car would be back by the first snow fall, so I assumed Ed would be back also. The snow came early that year and my car was back, but Ed would never be back as my husband. I still kept hoping and praying.

One night, as I walked through my dining room, I audibly heard the enemy taunt me with the words, "Look at you, I wanted to send you to New York and around the world, clothed in sable to your feet. I would have given you a limousine and chauffeur. You could have had anything you wanted, but you turned away from me to your God. What has He given you? Nothing! He has taken everything away."

I looked up to Heaven crying as I said to God, "He's right God," but He didn't speak one word in His own defense. Somehow I knew Who had given the most for me.

Shortly after that encounter with the enemy, another strange thing happened. I was preparing to go to sleep on the sofa and had just laid back on my pillow when out of the darkness appeared a huge being about eight or nine feet tall. It had a brown garment on and wore a crown that was muddy brown also. I couldn't see a face, but I heard it bellowing at me as it came toward me. It said, "You belong to me—you've been promised!"

I was paralyzed in fear, unable to speak a word as this being kept coming closer, screeching in a garbled voice, "You belong to me—you've been promised!" Somewhere in my spirit I finally screamed "JESUS!" Peace came with His name, even though I had not audibly spoken it.

About that time, a big mass of brightness without form and floating about a foot off the floor came around the door and headed directly for the being. The dark being stopped and flung its arms up over its head as if to shield its face, all the while saying "She's mine, she's been promised!" Although the bright mass had no form, I saw a sword of bright light come out of the mass and stay over the being's head. At that moment I knew it was the angel of the Lord, and I was safe.

The angel did not speak an audible word, but somehow the dark being perfectly understood what it was saying, and so did I. It said, "No, she is not yours! We gave her back her will and she chose God. You can never ever, ever, ever have her again!" Then the whole scene disappeared before my eyes.

I would like to say that I bravely went to sleep, but the truth is that I turned on the light for the rest of that night, and for many nights to follow.

People thought I was weird because of some of the things I would see and hear in the spirit realm, and I was just too naive to stop talking about them.

I was agonizing in travail for Ed on another occasion when, with my spiritual eyes, I saw Jesus walk up and sit down on the floor beside me and put His head over on my shoulder. He was sobbing softly and I thought it was for me and all my agony. I started trying to comfort Him, because I was becoming more concerned for His hurt than my own. I said, "Thank You for caring for my pain," and He said,

"Child, you don't understand. I'm not crying for you, I'm crying for Ed. You see, someday you will go on with your life and be healed and saved, and forget to even pray for Ed; but as long as Ed's alive, there is hope and I will hurt for his salvation long past your memory of him."

I knew I had received a divine visitation, and it gave me a deeper understanding of Jesus and His long suffering. That knowledge helped me grow a little stronger and a little less full of self-pity.

Times were tough. Food was often scarce and I didn't know who to turn to, but God. One time my eldest son looked in the refrigerator and said, "Look Mom, there is some macaroni and cheese that you can give the other guys and I can eat the last piece of bread. That's enough for me, Mom, really."

I just hung my head and wept in total desperation, "God, where are you?" I could almost hear and see the demons jumping around laughing and mocking me. Before it was time to eat, we heard a knock at the door. There stood a stranger with stuffed grocery sacks in her arms and a smile on her face. She asked, "Are you Janelle?" I said, "Yes, I am. What can I do for you?" She said, "You don't know me but God impressed on me that you needed food, so can I give you some of what I've got?"

I said yes and began shaking as I tried to hold back the tears of gratitude. She brought in sack after sack of food, then she quickly said her goodbyes and was gone. The boys and I exploded with excitement as we rummaged through the bags. She had even brought cookies for the boys. When God answers prayer, He answers prayer!

It didn't stop there. People all over brought food to us—including Ed's cousins and Mona. One man and his wife started supplying all our meat; he was a butcher and got special deals.

If I had any pride left, God was sure doing His part to humble me. When I had to go to a trustee to get oil for our furnace that year, I thought I couldn't make it through that embarrassment. I didn't know then, but now I realize that my flesh was dying and giving way to the spirit.

Do You Ever Wonder, "Can I Really Be Free?"

You may be one of the special people this book was written for, one of the hurting, abused or angry victims who feels bound in unbreakable chains of darkness and despair. My heart goes out to you, because I've been there.

The day came when my life changed drastically. Despite the hopelessness of my situation, God breathed the breath of life into my broken heart and tormented soul. I felt alive again.

Until my day of deliverance came, I lived in constant fear that the devil would take my life, or that I would end up as some old wreck of humanity. I didn't realize that God had already prepared the hearts of some of His servants for that fateful evening when I would walk hesitantly into that gymnasium to hear a preacher named Estie. God knew I wouldn't leave that place until I had finally, painfully, placed my burdens and chains at my Savior's feet.

God had already put some of His Champions on my "case," anointed Christians who knew how to pray and not let loose until the answer came. I believe God ordained that memorable night just for me. Jesus had you and me in mind when He said, "he hath sent me to heal the brokenhearted, to preach deliverance to the captives, and recovering of sight to the blind, to set at liberty them that are bruised..." (Luke 4:18).

After I surrendered to Jesus, and after His powerful words of deliverance were spoken over me, I was never the same. I was a new creature. The time had finally come when I truly *changed masters*—I chose to serve the greatest of them all: Jesus Christ.

Although I found my days and nights lonely at times, I was never really alone. I discovered that Jesus would talk to me during those times. He became a refuge for me when no one else was there or seemed to care.

When I openly made my decision to serve the Son of the Most High, satan saw to it that I experienced some discouragement and rejection. He hoped his "fiery darts" would make "serving Jesus" silly and unnecessary. God caused my faith to catch the pointed and sharp edges of those darts, and in time, I learned that He had truly freed me from my evil taskmaster of the past.

To the natural eye, it may appear that I went without, especially the times I stared into an empty refrigerator. When I look back, I see that God always supplied my needs, no matter what they were. His eye was on my children too. I've learned that my heavenly Father cares more about me and my needs than I ever dreamed.

My life changed because of a man named Jesus. Somehow, I don't care what it costs or what I lose by serving Him—He paid a very high price to set me free.

I began to discover that I could do something I hadn't been able to do since I was a child—I could let Janelle go free. I didn't have to live in the darkened places anymore. God helped me love again, and that was no small thing.

After I left the gymnasium, I began to fall in love with Jesus, and see all the beauty around me that had escaped me for years. Because of Him, I would never be the same. Because of Him, *you will never be the same!*

Chapter Nine

Intercession Begins at Home

I continued to pray for Ed, but by the end of the summer, the Spirit of God seemed to change my prayers. I began to agonize for my half-brother, Jay, who was almost nineteen and a drug addict.

Jay had been sent to boys' school a couple of years earlier, and when he got in trouble again, Mom and my stepdad had to put a mortgage on their home to keep him out of prison. He needed Jesus desperately and now my spirit was in agony for his salvation.

Suddenly, I felt I should stop praying, and I heard God say to my heart, "Jay is saved, just start praising Me for his salvation." I finally talked to Mom, and I looked forward to hearing her tell me about Jay's conversion. When I told Mom what God had said, she told me, "Janny, he's not saved yet, but I know he will be some day. God has promised me."

I was stunned. I knew I had heard from God, yet here I was looking like I had egg on my face. Who was I to think I had heard from God? I don't think Mom doubted me. I doubted myself. Every time I tried to pray for Jay after that, I still found I couldn't intercede. I could only praise God for him.

I spent the night at Marie and Terry's about two months later, and I received a phone call from Mom about four o'clock in the morning. I heard shouts and screams in the background as Mom wept loudly. My heart sank and fear ran through my mind as I wondered who had died and what's Jay done now? I just kept asking Mom, "What's wrong, what's going on?" Finally Mom said, "Janny, the most wonderful thing has happened. Jay just got home from a party and on the way home—even as drugged up as he was—he gave his heart to Jesus Christ."

As I began to weep with joy, I could hear Jay crying as he tore up his marijuana plants, pornography books, records and tapes. When he got it, he got it *good*.

This gave me even more hope to believe for my Ed! Jay and my oldest nephew, Kerry, were born just a few months apart, and they had been best friends all their lives. Jay's first burden was to get Kerry saved. He was deep into drugs and didn't really know much about Jesus.

About a month after Jay was saved, Kerry's younger sister, Ruthie, came to baby-sit for me. When I came home that evening with my girlfriend, Mona, Ruthie asked if she could share a dream she had, and of course we said yes. She began to weep as she shared the dream.

She said everyone was at her house in this dream, even friends and relatives that she had not seen for years. The kids decided to play hide and seek, and she was it. She said she was standing under a tree, counting to one hundred, when all of a sudden she realized the birds had stopped singing and the crickets were silent. A sense of eeriness came over her.

She said she turned around and looked up. There in the sky was one cloud in the shape of Jesus along with people dressed in white robes, and they were all praising Him. At that point, she knew the rapture was taking place. I asked her what she did, and Ruthie said, "Aunt Janny, I just fell on my face and begged Jesus not to leave me behind! Oh Aunt Janny, what can it mean?"

I prayed for God's wisdom silently, and answered, "Ruthie, I believe that one of two things were meant by that dream. Either it was a warning that you need to get your heart right with God, or it could mean that someone is going to die." Ruthie cried, "Aunt Janny, do you think it's me?" I told her I didn't know, and added, "Remember this: if you only have one breath left, and you ask Jesus to forgive you and mean it, the Bible says He is faithful and just to do it." Ruthie calmed down at this point, and I took her home.

Before Christmas that year, I asked God to send someone to me with a gift of a ham. I was hungry for ham and I couldn't afford it. God brought us so much food that year that I had to give food away, and He also brought us three hams! Praise God, we had ham for Christmas dinner at Mom's that year.

God just kept blessing me. Just before Christmas, I took my last five dollars to buy a tree for the boys, not knowing how I could ever get them presents. Along with the three hams and the flood of food, people brought so many presents for the boys that they got more than ever before, and we even received almost three hundred dollars in love gifts. We had a great Christmas, only we missed Ed. The other dark spot was my eighteen-year-old baby sister, Ruby, who was married and pregnant. She had a hard pregnancy and had been in and out of the hospital in false labor several times in the last two months before Christmas. We were very concerned about her and the baby. Even with our concern with her, we managed to have a joyous Christmas with the whole family that year.

Christmas was on Sunday that year and we went to church with Mother. After dinner, my nephew Kerry came down with another of his severe headaches (he had suffered with them most of his life). We checked him for fever, but he seemed not to have any, so he just took some more aspirin and laid down.

That evening, Kerry and Jay came to my house to spend a couple of days so Jay could prepare to give his testimony on a radio show. They went to church that night and I could tell Kerry was under conviction. Ed's cousins were visiting too, so we began to share some of the love and miracles we had experienced through our Savior, Jesus Christ.

Kerry had turned around one of my kitchen chairs, and sat with his head laying on top of his arms across the back of the chair saying, "Wow" to all the stories of God's faithfulness— not only to us, but to all mankind, even him. We moved to the front room where I played two songs for him, "Runnin'Away," from the movie sound track for *A Time To Run*, and "I Find No Fault In Him" by Tennessee Ernie Ford. Kerry and Jay went off over those songs and I knew Kerry was absorbing all of it.

The next couple of days, Kerry baby-sat the boys while Jay and I did what we had to do. Jay and Kerry left Tuesday evening, and Kerry hadn't actually made a commitment to Jesus yet. He said he wasn't going to drink anymore and would try to give up drugs. The convicting power of the Holy Spirit was all over him. On Thursday at about two in the afternoon, I was in town at Marie's when I received a phone call from Mom. She said Kerry had been rushed to the hospital in an apparent coma, and asked me to get over there as soon as possible. She was already committed to help Ruby, who was in the hospital again.

Marie and I rushed off to the hospital. When we entered the emergency room, I saw my oldest brother trying to comfort his wife, Betty, who was crying hysterically "My baby, oh God, not my baby!" Lee looked aged beyond his years as he shot me a pleading glance. I went over to Betty and held her as I tried to find out about Kerry. He was in the room with the doctor and that's all we knew.

When the doctor finally came out, he told us they had stabilized Kerry's vitals and were sending him by ambulance to a larger hospital in Fort Wayne, about thirty miles away. Lee and Betty got up as they wheeled Kerry out to the waiting amubulance, and Betty almost collapsed at the sight. There were tubes coming out of Kerry's body everywhere, and it was clear he was still in a coma. I stayed behind long enough to get Kerry's belongings. Then Marie and I started out.

On the way to Fort Wayne, we passed through the small town where Kerry had grown up. I was pretty calm until then, but as we passed through this town, Kerry's spirit overwhelmed me and I could hardly breathe—I felt him tell me goodbye. I started gasping and crying, and Marie asked if she should pull over. I finally regained my composure, but I was still unable to admit that Kerry could be dead or dying. We got to the hospital and wept as the results from the tests started coming in. Kerry had an aneurism of the brain—they would take one more test in the morning and if he still did not have any brain waves, we would have to make a decision concerning life support.

Even though I was screaming inside, I tried not to show it. I knew Lee and Betty were hurting much worse than I was, and they needed my support now more than ever. That was probably one of the first acts of true maturity that I'd ever shown.

Later that evening, Marie and I finally went in to see Kerry. I'll never forget the sight—he was in the same position that I had last seen him in, with his eyes wide open, showing no signs of life. He lay in a bed specially designed to regulate his body temperature.

I picked up his hand, and in the faith that Marie and I had, we began to pray quietly in the natural, but earnestly in the spirit realm. I bound up everything in heaven and earth, and entered into the Holy of Holies before the throne of God.

Remembering that hearing is the last sense to go, I spoke to Kerry in the presence of God, "Kerry, I think you are dying. You need to make peace with God. He is faithful and just to forgive you if you ask him, so I command your spirit right now to return to your body so you can do just that, in the name of Jesus Christ." Then I prayed, "Now, God You have to deal with him. You've promised Mom that none of her seed would be lost."

About then, a doctor and nurse came to Kerry's bed and started frantically working on him, so Marie and I went back out to the waiting room, clearly shaken. We told Lee that someone needed to check on Kerry because something was wrong. Neither Lee or Betty could handle it, so Mom's minister went in.

A few minutes later he came out smiling, saying "He's all right, his vital signs are normal for the first time since he went into the coma." Betty and Lee shed tears of relief, and we took Betty downstairs for a bite of food. As soon as we got our food, they came for us saying Kerry was worse. We rushed back upstairs and began the long night's wait.

The next morning, the doctor took us into a room and told us that Kerry was brain dead and we had to make a choice, to keep him hooked up to machines until his body withered away, or unplug him and let him live or die on his own. The doctor complicated the decision by asking Betty and Lee if they wanted to donate Kerry's kidneys.

Lee told him, "Yes, for my sister Janelle, because she only has one kidney and I hope that someone would do it for her should she ever need one."

I grasped for sanity inside, thinking of the unbelievable sacrifice of love my precious brother and sister-in-law were making on my behalf, as well as for the two young people who would benefit from Kerry's death.

Death could bring life, and somehow that warmed our hearts, knowing that part of our darling Kerry would live on. After we left the room, we scattered different ways to get hold of our emotions. I knew that I had to pull myself together for Lee and Betty—we still had to tell their other four children that their oldest brother had died.

I found a private place and cried out to God to show me why He had not allowed Kerry to live. Immediately, I saw Kerry in the spirit. He was walking up a luscious grassy hill toward a glorious city when he hesitated and turned back toward me. He lifted one of his gangly arms and smiled one of his wonderful smiles as he waved goodbye for the last time. At the same moment, God spoke to my heart and said, "I gave Kerry a choice. Rather than return to earth to live, he chose to come here with Me and I cannot go against his will." Somehow, peace came to me through all the pain and loss.

My youngest brother, Jay, had just lost his best friend and he wanted to be alone. We let him go because we knew that no one but God could touch the kind of grief he was feeling.

I left with Lee and Betty in their van to see their four children, waiting at their home with Valerie and her boyfriend several miles away. Lee's biggest concern was for his wife, Betty. She was overcome with grief for the loss of her first born. I watched from the back of the van as that amazing mother climbed out of her own sorrow in the short time it took to cover those few miles, and turned her love and concern toward her other four children who were anxiously waiting for news of their brother.

As we drove into the yard, four faces poked out of the door as each of them asked the same questions, "Where's Kerry? Is he dead? Please tell us he isn't dead."

They knew the answer by the tears and grief on their parents' faces, and the screams and cries that followed will echo in my heart the rest of my life. Each of us grabbed a child and tried to comfort them, but they were beyond comfort for the next several minutes, so we just tried to be there for them. The children were very close and they just didn't know how to face the sorrow they felt over Kerry's unexpected death.

After the initial shock, Ruthie called me into a bedroom and told me what happened the day before. She said Kerry suddenly slid to the floor by the sofa in excruciating pain, and her mother ran to the phone while her other brother ran to the machine shop at the back of the property. The youngest girl ran down the road to get her older sister at a neighbor's house.

Ruthie was left alone with Kerry as he began shaking violently. Fluid began to flow from his mouth as he tried to tell her to destroy the marijuana he had pulled out of his pant's pocket. She pushed it under the sofa and grabbed him by the shoulders and said, "Kerry, I think you're dying and Aunt Janny said if it's the last thing you do, and you ask God to forgive you and you ask Jesus to come into your heart, He is faithful and just to save you."

Then Ruthie fell into my arms sobbing, saying, "Oh, Aunt Janny, Kerry couldn't talk at all. He could only say 'fo...fo...fo.' " I gently held Ruthie and said, "Honey, in his heart he said forgive me and he's in Heaven with Jesus."

We buried our Kerry on a cold, snowy day in January. The weather was so bad we couldn't have graveside services, so we were forced to wait until later in the year to have a graveside memorial.

On Thursday, just two days later, I was called to the hospital again because my youngest sister, Ruby, was finally having her first baby. I met Mom, Ruby's husband, Bob, and Annie at the waiting room on the maternity floor. Ruby walked around during her early contractions, but was put in bed in the labor room when they became extremely intense.

Mom went with her, along with Bob, as the nurse examined her. Suddenly, I heard Ruby scream out, "Mommy, Daddy, Jesus, someone help me please!" Terrified, I began to pace, sensing something was wrong at this point. After what seemed like an eternity, my small-framed Mom came down the hall, looking pale and gray. I could tell she was about to explode in fear.

I asked her, "Mom, is Ruby all right?" but all she could say was, "I don't know, Janny. I'm so afraid. They are taking Ruby to surgery because the baby is coming bottom first and they don't know if they can save the baby—Ruby is in serious trouble."

We waited on Bob. Then we all went down to the main lobby to wait on the outcome of the surgery. Not knowing if we would be facing two more funerals or not, we prayed. Mom was so upset that the rest of us just tried to act very positive because we were concerned about her health as well. She just buried her oldest grandson and now her and my stepfather's youngest love child was in desperate trouble.

Finally, the doctor came out and Bob literally jumped up to meet him, "How is my baby?" he asked, meaning Ruby. The doctor smiled and said, "You have a baby girl and Ruby is doing just fine too."

Praises, hugs, and gratitude to God followed as we went back upstairs to see our precious little bundle. By that time, Lee and Betty had come in, and they were thankful that we as a family had a new life to celebrate—even in the shadow of burying one of their own. This new little princess named Kim became a special healing balm to all the family, and especially to Mom. Kim was and is truly a gift from God to each of us, as well as a gift back to Him. We sense a greatness in Kim that no one can define. We all just have a knowing that she was created for His glory and our joy, and we look forward to what the Father has in store for her as she grows into maturity.

For myself, the events of the past week only added to the sorrow of the six months before. Once again, the enemy convinced me that my heavenly Father was as uncaring as my childhood depicted. So on Saturday, I called some of my friends from work and said I wanted to go out with them. I told God I was just hurting too bad and I needed arms of flesh to comfort me. We went to a local club and I set out to get drunk, just to get rid of the pain I was in. I hurt so much that I couldn't even cry about it. I started out with hard liquor and finally went to beer, but I couldn't even get a buzz. Finally, I just ordered Pepsi and sat there, knowing that God was not allowing the booze to touch me.

As I sat there in a daze, a man tripped as he walked between the tables and fell right in my lap. He started to apologize, and when he saw who I was, he smiled and said, "I couldn't have timed it better." He had been my insurance man and he was now divorced. When he asked if he could take me home, I said yes.

We began a relationship of some sort. I can't speak for Cory, but I was just looking for arms to hold me and make me feel alive again. I was not going to be a hypocrite, so I seldom went to church. When I did, I never pretended to be right with God, or said anything or prayed out loud. I usually sat there, screaming within my soul asking Jesus to have mercy on me. Cory lived in a trailer, and the children and I went to his place on a few occasions. One time, Terry and Don (Ed's cousin) stopped by and made me feel like a jerk for what I was doing, but I was so numb inside that all I could feel from them was a self-righteous attitude, and that didn't impress me in the least, nor did it do a lot for my new boyfriend.

Cory's arms soon became hollow and empty to me. There wasn't any joy in my heart and I still felt dead inside. I was desperate to "feel something," even if it was wrong. I stayed with Cory through the blizzard of 1978, and he cared for our safety. Then I just sort of encouraged him to date others and just be my friend. It wasn't long before Cory stopped coming around, and that suited me just fine. I had already started repenting and going back to church. I will always be amazed when I think about how God kept on loving me and talking to me when I was in such a terrible backslidden condition. His love overwhelmed me when I realized it wasn't conditional, like all the other loves I had known. Wow, I didn't have to be perfect! His Son Jesus had already been perfect for me.

Somewhere inside my spirit, my new understanding of God's unconditional love brought life back into me. It also gave me a determination to never sin against that kind of love again. I no longer depended on fear to keep me from sin. It was *love* like I'd never known before, a freedom I had never experienced. With His help, I would serve Him with all my strength and all my heart. I was ashamed of letting Jesus down, but I am so glad that I experienced His mighty loving Grace.

The Home Is God's Greatest Workshop

Nearly every twisted thing that happened to me or that I did was somehow tied to my early life in the home, or to family relationships gone wrong. I think that's true for many of us. It's no surprise that the enemy attacks the home and family relationships so viciously, and it should be no surprise that God cares passionately about our lives at home with our families.

God brought a "settling" to my life once I submitted to Him. I was still human, with all the weaknesses and failings that come with the package, but God was still God too! He began to build a foundation in and around me that created peace.

The fast-paced life style I lived with drugs and witchcraft was now gone. Rather than trying to shove my children out of the way so I could have fun, I found myself learning how to be a real mother to my children. I learned how to love them more than myself.

As the Word of God began to dwell in me, I became an asset to my family, no longer a burden. As a single parent, I learned to rely on God. I was the only authority in a house with three healthy boys, and it was God who helped me create an atmosphere that offered some kind of security and stability for my sons. God knows it sure wasn't there before He rescued me!

God restored my relationship with my Mother too. Mom no longer had to go to her knees in prayer for her wayward daughter. I could now with her share my love for the same Lord she dearly loved and served. A special bond began to form that couldn't have existed if I had not been saved.

In time, I learned what it was to have a home, and a normal life. I had much to learn, and there were times of frustration and questioning. I didn't always handle my problems perfectly, as you have read in this chapter.

Through it all, the personal presence of Jesus was overwhelming to me. I even sensed angelic beings surrounding me even while I slept. For the first time in my troubled and tormented life, I knew what it was to dwell in peace, to sleep in peace, to raise my family in peace.

God began to show me why I have always been sensitive to the spirit realm. On many nights, I would be awakened to pray for people I barely knew. I look back on many of those strange situations and I'm thankful for the child-like trust in Him which He has given me.

Because of the strange manifestations of God's Spirit in my life, I have often been misunderstood by others in the Body of Christ, yet I had to obey His promptings. For more than four-and-a-half years, people came in and out of my home for Bible study, salvation, healing and deliverance from all kinds of bondages.

I have tried to obey my Savior, no matter what the cost. I have fallen in love with my Savior, and there is no turning back. If you have this same attitude, you will be free for life. You will see a new level of peace, joy and fulfillment permeate your life, your home and your family. If you have fallen in love with your Savior, there is no need to turn back to your past.

Chapter Ten

Divorce, Death and God's Provision

Once I made the decision never to look back to the things of the world and my past, God brought a healing to my emotions, especially concerning my control over sexual desires. I didn't realize that even in this, He was preparing me for challenges and opportunities I would face in the coming years.

My taste for new challenges was still occasionally running ahead of my ability to handle them. One day I decided to try my hand at tennis, so I signed up for lessons—and injured my back during the very first session! I was on sick leave for five-and-a-half months under a doctor's care. During this time, I relaxed and read my Bible as I listened to Christian music.

Ed's cousin, Don, found me an old Chevy and gave it to me. It ran and that was what counted. One Sunday, I got into my car to go to church and heard a funny hissing sound. I got out and stood there, watching in amazement as my tire went flat.

After that, I had eleven flat tires in the next three months, and the mechanics could never find a reason for it. In fact, one time I had just had brand new tires put on and they went flat! It got so bad that every time I called Marie, she would say, "Where are you stuck at now? I'll come and get you."

I was embarrassed and it didn't seem too funny to me; I knew that it was a form of harassment from the enemy. I was coming home from the grocery store with the boys once when we had a flat on one of the country roads. There were tornado warnings out and we were stuck in a horrible storm. I cried out to God for strength, and each time I pulled a scripture card out of my "daily bread" box, it said, "My grace is sufficient for you." One day I was so frustrated I threw the card across the room and cried out to God, "I don't need grace—I need food, money, a decent car, and yes, I still want Ed back."

I was pulling out of my driveway to go to church on a Sunday night when I had yet another flat tire. In total despair, I jumped out of the car, ready to get angry, when all of a sudden I remembered the preacher's message that morning, "Give thanks in all things, for that is the will of God."

I began to praise Him for the fact that I had a spare. I got out, jacked the car up (by now I was quite good at changing tires), and watched the last of the air hiss out of the tire. I still managed to praise God somehow, even when our litter of six-week-old puppies began to jump on me as I tried to get the tire off.

I'd made up my mind to give my God a sacrifice of praise, even if it was through clenched teeth! I finally got the spare on and let down the jack. Then I watched in horror as the spare sank flat to the ground! All my patience was gone. I just stood in the rain with puppy paw prints all up and down my back, and screamed my lungs out in anger to God about the situation, and about Ed leaving me in such need.

After I'd finally spent my anger, I walked in the rain about a half mile to our neighbor's house to call someone for help— they weren't home. Every fiber in my being was screaming, "Give up God, He doesn't love you," but I had no one else to run to but Him. I spent the rest of the year surviving and constantly hoping Ed would return. One evening, I found out that Ed was at his mother's with his girlfriend, and I decided to go over there to see for myself if he still cared at all for me. I also wanted to get a wedding ring back. It was part of our matched set, with crosses on them. We'd had them blessed by a Catholic priest and I felt they were holy and represented a lasting bond between us.

When I walked into the house, to my dismay I saw a lovely young woman sitting on the sofa wearing Ed's wedding band (the one that matched mine) as a "going steady ring." I looked Ed straight in the eye and demanded the ring, and he began to punch me in the chest with his finger and ordering me out of his mother's house.

I couldn't hold back the tears any longer, but I was determined to get the ring. Finally, his girlfriend said, "Ed, just let her have it. It doesn't mean anything to me. After all, I've got you." She gave him the ring, and he threw it at me and said, "Now get out of here before I make you sorry you ever came! I hate you, do you hear me? I don't ever want you showing your face around me again! Matter of fact, if you see me some place that you are heading for, you better turn around and go some place else, is that understood?"

I walked out in tears, realizing that I had truly lost him. I knew I should really try to get over him. At least now I could live without the heartache.

That summer, I went to a jeweler and sold all my gold rings for next to nothing to pay a bill and buy food for us all. A few months later, I had to sell off the antiques I had been given for the same reason, and again, I knew I was "getting took." I felt like I was at the mercy of everyone.

I went back to work and decided to try to stay around people I knew were Christians. At one point, we even started a Bible study at work, but we were forced to shut it down because people were offended by us. I was sure Jesus was coming soon. Ed filed for divorce, and I realized if I wanted to end up with anything, I would have to go against my own beliefs and cross file for the children's sake. That day in court was humiliating. Ed's lawyer asked him, "Did you buy a motorcycle?" When Ed said yes, the lawyer asked, "And what happened to this motorcycle?" Ed said, "I sold it." And then the lawyer asked his "punch line" question, "And what did you do with the money, Ed?" Ed answered with the line that was repeated many times that day, "I paid bills."

The second series of questions mimicked the first ones. Ed's lawyer asked, "Did you buy an antique gun?" Ed replied, "Yes I did." And once again the lawyer asked, "What did you do with the money?" Again, the damning punch line was delivered as Ed said, "I paid bills."

The handwriting was on the wall, and I was too shocked to realize it until we left with our divorce decree. No one asked me how Ed got the money for the motorcycle and gun— *I was still paying for them through my credit union.*

Again, I heard that inner scream of pain that always seemed to be lodged deep within me, the scream no one ever seemed to hear, crying, "It's not fair! It's just not fair!"

I left the courthouse and went directly to Marie's house. I came through the door and just looked at her, feeling sort of numb, when she grabbed me and took me into the front room. Leading me toward the stereo, she said, "God told me to play this song for you." I tried unsuccessfully to tell her I was just fine, and I wasn't bothered by the day's events. Marie, as usual, wouldn't let me skip out on her when she had heard from God.

I gave in and put on head phones as she set the phonograph needle and the song started. I heard Andrea Crouch start singing, and I suddenly broke, sobbing at the words of his song. He was singing, "God, I thought I'd given you my all, until I heard you ask for more." The Spirit of God reminded me that I was one of those described in Luke 12:48 where Jesus said "to whom much is given much would be required" (my paraphrase). I knew much had been given for my life. With a new perspective, I was able to let hope overtake the doubt once more, and I knew I would carry the cross proudly.

It was hard for me to face the boys with the news of the divorce. I knew how hurt and disappointed they were that Ed had left and never looked back at them. They had experienced so many devastating things in their lives that my heart broke as I told them Ed would never be back. Outwardly, they acted like it didn't bother them, but I knew that they had learned a long time ago to take care of their emotionally tormented mother, so they probably wouldn't show me how they really felt anyway. They were becoming just what I never wanted them to become—victims of my life. There were many nights when I didn't go to bed, I just prayed all night that tomorrow would not come. I figured it would be full of nothing but sorrow and problems that I didn't need. (I'm thankful that God is bigger and wiser than our circumstances, and that He doesn't answer our every prayer just because we think it's what we need. Otherwise, you wouldn't be reading this book and I wouldn't have been around to write it.)

That spring, the landlord asked me to move so he could improve the house and raise the rent. I felt that wasn't the real reason—he knew Ed wasn't coming back, and he didn't want the responsibility of a single mother with three children to worry over.

Fear almost sent me to the hospital. I didn't know what in this world I was going to do. I could barely afford to live, let alone rent some place with all the added expenses of a security deposit and fees to turn on the utilities. I had never faced responsibility very well, even with a husband, and now I felt like a scatterbrain, not knowing what to do and who to go to for help. Someone told me the government would build me a house if I met certain requirements. I had nothing to lose, so I talked with a man at the agency, not for one moment believing that I really had a chance to get a house. My credit wasn't that great and my income was really depressing. To my amazement, my application was accepted and the government agreed to build us a home! I even got to pick out the design and the colors I wanted inside and out. Even that presented a challenge to me: "wow, I had choices to make!" It was an exciting yet scary time for me because my decisions were hardly ever right up to that point in my life. The big catch in the deal was it would take them five or six months to complete the house, and I had no place to go. We had to split up for a while. My oldest son, who was always playing the "Mommy, I am the oldest" part, took it upon himself to be the one to stay with his Daddy, who was now married with two more children, and lived out in the country.

My firstborn felt he was stronger than the others and they needed to be with me more than he did, so he decided he would be the one to suffer the separation. I thought I couldn't take another day of heartbreak the day we moved, but with the help of Marie and some of our friends, we packed our belongings and put them in storage. I divided the two younger boys and myself between my parents and Marie's.

One day at Marie's, my oldest son stopped by after school to visit with me. As he walked through the kitchen where Marie's kids were playing games with my two other boys, they all began to mock him and say cutting remarks like, "What are you doing here? You aren't supposed to be here!"

My heart broke for him as he just kept on walking toward me with a smile on his face, "acting" like their remarks didn't faze him. Finally, Marie came into the room and I shared my concern for my son with her. I didn't realize the tension we were all under, but she said something that hurt me further and I accused her of not loving my son. After that, everything exploded into a bad scene, with Marie leaving and me packing up and moving in with my parents. My stepdad was older and most of the time he didn't feel well. He had very bad nerves and I was afraid that the boys would bother him, so I felt like I was walking on eggshells most of the time, trying to juggle everyone's emotions and moods. We stayed in the back bedroom, and the boys slept with me or on the floor beside me. They could have slept in the other room, but they just wouldn't leave me and I didn't want them to either. The best part of the arrangement was that my oldest son could come stay with me anytime he wanted to.

Dad and Mom were good to us during those difficult months, and they took extra care not to hurt me or the boys any more than we had already suffered.

Marie and I could never stay mad at one another very long, so it wasn't long before we were drinking coffee together again. She and I went to our house during the construction phase and anointed it with oil from the foundation up.

Sometimes I took the boys over there just to keep us mindful that we did indeed have a place we could call home soon. I would often drive to the construction site and just cry because I missed my son and my own home so much. I feared I would go insane with hurt. "Why was I born to a life that had such upheaval all the time?" I'd ask. "Was God mad at me?" One evening after work, Marie told me that the youngest brother of my old flame, Rob, had hung himself in his jail cell. No one knew why he did it; he was a good-looking teenager who was in jail for a minor offence.

The first thought I had was for Rob, and I asked Marie, "How is Rob doing? Have you heard from him"? Marie said, "No, but we are going to the funeral home tonight if you want to go with us."

As we entered the funeral home, Rob saw us and came right to us, crying and hugging us to him, grateful that we were there. I felt like an emotional wreck. The old feelings of intense love resurfaced that I thought were gone. It was as if we were still with each other. I was pretty sure he didn't share the same feelings about me, so I just went on my way.

However, when I returned home, I went directly to the phone and called my spiritual mother, Carla, and started crying on her shoulder about my hurt and fear of still being in love with this man. She prayed and talked with me for hours, encouraging me and lifting me back up where God wanted me. Carla sounded raspy, so I asked, "Do you have that sore throat again?" She said, "No, in Jesus' name," and then we said goodbye.

The next day at work, I told another friend, Jackie, about talking to Carla and how bad she sounded. Jackie looked at me funny and said, "Didn't you know that Carla has cancer? She will die if the Lord doesn't intervene." I was so shocked I almost fell off the chair, and I cried "No!" so loudly that everybody looked around to see what was wrong with me. After work, I headed straight for Carla's house trailer. When I came in, I saw her sitting at the kitchen table in a beautiful robe with her blonde hair done perfectly. She had that same sparkle in her eyes as she smiled and asked how I was doing. I talked to her as she sat with her head hung over a saucepan of hot water laced with Vick's salve, trying to breathe. Somehow I knew that the night before, when she was so loving to me, that she was probably suffering with every breath she took, just as she was now. I felt totally ashamed of my self-centered conversation the night before. I learned that Carla had been fighting breast cancer for over a year and was trusting in God for her healing. She was going to a doctor, but refused to take any treatment or have surgery because she believed God was going to heal her. I remember the time I was talking with Carla and her husband, Mick, when Angie came to the door. Angie was one of my best friends and a professional hairdresser. She came to see to Carla's hair. As soon as she sat down at the table we started to pray in unison for Carla's healing.

I asked the Holy Spirit to come in and minister to Carla, and at that instant, an explosion of wind inside the trailer popped the windows open and an eerie howling started. We each felt the presence of the Holy Spirit so strongly that it sent us to our knees in awe of the moment—we didn't know what might happen in the next few moments.

Angie fell to her knees, layed her hands on Carla's feet and began to pray at the same time I put my hands on Carla's head—we fully expected to see the manifestation of her total healing. Nothing happened at that moment, other then Carla getting total peace and strength, but we knew that God had heard our prayers and we waited on His will.

After that evening, I couldn't stay away from Carla and Mick's trailer. Later that week, Carla told me that if I would bring my cigarettes to her house, she would pray for my deliverance from smoking and God would heal me and deliver me from even the desire to smoke.

On a Thursday evening, Marie and I went to see her. I confess that I smoked and smoked all day long—I was a driven woman determined to smoke all I could. I even bought an off-brand of cigarettes because I didn't have the heart to tear up my favorite brand. I only had three cigarettes left in the pack by the time I got to Carla's, and I only half-expected to walk out of there healed and set free. That was because I only half-way wanted to really give them up, and God knew it.

Carla had me kneel in front of her and tear up what was left of the pack of cigarettes. Then she asked God to heal and forgive me for harming my body, His temple. All of a sudden, I found myself agreeing with her from the heart, and it didn't take long for me to realize that God had set me free—I just "knew that I knew" I was healed.

Then Carla turned to Marie and asked her if she needed prayer, and Marie said, "Yes, for my back." Carla reached up from where she sat on the sofa and laid her hand on Marie's head, anointed her with oil and began to pray for her healing. Suddenly, Marie was knocked completely off her feet and landed on the floor in a sitting position. Marie was so touched by God that she couldn't do anything but laugh, lost in wonderment and love. Yes, she was healed.

We left that night praising God and fully believing that God would heal Carla, just as He had healed us through her. But in a few days, I found out she had entered the hospital. I hurried out to the hospital to see her, and when I entered her room, I saw her sitting alone in a wheelchair with her head hanging down. She raised her head and looked at me with those wonderful big blue eyes and never flinched when I asked her, "What are you doing in here, girl?"

Carla softly whispered the answer she motioned upward with her head, "Ask the Father," and then her head dropped back down. I sat beside her and began to talk all the faith talk I knew. A couple of days later, Carla was in a sitting position with oxygen tubes in her nose, and I could tell she was much worse. I knew that if God didn't do something fast, we would be saying our goodbyes to our dear sweet Carla soon. My friend Angie had spent the night with her, and she said Carla had fought demonic powers all night, seeing things that were not of the natural realm. She also said Carla had prayed for several nurses during the night for their healing and salvation. What a witness she was for Christ, never thinking of her own need—only the needs of others!

All that day, she sat in that bed trying to breathe. At times, she would begin to hyperventilate and Mick would remind her, "Carla, breathe through your nose and blow the air out of your mouth." She'd take in a big breath of air and hold it as she looked around the room at everyone there until her eyes met mine and then she would smile and blow the air at me. It seemed as if she was giving me something precious, with each gust of air. On several occasions, I moved different places in the room just to see if I was making something out of nothing, but she always found me.

Finally, I left to check on my sons at Marie and Terry's house. Just a short time later, someone called to say Carla wasn't doing too well, but I already knew that. I had just left her, but something inside told me to get back to the hospital immediately. As I stepped off the elevator, they told me she was going fast, and I hurried to her room.

When I entered the room, Carla was lying flat in her bed, gasping for her last breath. I gently kissed her on the forehead and cried softly, as I said, "Go to Him, beloved, the man called Jesus that you have waited to see, and tell Him I love Him—your Bridegroom cometh." Then I left her room and went into the waiting room. I just sat and listened as some of the others told how Carla had been sitting there trying to breathe, when all of a sudden she sat straight up in bed and looked up into Heaven and said, "Oh my God, my Savior!" After that, she simply fell back on the bed in a coma.

I sat with tears streaming down my face, not in sorrow but total joy, knowing our sweet, dear Carla had seen her Bridegroom coming for her. Mick came in about that time and said "She is gone." (I'll see you later, Carla, in Jesus' name.)

A few days after her funeral, I went out to the trailer to say goodbye to her best friend, Betty, who would be leaving for home the next day. Mick and his son were sitting with Betty at the table, reminiscing about old times with Carla and how very special she was to so many.

Betty wanted the coat that Carla wore, since she had bought it for her to wear in the ministry she was in. It was a black coat with a sable collar, and Carla had loved that coat and cared for it carefully. She'd had a very rough time of it before marrying Mick.

As they sat there, Betty suddenly changed her mind and said, "I feel like Carla would want me to give the coat to you, Janelle." I almost fell off the chair because I knew what that coat represented to Betty.

I protested, but the three of them felt it was God's will. Then Mick went into the bedroom and brought out a box. As he held it, he said, "Carla never bought anything foolishly in her life, but she saw this and couldn't resist it. I feel she would want you to have it too, Janelle." He gave me the box, and in it was a magnificent felt hat with a long feather in the head-band. I didn't know what to say, except thank you.

Then Mick went back into the bedroom and returned with a box of shoes and said, "I want you to have these also. Maybe some of them will fit."

When I got home, I started crying and told God, "If I didn't know any better, I would think that Carla was handing down her mantle to me. Lord, if they would have given me her gloves, I would really believe that's what has happened."

Several days later, I took the coat out of the closet and guess what—Carla's gloves were in the pocket. I don't know how it all happened, but I knew God had ordained something I was not yet to know.

Have You Failed God? Do You Feel Life Is Hopeless?

Thousands of Christians like you and me discover every week that they can still make mistakes, feel pain and suffer hardships—even after they have received Jesus Christ as Lord and Savior.

Our "valley experiences" make us appreciate those times when we make it to the mountain top. Through all of my disappointments, I learned that God never let me get to the place where I would totally give in or give up. I look back at the painful memories of the times I lost loved ones, and I know I can rejoice that these loved ones belong to the same Jesus I serve. It was through the valley experiences that I learned much about sorrow and restoration.

I learned about death through my experience with Carla at the hospital. When she passed away with cancer, she didn't leave this earth empty or wanton—she had a Savior waiting for her. After she closed her eyes, her last breath sent her into the very arms of Jesus Himself, to behold beauty and glory unimagined by the human mind.

Even while I hurt because I knew I would never again look into Carla's beautiful blue eyes on this earth, I was comforted by knowing that my life had been deeply touched by this godly woman. And somewhere in the quietness of my mind, I heard the words, "Death is swallowed up in victory!"

Through Carla's death I learned that even in death, we need not fear.

It was through struggle and hardship that I learned that my God actually delights in taking care of my needs and watching over me. God's goodness has been overwhelming at times, as He saw to it that my needs were more than met—thanks to my heavenly Father, I had the privilege of becoming a bona fide homeowner.

While I was struggling to raise three sons alone, as a single mother, I discovered that God was clearing the path and making the crooked places straight—in me as well as in my circumstances.

As I learned by following the Master, even as I stumbled and fell, as I was lifted up by the Holy Spirit, I found a new strength being poured into me, and my faith began to soar. I even found I could have faith for others as well as myself. God had ignited a spark in me that could not be extinguished. I was growing and quickly becoming a woman of God—leaving the tell-tale signs of the past with its hurts, failures and shame far behind.

I've written this chapter to illustrate how human I am, and how loving our God is. He knew I'd reach the point where I'd stand in the rain with a litter of puppies, shaking my fist in anger and ask Him why my tires always went flat. He also knew I'd write these words for you....

Never underestimate God's love or His ability to salvage the people He loves—His eye and His love are upon you this moment.

Chapter Eleven

Discipleship: Learning to Overcome

Our new house was finally finished just before Thanksgiving, and Marie and some friends moved us in as we joyously praised God for His good gift to the children and me. Even some of the church people stopped by to share in our joy. We were so excited that first night in our brand new home that I doubt if we could have slept had we not been so tired from moving all day. That Thanksgiving and Christmas were equally wonderful for us. I managed to get off to a bad start though. While the boys were at their grandparents' on Christmas Eve, I just drove around the town looking at all the cars parked in front of home after home, and I began to cry out of sheer loneliness. I stopped at a friend's house to share in their family's time of closeness, only to return home in tears.

It didn't take long for me to change my attitude once I got home. I looked around at what the Lord had done, played some Christmas music on the stereo and started baking cookies. The boys soon came home and we had a party of our own as we baked cookies together and played games.

A few months later, our pastor was exposed and dismissed for committing adultery with several women in our congregation, including some of my friends. I was shocked—I had been raised to believe the pastorate was sacred and pastors were next to God (and almost as perfect). The pastor's wife was Marie's best friend, and I felt she was becoming one of mine too, so the evidence broke our hearts. Marie was so broken I couldn't even help her. We just sat and cried together.

We suffered through the pastor's resignation and Marie and Terry, along with others, helped them move. The loss was great to us, and it became even greater as we watched many of the congregation leave over it all.

People at work asked me if I had been one of the pastor's many conquests, and if I knew how many he had. They called him Jim Jones and taunted me as they mocked Christianity until I wanted to crawl under the table. Our church became the laughing stock of the whole town, and it was hard to take because I had become very involved in all aspects of the church.

I was a young Christian just delivered from demonic insanity, never knowing just what might happen next, yet never able to give up on my salvation experience. Everyone kept telling me that trials come only to make us strong. Well, I didn't want to be strong—I wanted peace and security.

I had just left hell as a non-Christian and here I was in a church with big problems. If this was a joke, I wasn't laughing. Things just kept getting stranger, and every day, I thought I couldn't take one more thing. But troubles just kept coming. Just when I thought that surely it couldn't get any worse, it did.

Things finally got to me and I went to my doctor to see if he could give me any insight or solutions to this problem. He just put me in a private hospital isolated on a long corridor of a new wing. He said that I was suffering from nervous exhaustion and needed to get away and rest where I wouldn't be bothered. He even put a no visitor sign on my door. (I could see family members, but only the ones I wanted to see.)

I'd settled down in my hospital room when my sisters came in to tell me Aunt Helena was in a room directly above mine. She had suffered a heart attack and they didn't expect her to live. My heart broke for her, and I asked my sisters if I could see her. I noticed that they seemed a little embarrassed, but I thought it was because of their concern for my well being. Later that day, my cousin Wheezie, Aunt Helena's adopted daughter, came to see me and she was acting strangely too. Finally she looked at me and told me what was going on.

The year before, God showed me I had bitterness and unforgiveness toward Aunt Helena, and He wanted me to apologize to her for it. I remember screaming that it wasn't fair—after all, she had been the one that had done so much damage to me. I wasn't guilty of anything but loving her...I even reminded Him that I was the one who took care of her when she was sick. All I heard in response was silence. I always hate it when God is silent because I know He is always right...it isn't necessary for Him to argue with us.

Finally I halfheartedly said, "Okay God, if You want me to, I will apologize, but you will have to set it up. She lives in another town that is too far away to get to." I felt real safe at that point, but I started to get concerned when Mom told me Aunt Helena had moved to her son's farm and was living in a trailer they had purchased for her. Now she was only about ten miles from my Mom and Dad's house.

I began to just put it out of my mind. Several months later on Mother's Day, the boys and I went to church with Mom in the town where I had been raised as a child. No sooner had I slipped into the church than I saw Aunt Helena sitting there. I walked up and gave her a kiss on the cheek, and we sat down. I couldn't believe she was there. She never went to Mom's church.

The Lord began to work on my memory and heart. I had nearly forgotten my promise to Him concerning my aunt. During the service, I said to God, "If You want me to talk to her, then let her go to Mom's and have coffee and I will know that this is the right time." I had already heard Aunt Helena tell Mom she was going to her son's house for dinner, so I figured I was safe. I helped her take her flowers out to the car after the service and hugged her, saying, "I love you, Aunt Helena." To my dismay, she told me she was going to drop something off at Mom's, but she couldn't come in or stay. I was relieved.

When we got to Mom's, my aunt started to get out of the car, and I thought, what is going on? When she said, "I have time for one cup of coffee, and I need to ask you something, Janny." I was horror-stricken. I made my way to the house, feeling as I had as a little girl, with fear overtaking all sanity once more.

Once we were settled at the table with our coffee, she look at me sternly and said, "Janny, you haven't come to see me, and God had shown me that you have something against me. I want to clear the air, now."

As I felt my body begin to shake, I summoned all the strength I had, and told her how much she hurt me. Then I asked her to forgive me for holding bitterness and unforgiveness toward her. I told her how afraid I had been of the cat-o-nine tails she had. At this point, she couldn't even remember having it, and said she would never have used such a thing on us.

Mom sat down at the table and spoke up, "Helena, you did have a cat-o-nine tails, don't you remember?" That was all that saved me that day. Mom finally stuck up for me to my aunt. Mom didn't remember all the abuse I had described, but she agreed that I knew what I was talking about, and that was a glorious feeling.

My aunt sat there, stunned that I could ever believe she hated me, or that I had anything to fear from her as a child. In her hurt, she said, "After all, didn't I take you in when no one else wanted to help you?"

Suddenly, I realized I was standing between Mom's stove and the cabinet with my hands clenched tightly to each of them, my back against the wall. I began to sob uncontrollably as I said, "See, Aunt Helena? I'm thirty-seven years old now, and look how afraid I still am of you and your disapproval of me!"

She looked at me sternly and said, "Janny, I don't remember ever doing those things to you, but I accept your apology and I'm sorry that you don't think I love you, because I do. I really do." I told her I really did believe she loved me. Then I said, "I'm sorry if all this has hurt you, Aunt Helena, because I love you dearly."

She left a short time later and I truly thought all was well, and I hoped that she and I might have a new relationship one day soon. Now it looked like that time would never come—she was now dying in the room above me.

My cousin told me that after our conversation that Sunday at Mom's, Aunt Helena went to her son's house in tears. She said I had hurt her badly by saying how much I hated her. Supposedly, she didn't stop there; she told all her kids how cruel I was. Now they were telling me she wouldn't want to see me, and that she would flinch at the mere mention of my name.

I had no idea Aunt Helena was so hurt and felt so badly toward me until that moment in the hospital. I'm thankful that Glendon came to visit me though. He was one of Aunt Helena's sons who lived in another state. He was very sweet to me and I will ever be grateful to him. I found out Mom was staying in Aunt Helena's room most of the time. When she only came down to see me twice that week for only a few minutes, I figured she was on their side also. (So much for nervous exhaustion—now I was just plain nuts.)

Aunt Helena died and I cried for the loss. I was to be released the day of her funeral, but I had been warned that I should not, under any circumstances, show up for her funeral.

My sisters picked me up early that morning and slipped me into the funeral home to pay my respects to my aunt, while they watched at the door for any family members. I stood alone and silent over the coffin, wondering how I could have proven my love to this woman. I had loved her in spite of the abuse and fear; after all, she had been there through my formative years and was like a second mother in some ways. With hot tears flowing down my face, I said my good-byes and left.

Why are abused children or adults who dare to reveal their torment and tormentors regarded as whiners and pity-seekers? Why do we feel guilty for telling others about our pain when the guilt should fall on the person(s) causing the pain? Why do the abusers sleep at night, free from guilt, while the victims beat themselves to death for their "sins?"

I have never figured out why truth hurts people so badly that they will believe a lie—even if the innocent little ones must pay the cost of their denial.

As I stood before my aunt's coffin, it seemed like everyone in my life who ever hurt me sexually or physically were supposed to go free, but I was never to talk about it or tell the truth at their expense. "Well, what about me?!" I cried out, "what about the cost I paid to survive: a life full of nightmares and emotional upheaval on every breaking wave of reality!"

Perhaps my past made me want to help others like me. After much prayer, I opened up my home for prayer meetings on Friday nights. Thirty-eight people showed up for the first meeting. There were people everywhere, in the kitchen, down the hall and in the laundry room as well as the front room. No one talked. We just prayed, and if anyone had to leave, they just slipped out quietly. Sometimes a few people stayed to pray after that, and often the house was full of people praying. During the trouble at church, I was grateful for the fellowship of the people at the prayer meetings. Most of them didn't go to my church and they ministered healing to me. Carla's husband, Mick, had become a very dear friend to me since her death. He was always there to talk to me on the telephone or in person, no matter what time of the day or night. He was my friend and mentor.

During the prayer meetings, we saw people come into my home sick and leave well. Some came in possessed and left saved, as new creations in Jesus Christ. Total strangers came to my house for ministry, and I don't know who they were or where they came from them to this day. It was a miraculous time.

Once a Jewish lady came in to give each of us a message from the Lord and left—I think she was an angel. On many occasions, several of us prayed half the night away, and as the last people left, we would stand outside the house talking, not wanting to separate.

On several occasions, I looked up in the sky and literally saw angels flying away from the house. They were transparent but visible, and without forethought of what my friends would think, I would say, "Look, there go the angels we have sent to make war on the enemy." My friends looked at one another, and then looked at the sky in puzzlement at my words, when all at once, they too would see them flying away and stand in awe at the sight.

One time during a church service, I saw an angel hovering prostrate in the air over two of my dearest friends, and facing the podium where the pastor and three other men were singing. I didn't say anything to anyone about it, though, because the people already thought I was weird. (The pastor would introduce me by saying, "This is Janelle, strange but nice.")

That afternoon, I felt impressed that Jesus wanted me to share the experience with Marie, but I needed to clean my house. After getting the house in order, I felt so relaxed that I decided to stay alone and enjoy the afternoon in my nice clean house. I made a cup of coffee and started down the hallway to my bedroom—fully aware that I had no plans to call Marie or go see her. (After all, I reasoned, she always rests on Sunday afternoons and she's probably asleep.)

No sooner had I started down the hall than someone rang the doorbell and walked in the door. I turned to see Marie in her house slippers as she said, "I just thought I would do something different today, and I was bored anyway, so I thought I would come over to see you and have a cup of coffee." I just stood there in amazement—I had heard from God and He was making sure I was not a disobedient child.

We took our coffee and went back to my bedroom to be alone and talk, and I began to tell her what I had seen that morning in church. To my surprise, she believed me and became very excited. I sat there amazed as she told me she had heard high-pitched singing while the men were singing. Now I didn't tell Marie *when* I had seen the angel, only where it was positioned. Her perception of the heavenly music at the same time the pastor and the three men sang coincided perfectly and independently with what I saw.

When we realized that our church had a visitation from an angel, it was almost more than we could comprehend. That evening as we entered the church, Marie and I shared our experience with one of the men of the church and she decided to give a testimony about it during the service. (That was okay by me. Our church was conservative on many issues and I was tired of being thought of as weird. Besides that, Marie and Terry had a good reputation with the people there).

As Marie began to share the details about the angel I saw and the music she heard, one of the older ladies cried out, "I heard it too! I was down in the nursery and I heard it through the intercom. I wondered what woman with that lovely high voice was singing with the men." The church was stunned, unable to fully comprehend the situation. Some of them got very excited about what had happened, and one dear lady went home and wrote a poem about it. I knew I was different. I just didn't know how or why. I wanted to be a part of all of them, but I always felt like they held me at arm's length. Marie told me that I should be careful about telling other people the things I saw in the Spirit—it just scared people too much. I told her I would try, but it would be hard, because I couldn't distinguish between normal and strange. The life I had was always strange compared to everyone else's that I knew. What was normal?

God had a special work He wanted to do in me, and he used a man who came into the church to conduct Bible college classes. He was the founder of a Bible institute that held classes around our state wherever a door was opened and an interest was shown. Our church purchased a monastery from the Catholic church and now we had more than enough room for our own needs. The church made it a practice to rent out rooms for various retreats and meetings, and that is how this institute began meeting in our church.

About fifteen people attended classes at the institute, including me. I learned more from that man than I knew was possible to know about the Word and the ways of God. I learned that the closer you get to God, the stranger you will seem to man. He taught us that "strange" was all right as long as you could back it up with the Word of God and remain balanced in what you did. He taught a class on memory healing that took me through a valley of despair, but by the time we finished it, I had a deeper understanding and more wisdom about all I had been through than any psychiatrist ever showed me. I was healed in places I didn't even know or understand I needed healing in.

I spent two years at the institute, learning things about the major and minor prophets, and taking in-depth surveys of the Old and New Testaments. There was such in-depth learning and rich fellowship there, that I can honestly say I've never been the same since that time.

Invisibly, almost overnight, it seemed the Lord began giving me my orders. I was becoming a servant of the Lord. I wasn't in any recognized ministry, yet the Lord began sending people my way who were in need of healing or deliverance, or sometimes, just in need of love.

Although I had serious moments of doubt when I would question whether God could really use me, I was learning that the pain and abuse I suffered as a child gave me the ability to relate to countless hundreds of others who had been hurt and abused as well.

Every time I attended meetings outside my church featuring guest preachers or speakers—whether I was buried in a crowd of fifty or three thousand people—they always seemed to pull me out of the crowd and give me a message from the Lord.

After a while, I tried to ignore them by not making eye contact with them. I would even hang my head down, as if I was reading my Bible, but they always had something to say to me about me being special. Time and again I was told that God was doing something in me that I could not yet see, or that a great mystery was unfolding in my life and someday I would understand why things happened to me as they had. I still didn't care about being special—I just wanted to be "normal."

During the next year or so, I started having dreams that would come true, and sometimes I saw things in others that would end up being true—things that no one else could see.

Even Marie was beginning to wonder about me. I started having a recurring dream about a boy named Kirk who played on my son's farm league team. I hadn't seen him for several years, but then within two months, I ran into him several times. He was a wonderful young man from a good Christian family who seemed to have everything going for him.

He had long blonde (almost white) hair, beautiful blue eyes and a great personality. I couldn't understand why I was being awakened nightly to pray for him. When I went to sleep, his face would zoom in at me, causing me to sit straight up in bed. I would get out of bed and pray for him until I fell asleep on my knees. This went on for a couple of months without me thinking anything of it except that I was called to pray for him.

One day I went to Terry and Marie's, but I couldn't enjoy the fellowship because my spirit was alive with urgency that day—I didn't know whether I was under demonic attack or losing my mind or what! I didn't say a word to anyone there, but I was screaming inside because it felt like total chaos was overtaking my mind and emotions. Finally, the phone rang and it was for me. It was Mona. I took the phone and pulled it out of earshot of everyone there, said hello, and began to cry. Mona asked "What is wrong?" and I couldn't even talk. I just started mumbling something like, "I don't know. I think the demons are back inside me. I'm so scared." Mona had heard enough, and said, "I'm coming after you now, okay?"

I hung up the phone and slipped out the back door to wait. I began to realize how odd this day had been. I couldn't stop praying—even though I had no idea who or what I was praying for; and Mona had called me out of nowhere, and she had never called me at any of my friends' houses before for fear of bothering me. It just seemed strange, but then again I guess normality has never been part of my life. I didn't have to wait on Mona for long. As I slipped into her car, she said, "You look awful. What is going on"? I looked at her and said, "I don't know, but you've just got to help me—please." She said, "Where do you want to go?" and the only person I could think of who might be able to help me was Mick, so I said, "Mick. Hurry! Get to Mick's house."

By the time we got to Mick's trailer, I was sobbing and crying. Mick took one look at me and asked Mona, "What in the world has happened to Janelle?" All Mona could say was, "I don't know. She was like this when I picked her up—she asked me to bring her here to you."

Mick cleared off the coffee table and said, "Kneel down. We better pray." We had only prayed a few minutes when we were interrupted by the phone. Apologetically, Mick answered the phone. All I heard him say was, "Hello. Oh no, Sister Laura—how are John and Judy doing?"

That was all it took. I knew something horrible had happened and somehow it involved Kirk. I began to scream, "Kirk, oh God, not Kirk!" Even though I barely knew John and Judy, I knew they had four children, and one of them was Kirk. Somehow, I also knew who Mick was referring to on the phone—Kirk was dying or dead.

I turned to First John 5:16 where it says, "If any man see his brother sin a sin which is not unto death, he shall ask, and he shall give him life for them that sin not unto death." Then I began to intercede for Kirk to God, begging Him for Kirk's eternal soul, not knowing if Kirk was dead or alive—I just stood in the gap for him anyway. Mick got off the phone and said "Sis, we have to pray for John and Judy—Kirk has just been shot and killed in front of the police station."

Finally, Mona dropped me off back at Marie's and I shared the sad news about Kirk. They were shocked at the news, and they weren't sure what had happened to me, but it seemed to be tied to Kirk's death. I just know that again and again, God talks to His children; we sometimes don't know what He is saying, but I am thankful for the spirit of travail. I found out later that Kirk went to the police station and passed cigarettes through a hole in a cell screen to an inmate inside. He didn't know it, but three times that day, the police had received reports of an attempted jail break planned for that night. The police hired some men to come in and help protect the jail.

One of those men ordered "Halt!" to an unarmed seven-teen-year-old blonde-haired, blue-eyed boy who took off running in fear, and shot him in the back—when he was only a few feet away. I guess no one but God truly knows all the details of the shooting, but God made provisions of prayer for Kirk. He knew what the future would hold for him. I've long since found peace in that fact.

I've learned that many people don't understand me and or what I feel and see in the spirit realm. Sometimes I wish I didn't know either—the Word of God has taught me that the devil is a counterfeiter and that there is no new thing under the sun. So if God is the creator of all, then He must also have a prophetic power for His children from which the devil crafted his counterfeit: the medium or "channeler." The Old Testament prophets offer us a glimpse of this divinely ordained power.

When I see people wonder about me, I want them to like me so much that time and again I have prayed, "Please, God, let me be like them, please!" Silence.

After Kirk's death, I met a Christian lady named Lois, who had a foster home. We seemed to hit it off right away and I sure was in need of an encourager. At one point, she asked me to go to the headquarters of a Christian television ministry to attend a series of meetings, and I agreed to go.

I had never been to anything as wonderful as those meetings, nor had I seen people so loving and kind. It was like going to heaven for a week. There were people from every denomination there, praising God with a freedom of oneness like I had never seen.

One day on the way to the meeting, I saw this wonderful black man who was a bus driver, and God put it on my heart to tell him something. I wouldn't listen, because I was sure it was just "dumb old me." That night, when I went into the meeting, the Lord prompted me as I saw the man again that He wanted me to say something to him. I refused to do it again, even though by now I knew it was the Lord talking to me.

As the meeting was about to end, I felt the urgency again to go, and this time I obeyed. I slipped out of the pew and down the long aisle, and headed for the doors. I saw him outside, standing just inside the open door of his bus. It was misting rain pretty heavily and I didn't even notice it—all I could do was hurry across to that man.

He saw me coming, and he kept looking around to see who I was heading for. I finally reached him and took his hand, looked straight in his eyes and told him, "God has told me all day to come to you and tell you that out of all these people, He has his eye on you and you are so special to Him. He wants you to come to Him and let Him love you." Then I said, "God loves you and so do I, and I will ever pray for you." At that point, I hugged his neck and told him goodbye and God Bless. I'll never forget the tears in those brown eyes, and somehow I know I will see him in Heaven.

People were getting on the bus by then, and I went to find Lois and her foster son, Peter. As we walked back outside, a bus was just pulling out and I saw my "friend" wave, as he drove up the hill and out of sight. He honked his horn all the way, as if to say goodbye and I will see you later. As I was drying out from the rain and complaining about being wet after that, the Lord reminded me that had I obeyed Him when He first prompted me earlier that day, I would not have gotten wet. I could almost see a loving father with a knowing smile.

Of the many things that happened on that trip, two stand out as spiritual landmarks for my life and future ministry.

One evening, at the close of the service, the Lord told me to put my hand on the lady in front of me. As usual, I debated with the Spirit. He told me that she had a severe back problem and that He would heal her if I would put my hand on her back. Finally I obeyed. The woman didn't even turn around or look at me as I prayed, but her friends began to praise God and cry. After I finished, she turned around and I saw one of the loveliest black women I had ever seen. As soon as she composed herself, she explained why her companions were so excited.

She had been confined to a hospital in Georgia. She knew if she could just get to these meetings with her friends, that God would heal her. When she learned that all the seats on the bus were taken (that was her only means of coming), she prayed for God to make a way. Then a friend stopped by the hospital and told her there had been a cancellation on the bus. She sat up in bed and removed all the weights they had on her and told the nurse she was leaving. The miracle didn't stop there! The night before, she had a dream of a white lady with dark hair who took her by the hand and led her down into a pool of water and submerged her, as hundreds of people watched her get healed.

That's why all her friends were so excited—even though there wasn't a physical pool of water, it happened just like in her dream—she was instantly healed! Several days after we returned home, this lady called me and said the Lord had truly touched her—even her doctors were amazed. All I could think was, "Lord, why am I so weird?" I couldn't understand why God would use somebody like me.

The second landmark for me happened on the day we left. I still remember the service. There was an altar call given "only for those who felt like they had a call to the ministry." The minister said God was going to anoint them for special ministries. I waited and waited, trying to ignore the voice within that was urging me to go forward. Finally, Lois looked at me and said, "Why haven't you gone? Do it!"

No one laid hands on anyone or anything like that. There was just a sweet spirit there. I stood there just breaking and breaking. I was crying, as I envisioned a big angel pouring oil onto my head from a pitcher, but only a drop came out. When it hit my head, it just melted all down my body. Suddenly I noticed someone about four feet to my right who was sobbing uncontrollably and saying, "Thank you Lord. Thank you for letting me live to see this, and to see her."

About that time I looked at her, but I couldn't really see her for the tears. All I could do was shake my head yes as she came closer saying, "Do you see it? Do you see the angel pouring oil on your head?" I was only seeing it in the spirit, but she was seeing it in reality, and both of us were awed by the experience. I have no idea who she was—she just disappeared in the crowd. Was God preparing me for something?

After returning home, I was asked to help with the youth group in our church. I helped the youth pastor with about forty teenagers as a youth sponsor. I had found a nitch, I loved teenagers and felt a real rapport with them.

Then I was asked if I would consider becoming a deaconess, and again after much prayer, I said yes. Doors were beginning to open to me for ministry, and it was happening so fast that I never even realized what was going on.

When the church decided to open a wing of the building for a counseling center and community pantry, another staff pastor was hired who was in his last year of training to become a doctor of psychology. It was exciting to be a part of the vision. I was on the board and served as secretary to the "Outreach Center."

The pastor asked me to sit in on counseling with him and attend seminars with him and his secretary. I was humbled at the opportunity to serve. I would never have believed that I would be asked to serve on anything, let alone teach kids in Sunday school and the teen group. I don't know what God's got in store for me, but I'm His and He can do anything He wants with me.

Chapter Twelve

Epilogue: Living Beyond MyYesterdays

God loves to ask us, "Is anything too hard for Me? Will you be made whole?" As I look back, it's hard for me to fathom all my Savior has brought me through. I sometimes wonder why He even bothered...but God's love never leaves me wondering long.

I still marvel at God's love for "impossible cases." To think that someone who had been a drug-addict, a messed up witch, and someone who could never seem to "get it together," could be transformed into a godly woman and a chosen vessel of anointed ministry—it is overwhelming to me.

My natural mind continued to revert back to its unredeemed thought patterns long after I was rescued from darkness by Jesus Christ. The enemy had used my painful and shameful memories as weapons against me after I was saved—until I finally realized that as long as I held onto unforgiveness and bitterness, I was still a victim.

Again and again, I battled the thought, "Give up! You're too messed up and you're certainly not any good for Jesus." One day, I read a statement in one of Kathryn Kulman's books that I hold dear to my heart. She was being interviewed by some reporters who kept bringing up her past failures as a Christian. Instead of being flustered or angry, she just calmly looked at them and said, "If I live in all my yesterdays, I will have no tomorrows."

That made sense to me, and right then and there, I made a quality decision that I wanted tomorrows, and that I would let Jesus take care of the yesterdays.

Up to that time, my yesterdays kept coming up in my todays and ruining my chance for a future. Like most abused persons, I usually denied the truth because it hurt me to face it. It almost caused me to relive the horrors I'd suffered.

My denial was often fueled by negative reactions from other people too. Whenever I dared to tell the truth about an abusive act I'd suffered, I always heard statements like "it didn't hurt, it didn't happen, you're wrong," or "your reality isn't accurate."

As a child, I quickly modified my thinking to accept what I was being told—the truth became a lie and lies became the truth. The people who abused me also tried to convince me that it was my fault, that I made them hurt me, or that I wanted it to happen. Only the light of God can expose all the lies and help people like me see the truth. Abuse victims must always be careful not to believe a lie concerning what really happened, because self-pity will try to get us to make it worse—especially when we so desperately need for someone to care that we have indeed been hurt.

I found that many adults I've ministered to have continued to suffer in their adult lives. Abusers will often use new tactics to control their now-grown victims.

I knew a young woman who was raised by a domineering father who beat her viciously with a belt or whatever he could find at the drop of a hat. The father wanted to control this young girl and did. She grew up and became successful in leadership, but her father never gave her a compliment and verbally knocked her in front of people.

She couldn't understand why her father couldn't see her in leadership, and was always knocking her. As we prayed, the Lord showed us that as long as her father could still affect her with his words, he was still abusing her, and he knew it by her reactions. He still whipped her as if she was still a little girl, only this time he did it with words instead of his belt. As long as his words could keep her in control, he had no respect for her as a woman in leadership, because he could only see her as a little girl.

As soon as she stopped bowing down to his abusive authority, and began to walk away telling him in love and without fear that she didn't have to take it anymore, she then—and only then—found a measure of the respect from him she had so longed for.

Through the years, I've discovered that our memories don't go away. They stay with us until death. With the help of the Holy Spirit, I've learned the secret to living with them. I use them for good.

I found out there are thousands of people in the world who have been hurt much worse than me. I use the little bit that has happened to me as a "school of experience," and I use the knowledge gained from these memories to heal mountains of hurt in others. It makes the devil real mad, and that makes me real glad—it makes me feel like I'm getting even somehow.

God began to develop my gifts and perfect my ministry abilities in the safety and supportive atmosphere of a local church. Under the guidance of my pastor and other seasoned believers, I began to reach out to hurting people. My first area of ministry was my family and the circle of friends God had given me.

There was the time God gave me the same intense burden for Mona's husband as He gave me for Kirk, the teenage boy who was shot at the police station. I would often wake up in the middle of the night and see his pleading eyes asking me to pray. There were times when he saw me on the street and would beg me not to stop praying. I said to him, "Manny, I do pray for you, but God's telling me it's time for you to pray."

When Manny said, "I do pray all the time, but I don't think He hears me," I told him, "Manny, God hears you, but you need to change your life style." He just hung his head and said, "I know, just continue to pray, okay?"

As I slept one night, I saw a vision of Mona crying out to me, with her baby on her hip, saying, "Please Jan, get up! Manny has been shot and killed just three blocks from here. Please help me!" I awoke with a start, in a cold sweat and already crying out to God for Manny. This time, it wasn't just a dream—Mona and her baby were really there and I found out that Manny had been killed just a short time earlier. From that time on, I began to ask God to please release me from that kind of knowledge and travail, but all I heard Him say was that I would be the "midnight cry" for many people. I couldn't even comprehend it, but I was just grateful to be His.

Sometimes when I was in my greatest agony, I would hear Him say, "Lovest thou Me? Then feed My sheep." God seemed to have given me a heart for what the world calls, "throw-away people." Marie always told me that I was able to love the unlovable, and I had trouble accepting that as a compliment, even though it was fact. I just thought that when I became a Christian, everyone became my problem and that I was to lay down my life for everyone.

My house was like Grand Central Station, because someone was always there. God put it in me—I loved people.

In the years to come, I returned to school to get my high school diploma. I followed God's leading and established J.B. Ministries (the J.B. stands for "Just Believe").

God gave me one of my deepest desires when He gave me a godly husband. Together, we moved our home and ministry from Indiana to Virginia. We minister to countless hundreds of people who cross our path—people whose lives have been destroyed and damaged by abuse of some kind.

Many are healed instantly by the power of God, and others have to press in like I did, through a painful step-by-step process of healing and restoration. For all of them, God is always faithful and ever present.

There is a great need today for deliverance and knowledgeable ministry to people who have become trapped in various kinds of demonic oppression, possession and bondage—whether it involves drug addiction, satanism, witchcraft and the occult, or sexual and physical abuse.

Most of the people who come to us are desperate for someone to understand their pain and simply believe they are not suffering from mental illness. Others simply need a very special touch from the Savior.

As I have tried to fulfill my calling to feed my Master's sheep, I continue to see the need and hear the cries of many wounded hearts who are desperately looking for a way out of their darkness. I want to show them the way out—I want to show them Jesus.

I have had the opportunity to appear on various Christian and secular television programs, including the Geraldo Rivera Show, and the 700 Club with Sheila Walsh; and I've also ministered on numerous satellite TV programs and countless radio talk shows. The message is the same: Jesus is the answer, no matter how deep or dark our sin may take us, no matter how abused or victimized we are.

The Lord has opened the doors so I could work hand-in-hand with many doctors and ministries to help set people free from the occult and other dark realms of bondage and fear. Many people in this type of bondage need to be relocated during their restoration period. (We call this our "spiritual I.C.U." or Intensive Care Unit.)

I've been blessed to work with many police and law enforcement agencies in the area of occult worship and dangerous satanic rituals.

My husband and I hold evangelistic revivals and seminars across the country. My husband is a gospel singer and song writer, and we have recorded and released two singing tapes.

I especially enjoy speaking at colleges across the country. I have a great love for young people, and I consider myself blessed to be allowed to communicate with them and minister to their various needs.

I left hundreds of stories out of this book, partly because they would make this book too heavy to carry, and partly because I want to present Jesus to you and my other readers more than I want to present my problems from the past. Above all, I want you to understand that nothing is too great for our God. He can set you free from any bondage that man or devil can dream up—He is the Almighty One, and best of all, He loves us!

May God bless you, and may you walk in His blessed freedom and light all your days. And as you go, take His light into the world with you—there may be a Janelle out there who desperately wants to meet your God and be set free too!